REMAKING
LAW FIRMS

WHY & HOW

GEORGE BEATON
IMME KASCHNER

Printed in the United States of America.

20 19 18 17 16   5 4 3

Library of Congress Cataloging-in-Publication Data

Names: Beaton, George (Consultant), author. I Kaschner, Imme, author.
Title: Remaking law firms : why and how / George Beaton, Imme Kaschner.
Description: Chicago : American Bar Association, [2016] I Includes
    bibliographical references and index.
Identifiers: LCCN 2016004286 I ISBN 9781634253963
Subjects: LCSH: Practice of law—Economic aspects. I Law offices. I Law
    firms. I Lawyers—Marketing.
Classification: LCC K129 .B43 2016 I DDC 340.068/4—dc23
LC record available at http://lccn.loc.gov/2016004286

Discounts are available for books ordered in bulk. Special consideration is given to state bars, CLE programs, and other bar-related organizations. Inquire at Book Publishing, ABA Publishing, American Bar Association, 321 North Clark Street, Chicago, Illinois 60654-7598.

www.ShopABA.org

To the lawyers everywhere
who strive to serve their clients ever better.

Table of Contents

Foreword

I like the dreams of the future better than the history of the past.

—*Thomas Jefferson*

Change does not come easily to the legal profession. We are trained to be skeptical, cautious, anchored in precedents and tradition. Yet, disruptive change is here. And that change is growing and accelerating, persistent and threatening.

The evidence of this abounds in our changing vocabulary. There was a time when we mostly worried about advising clients and billing time. Today, we deal with disruptive technologies, commoditization, unbundling of legal services, and globalization of firms. We now use neologisms like BigLaw and NewLaw, and "co-opetition." These terms reflect changes. Changes of a magnitude and variety our clients and our profession have not previously experienced. Changes that challenge many of the ethical foundations of what makes ours a special, regulated profession.

Cost-conscious clients (empowered by new tools and technologies) are challenging us to manage projects better, improve efficiencies, control costs, and assure quality. They want the right people doing the right things the right way, at the best possible cost, and as quickly as they require.

These are not the challenges many in our noble profession signed up for. But they cannot be avoided. And, truth be told, they are making what we do far more professional, and more exciting and rewarding for those who embrace and adapt to change and the opportunities it brings. They are pushing us to remain relevant to our clients, our people, and our communities, as these also change.

As chief change agent for one of the world's largest law firms, I am constantly looking for insights and advice to help us make sense of change, and to make those changes necessary for us to remain one of the world's leading law firms. That is why I am delighted to introduce *Remaking Law Firms: Why and How*.

In this timely, state-of-the-art, and thoughtful book, Dr. George Beaton and coauthor Dr. Imme Kaschner describe where the profession and its corporate clients are heading, and how law firms can navigate and prosper in this future with confidence. The authors explain why this is happening at such a fast pace and offer practical advice on what every law firm anywhere in the world should be doing in response.

Last year I had the privilege of first hearing Dr. Beaton talk about his scientifically developed scenario depicting the year 2025. He painted a picture describing how corporations and governments will be meeting their legal needs and how a heterogeneous variety of legal services providers will be competing in ways undreamt of before. The story he told was thoroughly researched, convincing, and grounded on advisory and market research experience. Appropriately, chapter 5 is titled "The 2025 Kaleidoscope Scenario."

Whether you are leading a global law firm or simply trying to make sense of a profession in transition, *Remaking Law Firms: Why and How* will make you think and encourage you to act. Because the future belongs to those who embrace tomorrow today.

Eduardo C. Leite
Chairman of the Executive Committee
Baker & McKenzie International

Preface

The origins of this book go back to October 7, 2013, when George Beaton published a seemingly innocuous blog post titled *The Rise and Rise of the NewLaw Business Model*. It discussed changes in the legal services industry, with a focus on legal services providers that are different from traditional law firms. The post kicked off a lively and passionate exchange between lawyers from traditional and unconventional firms, in-house departments, professionals from consulting with backgrounds in law and other disciplines, and academics.

Contributors came from Australia, Canada, Hong Kong, Spain, the United Kingdom, and the United States. The wealth of expertise and thought leadership about changes and innovation in the legal services industry was too valuable to languish in its fragmented online format, and this provided the incentive for George's first foray into the e-book space. *NewLaw New Rules: A Conversation About the Future of the Legal Services Industry*, a structured and amended version using much of the material initially posted on the blog, was published in December 2013. Since its publication, the neologism "NewLaw" has entered the lexicon, and the e-book is being used for teaching purposes by academics educating "tomorrow's lawyers."

Based on George's extensive experience in researching clients' needs and advising professional services firms, and considering themes raised in *NewLaw New Rules*, the time was right for a closer look at the traditional law firm business model. The result is *Remaking Law Firms: Why and How*, which examines the historical strengths of the traditional business model with its approach to technically excellent service at seemingly whatever cost, and its many present day weaknesses. Law firms around the world have relied on this business model for decades because it provided a blueprint to deliver excellent service to commercial clients and handsome profits to partners. But the times have changed, with the global financial crisis only accelerating the maturation of the legal services industry with its attendant price-down pressures, commoditization, and increasing client demand for efficient, business-relevant services. To respond, law firms will have to go beyond cutting costs while preserving the general way they win work, produce work, and govern themselves. Law firms need to look for business models that are better adapted to serve their clients not just today, but well into the future. What we call remade law firms and NewLaw providers are based on such innovative business models, and therefore now provide a better blueprint.

It is frequently asserted that legal services are different from other professions, and from other industries (if anyone is willing to go so far as to acknowledge that law is indeed an industry). Our own work has confirmed this in one respect only—lawyers as a group are more risk-averse, and less willing to innovate and take chances by diverging from established methods and processes, than other professional groups. And since culture is the sum of the behavior of individuals in a group, the culture of traditional law firms is more change-averse and less innovation-minded than that of other industries. The result is a conundrum for any group of lawyers seeking to position their firm ahead of others: Being better by default means being different, but who would dare to venture where no firm has gone before? This is compounded by the inherent inertia in any large, complex organization, which means that law firms need to start changing well ahead of any actual need to have completed the change—but what self-respecting group of lawyers would be prompted to start making rash and risky changes without a clear and compelling need to do so? It's Joseph Heller all over again. The only possible answer is simple—start somewhere, start small, keep building from there—and don't stop.

To succeed under the changed circumstances, law firms need to remake their business models to improve alignment with the job that commercial clients need to be done. Examples of innovative and successful business models from remade law firms and NewLaw providers in this book go beyond theoretical concepts and provide proof of principle because, to borrow from a Peter Drucker aphorism, "Business models [sic] are a commodity, execution is an art." Our book provides a wide range of innovation examples and case studies from legal services providers and other professional service firms that illustrate what a remade business model for a law firm might look like. We hope that *Remaking Law Firms: Why and How* will fuel a desire for change in law firms that goes beyond thinking and planning and leads straight into the messy, frustrating, exciting world of implementing change, and ultimately to better client service.

Acknowledgments

Remaking Law Firms: Why and How would not have been written without our more than 40 contributors who are professional and thought leaders in legal services, other professions, and cognate fields. In spite of their many commitments, all of them generously gave their time and insights through interviews and written comments. We are deeply indebted to them for allowing us to benefit from their experience, expertise, and opinions, and to share this material with our readers. They are proof of the spirit of innovation that is starting to pervade the legal profession around the world. So thank you to our contributors for making the book possible, and for being the inspiring people you are! Any flaws in the reasoning and analysis are, of course, our own. Thank you also to Encompass Corporation and Seyfarth Shaw LLP for allowing us to use their proprietary graphic material to illustrate specific points as acknowledged in the figure legends.

Our special gratitude goes to Eric Chin, an Associate with Beaton, who has been part of the *NewLaw New Rules* and *Remaking Law Firms: Why and How* team from the beginning. Eric's analytical skills, knowledge of the legal services industry, and considered approach to complex problems have guided us through countless whiteboard sessions, and have left their imprint on many of the figures, and on the book as a whole.

Then there is the rest of the team to thank: Julian Jones of Wellmark translated our visions of figures into graphic realities with unfailing patience. Scott Colvin heroically shouldered the task of working his way through the Bluebook to bring our Australian footnotes in line with American referencing style, venturing boldly into citations of electronic material where no citation guide had gone before, and assisted with proofreading. Anna Bornemisza provided research assistance. Lynda Dean rendered expert administrative assistance throughout the writing process.

Finally, we thank the editorial team, and most importantly Rick Paszkiet and Sarah Forbes Orwig Ph.D. at American Bar Association Publishing, for their support in bringing our book to life.

A Personal Note from George

A school career counselor advised my father and me that I had talent for writing and suggested I aim to become a professor of English. He was half right. I have been a professor in two disciplines—medical education and business management—and I have taught management in a law school. For the last 30 years I have worked with lawyers of many stripes, but most particularly those in private practice in larger firms on several continents. My colleagues and I have surveyed tens of thousands of clients of these firms and rigorously analyzed the legal services industry. Coauthoring *Remaking Law Firms* draws on my respect for the scientific method, business strategy frameworks, the noble profession of law, and a Hippocratic duty to teach others. I thank Margaret, my wife and business partner, for her love and unfailing support in this and all my endeavors.

A Personal Note from Imme

Despite appreciating the convenience of electronic sources of information, I have always loved the smell of libraries. I hope that some things never change. I want to thank my husband Piers for his love and support through a change of continents and careers, and our daughter Hazel for being a joy and never letting us get away with easy answers. I also want to thank my teachers in the JD program at Melbourne Law School for opening my eyes to the beauty and complexity of law, and the lawyers who have taught and are teaching me about the privilege of belonging to this profession. In addition, my thanks go to my former PI at Boston Children's Hospital, Francis McGowan, MD, a pediatrician of outstanding passion and kindness, for teaching me about the joys of (medical) research a long time ago. Finally, I would like to thank my mother, Dr. Maria Kaschner, who still enjoys learning new things, and gave us children wings to fly.

About the Authors

George Beaton MD MBA PhD has guided clients through a wide variety of business and strategic decisions in his 25 years as an advisor and researcher working with law and other professional services firms. Evolving from his medical degree and advisory work in the health care sector, today his practice is focused on corporate advisory, client-centric performance improvement, and trouble-shooting engagements for firms.

George's background in teaching business strategy at Melbourne Business School and Melbourne Law School, both in The University of Melbourne, combined with his work in public and private companies, professional service firms, universities, and governments, has given him deep insights into the challenges and opportunities facing law firm leaders and their firms. He frequently shares his insights through social and print media, and published the e-book *NewLaw New Rules: A Conversation on the Future of the Legal Services Industry* in 2013.

He is widely regarded as a leading independent authority on professional services firms, and law firms in particular, reflected in his frequent keynote and media appearances. Based in Melbourne, Australia his work now covers Australia, Canada, China, Hong Kong, the U.S. and the U.K.

Imme Kaschner JD, MD was admitted as an Australian lawyer in March 2015, following her graduation from the Melbourne Law School JD program in 2013. She now works at commercial firm Hive Legal Pty. Ltd. Her interest in how complex systems, including the legal services industry, work and change, led to the cooperation with George, first project managing the compilation of the e-book *NewLaw New Rules: A conversation on the future of the legal services industry,* and now coauthoring *Remaking Law Firms: Why and How.*

Imme has tutored Marketing Law at the Department of Business Law & Taxation at the Faculty of Business and Economics, Monash University. She is also a member of the Intellectual Property and Information Technology Committee of the Law Institute of Victoria.

Prior to her move to Australia with her daughter and husband in 2010, Imme worked as a researcher and medical doctor at Boston Children's Hospital and Brigham & Women's Hospital in Boston, MA.

PART I
Why

Chapter 1

Introduction

LET'S START AT THE VERY BEGINNING

This is not yet another book on business strategy for law firms to keep on the shelf. *Remaking Law Firms* is about innovation in law firms in the United States and other common law jurisdictions, mainly Canada, the United Kingdom, and Australia. We also intend it to be good reading. To these ends, we have talked to legal practitioners and other professionals and thought leaders in several parts of the world, and examined a plethora of sources. The book is the result of studying players in the legal services ecosystem in the United States and elsewhere for two decades. It offers a probing look at the trends and developments in legal services, and a well-formed and practical view of what larger law firms should be doing now to prepare for their futures.

Going far beyond the conventional and a description of the status quo, *Remaking Law Firms* sets out a compelling scenario showing how client demand will drive deep changes in the legal services industry. Our analysis of the present and narrative on the probable future (the *why*) leads to a comprehensive assessment of how firms can—and must—adapt to the new normal by changing, that is, remaking, their business models. Remaking, in the sense in which we use the word, is done in ways that include learning from, and cooperating with, newly established nontraditional legal services providers (the *how*). The underlying concepts are brought to life in examples and case studies from innovative law firms, as well as in-house departments, nontraditional legal services providers, consultants, and other types of professional services firms.

For us, the most striking insight to come out of the research for this book is an understanding of how the professional values of bespoke, technically excellent client service and perfectionism in a law firm can have the effect of compromising the delivery of excellent value, as defined by a firm's commercial clients. The upside of this conundrum is that the professional service ethos of practicing lawyers also provides the strongest available lever to drive cultural adaptation in law firms, if it can be demonstrated that clients want their legal services providers to change—though firms must not fall into the trap of changing solely in a reactive manner based on explicit client demands.

Remaking Law Firms is about firms and other legal services providers serving corporate and commercial clients. It is not primarily addressed to small firms and individual lawyers that mainly serve consumers, because a number of the challenges that we discuss and the innovation examples that we highlight relate to the complex structure of large firms. Sole practitioners and those practicing in smaller firms, whether they serve consumer or commercial clients, may nevertheless find the book helpful. This is because challenges, such as clients demanding more predictability of time frames and costs, resulting in a need to practice more efficiently, and the need to meet increasing service commoditization by differentiation, diversification, and branding, similarly arise for those practitioners. And the implementation of solutions to address these and other challenges always necessitates the core competency of change readiness as addressed in this book.

BIGLAW AND NEWLAW

As defined in *NewLaw New Rules*, an earlier e-book collaboration of ours, the terms "BigLaw" and "NewLaw" that are used throughout this book do not designate the size or the founding date of the entities to which they collectively refer. Rather, they denote firms or corporations that share a business model with certain characteristics:

> The phrase Big Law (two words) has been in use—mainly in the USA—for some time. It describes large law firms and by inference their business model. The late Larry Ribstein of the University of Illinois College of Law wrote *The Death of Big Law* in 2010. This major paper captured the prevailing understanding of the concerns about Big Law. [George Beaton] adopted the words Big Law and removed the space between them to create "BigLaw" as a mnemonic for the business model underpinning the operations of traditional law firms.
>
> . . .
>
> Eric Chin coined "NewLaw" in his provocative post *2018: The year Axiom becomes the world's largest legal services firm*. Eric's NewLaw neologism is a collective noun describing legal services providers with new business models.[1]

As participants in the discourse on BigLaw/NewLaw, we are excited to see that the occasionally antagonistic debate about the necessity to find new ways of serving commercial legal needs is giving way to nuanced discussions about the evolution of a legal services ecosystem, and the ways in which different legal services providers (law firms, in-house departments, and NewLaw corporations) with different business models and different focal points can interact for mutual benefit. This

---

1. GEORGE BEATON, NEWLAW NEW RULES (Beaton Capital 2013) (quoting Eric Chin, *2018: The Year Axiom Becomes the World's Largest Legal Services Firm*, BIGGER. BETTER. BOTH? BLOG (Sept. 13, 2013), http://www .beatoncapital.com/2013/09/2018-year-axiom-becomes-worlds-largest-legal-services-firm/).

book adds to the dialog by collating and describing a number of those forms of cooperation.

THE LEGAL SERVICES INDUSTRY

Throughout this book, we will refer to the legal services industry and legal services providers. These terms necessitate some explanation. We prefer "legal services industry" to "legal industry" because it is more accurate in capturing not only the service-based nature, but also the competitive dynamics. We include in this industry traditional law firms, in-house legal departments, other entities providing legal services, and those directly supporting legal processes—specifically legal services outsourcers and legal knowledge providers. "Legal services providers" by analogy include enterprises and individuals that provide various building blocks of legal solutions, and that sell to clients who may or may not be lawyers. They may be affiliated with law firms, in-house legal departments, or corporations without internal legal services.

The size of the U.S. legal services industry is considerable, with numbers in the range of $300 billion frequently cited.[2] We acknowledge that the actual share of this market held by nontraditional legal services providers is quite small at this point in time. We believe that worldwide, their share is less than 1 percent, based on a crowd-sourced estimate undertaken in late 2014. The importance of the alternative legal services providers at this point lies in their successful proof of concept and their enormous growth potential. Conceivably, every in-house department and every law firm that has not already reviewed its internal processes, especially those related to work of lower complexity, and has not allocated that work to the most efficient way of sourcing, is a potential customer for the nontraditional providers.

WHAT THIS BOOK DOES NOT COVER

The legal profession does not exist in a vacuum, and it is subject to a large number of normative influences including direct regulation, the structure of court systems, and other established dispute resolution processes. *Remaking Law Firms* does not address how these systems in the United States and elsewhere might contribute to law firms providing services in ways that have fallen behind clients' expectations, and how they, too, would benefit from being remade to deliver services better, faster, and cheaper.

The book also does not discuss how changes in the legal services industry, particularly increasing digitization and commoditization, need to be reflected in legal education. Across the United States and other common law jurisdictions legal education by and large still focuses on building individual, legal analytical

---

2. *See, e.g.*, Frank Strong, *What Size Is the Addressable US Legal Market?* Business of Law Blog (Jan. 15, 2015), http://businessoflawblog.com/2015/01/addressable-us-legal-market/.

and research skills, neglecting a need to train lawyers in systems theory, multi-disciplinary cooperation, people skills, computer science, general business and economic concepts, and real-world application of academic concepts (comparable to medical schools, which now increasingly expose students to patients and communities in a carefully controlled manner from the very beginning of their studies). Nevertheless, for "tomorrow's lawyers" in the sense coined by Richard Susskind (who might singlehandedly have done more than any other thought leader to put the need for innovation in legal services firmly on the agenda),[3] this book is a useful tool for understanding the trends and forces that have shaped and will continue to shape the legal services industry, and for understanding the resulting challenges and evolving opportunities.

Similarly, beyond some material in chapter 2 on legal services deregulation in the United Kingdom and Australia that could possibly be a portent for what may lie in store for the United States, and the new technological competency requirement in the comment to the American Bar Association bar rules, this book does not address the need for regulatory or professional conduct rule changes that might arise from developments in the legal services industry.

OUR CONTRIBUTORS

This book was inspired by the exhilarating experience of crowdsourcing the e-book *NewLaw New Rules*, which brought together a large number of thought leaders from around the world to share their unique vantage points on what is happening and what may occur in the legal services industry. We wanted to capture that breadth of expertise from all walks of corporate and commercial legal and other professional services to supplement our own analysis of how law firms need to change to remain relevant in meeting their clients' needs. To this end, the team, including Eric Chin, conducted semistructured interviews and corresponded with over 40 invited commentators between July 2014 and February 2015. We are very grateful to all our contributors (as listed in the Appendix) for generously volunteering their time. In providing material for this book, they guided our understanding of how they strive every day to serve their clients and manage their firms ever better in various direct and indirect ways. *Remaking Law Firms* would not have been possible without them, and they are proof of how members of the legal profession and other disciplines have taken up the challenge to remake legal services.

THE STRUCTURE OF THE BOOK

The book consists of two parts, the *why* and the *how* of remaking law firms. The first part commences in chapter 2 with an overview of the legal services industry

---

3. See Richard Susskind, Tomorrow's Lawyers: An Introduction to Your Future (Oxford University Press 2013).

today. It describes the prevailing traditional law firm business model and some of its challenges, and contrasts it with other entities providing legal services. The taxonomy of legal services providers in the market today provides a concise description and basis for understanding the essential differences between types of providers (see Figure 2.1).

The legal services industry as such is analyzed using Michael E. Porter's five forces framework in chapter 3, reaching the conclusion that it displays all the signs of being mature. The consequences of maturity are explored and explained. To highlight the plight of most law firms, a case study describing a mid-sized firm that in spite of strong post-financial crisis performance has "maxed out" on the profit levers (as described in David Maister's profitability equation) concludes chapter 3.

Chapter 4 provides a detailed picture of the clients of the future—the main drivers of change in the industry, partly by increasing their own capacity to meet more of their internal clients' legal needs. The chapter starts with key demographic trends and provides evidence of continuing growth in in-house legal departments in order to increase the volume and complexity of legal services they provide to their internal clients. This trend is coupled with a decrease in external legal spend and a demand for external legal services to be priced and delivered in alignment with clients' business goals. The increasing consolidation of panels to maximize buying power and application of professional procurement processes are additional manifestations of this trend. Corporate clients, both those with and without in-house legal departments, are starting to use retainer-based services from New-Law providers. Sourcing options for in-house legal departments have evolved far beyond traditional law firms, and can involve captives and collaboration with New-Law firms. Clients' successes with bringing work in-house and using alternative legal providers are fueling a positive feedback loop.

Chapter 5, The 2025 Kaleidoscope Scenario, builds on the state of the legal services industry today and how clients' demographics, needs, and behavior are changing to provide a scenario of what the legal services industry might look like in ten years' time. Scenario building is a tool for firms to use in strategic planning in the face of uncertainty. It can be used to formulate and assess the business model changes and strategic options a firm must consider to sustainably serve its clients and at the same time achieve professional and financial success. Our analysis of the legal services industry makes a multifaceted scenario most likely, hence our use of the term "kaleidoscope" to describe it. Many forms of legal services providers will coexist, compete, and cooperate in ways that depend on clients' preferences, industries, and jurisdictions.

Chapter 6 is about diagnosing your firm's readiness for change. It contains a self-assessment tool (see Figure 6.1) to gauge levels of awareness of changes in the legal services market; to assess to what degree a firm is ready to remake, or is already remaking, how it wins work and does work; as well as to consider its overall readiness for change. Such a self-assessment is a starting point to direct change efforts based on an identification of strengths and weaknesses in specific areas that are important in remaking the firm, and can also guide readers to areas of particular interest in the book.

Chapter 7, Designing the Business Model, provides a link between chapters 2 through 6, which illustrate *why* law firms need to remake their business model to meet the present and future challenges in the legal services industry, and chapters 8 through 13, which set out *how* this remaking is to be done. The chapter examines *what* is to be remade. It details the concept of the business model and applies it in the context of legal service providers. A business model encompasses both the narrative of how a business works and the quantitative considerations, including modeling, to provide evidence that if the underlying assumptions are correct, the business will be profitable. The business model of a law firm needs to articulate how work is won, how work is done, and how the enterprise is governed. Each of these dimensions can be further broken down into specific hallmarks. The business models of BigLaw and NewLaw firms are quite different in regard to each of those hallmarks, and individual firms lie on a continuum or spectrum, extending from BigLaw to NewLaw for a given hallmark (see Figure 7.1). Remaking a firm means designing its business model to move toward the more client-centric, more efficient, and more agile manifestations of hallmarks that characterize the NewLaw business model.

Chapter 8 is the first of the chapters detailing how the business model can be remade. It focuses on brand, marketing, and business development, because brands make legal services providers stand out in commoditized markets, and law firms are missing opportunities by focusing too much on personal partner brands rather than on a compelling, distinctive brand for the firm. Building a credible brand around differentiated and, for some firms, diversified offerings needs to proceed from an assessment of market- and client-derived insights. "Expert evidence" illustrates how this works in practice. These insights need to be matched with the particular strengths of the firm to define and execute its brand purpose, thereby contributing to a sustainable business model and creating a competitive advantage. The example of a NewLaw firm and its branding strategy demonstrates this point. Dedicated, professional business development staff add value by enabling more cost-effective business development, better quality client relationships, and more responsive client service, illustrated in a case study on the development of a professional sales force in the diversified professional services firm PwC.

Chapter 9 discusses pricing and fee arrangements as another crucially important component of a remade business model. The billable hour has long been a cornerstone of the traditional law firm business model, but in the interests of clients and firms, law firms need to move away from six-minute units as the dominant form of pricing. An overseas case study about a local council in-house department in the United Kingdom (Kent county) that initially moved to billable hours as a pricing mechanism, and subsequently on to Alternative Fee Arrangements (AFAs), both times in order to improve client service, provides a powerful illustration. There is quantitative and anecdotal evidence that AFAs can be employed in a profitable manner, particularly if offered to clients proactively. AFAs also provide a way to increase realization rates if linked to prudent resource allocation. Sustainable and profitable pricing is a multidisciplinary challenge that needs involvement and data input from all parts of the firm as well as external sources. Fee arrangements that demonstrate alignment with and value to clients include fixed fees; bonus or hold-back components around client-defined metrics; and outcomes-related fees, retainers, and contingency fees.

Chapter 10 covers sourcing and outsourcing, because clients are increasingly becoming self-sufficient by bringing work in-house, and also sourcing from New-Law, or expecting their law firms to cooperate with NewLaw providers to ensure work is done at an appropriate cost. Beyond that, cooperation with legal services outsourcers opens up the possibility for law firms to benefit from the significant investments in people, process, and technology, as well as economies of scale, that these corporations offer. The chapter contains examples of how cooperation between BigLaw and NewLaw firms can work, and also provides the perspective of a major client assessing sourcing options for its firm. Sourcing alternatives, including on-demand workers, captive entities (as an increasing number of law firms in the United States and the United Kingdom have set up), and third-party outsourcers are discussed. The most relevant considerations for the make versus buy decision by law firms are summed up elsewhere (see Figure 10.1).

Chapter 11 explains the rationale behind using legal process management (LPM) and process improvement as structured approaches to more predictably meet clients' and firms' expectations about quality, time, and budget for a matter. Technology enables effective and efficient project management and process improvement, but, as an expert points out, firms must not neglect the significant behavioral challenge in getting lawyers to work differently and adopt new approaches. The challenges and milestones in implementing a comprehensive technology-supported LPM initiative in a law firm are captured in a detailed case study about "Gowlings Practical" at a large Canadian firm.

Chapter 12 makes clear how technology, knowledge management, and analytics contribute to the success of a remade law firm business model. Given the significant spend law firms make on information technology (IT), it is important to derive maximum value from this capability. This can be achieved through an appropriate operating model, by structuring IT governance through senior management accountability and oversight, and by creating seamless IT integration with the operations of the firm.

Knowledge management is enabled through technology, and tools that optimize search and retrieval can increase both quality of work and margins. Expert systems are considered a specific type of knowledge management that allows firms to broaden their services and leverage their expertise beyond custom-made individual advice. Analytics is one of the next big challenges for law firms, since much of their business is to provide information relating to legal risk management. Applying analytics to their internal data also enables law firms to improve internal processes.

Chapter 13 completes the *how* part of the book, discussing partners, innovation, and change. In our view, the implementation of plans to remake the business model of a firm is the most significant remaking challenge. As the saying goes, "culture eats strategy for breakfast."[4] The firms that intend to remain as successful as they are today in serving clients and making profits must welcome and embrace the changes discussed in the earlier chapters. Lawyers tend to be conservative and risk-averse, and their quest for perfection is at odds with an experimental approach that sees circumscribed failure as a necessary part of development and change. Very considerable resources are necessary to design and execute meaningful change initiatives in a law firm. This chapter provides examples of how firms have nevertheless successfully remade and/or added new facets to their business models, or have formalized processes for enduring innovation. Commentators point to the importance of tapping into the professional ethos of client service to drive change, and the importance of starting with small change initiatives that can be scaled up and modified if successful, possibly outside the parent firm. In this way, a firm can take the first strides on its change journey, simultaneously building specific initiatives and the crucial capability of change readiness.

Chapter 14 briefly sums up our insights and reaffirms our call to action for traditional law firms to start remaking their business models now. By the way, have you ever considered that today is the first day of the rest of your law firm's life?

---

4. Apocryphally attributed to Peter Drucker.

Chapter 2

The Legal Services Industry Today

Key Points

- Today's law firms share a business model that we style "BigLaw." BigLaw has been immensely successful for clients and partners over many decades, but the model is now less well suited to competing in an industry characterized by buyer power, cost-down pressures, increasing use of technology and digitization, and substitute services.
- Traditional BigLaw firms and competing NewLaw providers may be compared in how they win work, how they produce work, and how they are led and governed. NewLaw is much closer to the business model of client companies than traditional law firm partnerships. Remade law firms are those that have changed and diversified their business models, and in some respects are similar to NewLaw entities.
- The industry is experiencing a number of pervasive trends: a demand to "do more for less"; a need to "do the right law"; an ongoing shift of work from law firms to in-house legal departments; the rapidly growing role of information technology and digitization in all aspects of practice; a move away from artisanal, one-off practices to commoditized services; globalization; and possibly even deregulation.

INTRODUCTION

Today's legal services industry is in a state of change. Margins are shrinking. Alternative fee arrangements are on the rise. Providers with novel ways of delivering legal services are hungry for business. There is a great deal of uncertainty about where legal services are heading and how firms should react to these changes. Things are, in short, "excitingly unpredictable" (a phrase used by the Australian High Court in the iconic intellectual property law case *National Research Development Corporation and Commissioner of Patents* to refer to the purpose of section 6 in the 1623 British *Statute of Monopolies* that was "to allow the use of the prerogative to encourage national development in a field which already, in 1623, was seen to be excitingly unpredictable" through the grant of letters patent).[1]

It might be a cold comfort that what the legal services industry is experiencing is by no means unique. Harvard Business School professor Michael E. Porter published his influential book *Competitive Strategy: Techniques for Analyzing Industries and Competitors* in 1980, describing the dynamics that predictably occur in *any* industry when it matures. How this applies to law today will be considered in detail in chapter 3. The endgame is a hypercompetitive market with fewer consolidated and many more fragmented players leveraging economies of scale and niche positions, respectively. As much as some lawyers may fervently wish to deny this, law is no different. As MIT's Peter Weill described in *Place to Space: Migrating to eBusiness Models* in 2001, the effects of digitization—that is, moving away from bespoke services delivered from brick-and-mortar offices to mass-customized, online services—are similarly predictable (and adverse to traditional practices) unless they adapt.[2] The companies buying services from large commercial law firms demand the same level of quality, predictability, and price certainty from those firms as they do from all other suppliers, and they are becoming more experienced in negotiating how that can be achieved. The question that law firms need to ask is not how they can avoid these challenges—they cannot. It is how they can best position themselves to emerge with a clear value proposition to attract and profitably serve or even expand their share of client demand.

EVOLUTION

In order to understand how the legal services industry reached this point, it is helpful to look at the evolution of the business model of today's commercial law firms in the United States, which similarly applies to many other common law jurisdictions. The concept of a business model will be discussed in more detail in chapter 7. The business model (BigLaw) is characterized by:

- attraction and training of top legal talent (frequently defined almost exclusively by alma mater);
- leverage of employed lawyers to do the more routine aspects of the work of serving clients, resulting in a pyramid-like structure in the firm, with a tightly restricted number of equity owners at the top;
- creation of a "tournament" to motivate junior lawyers to strive to become equity partners (the idea of a tournament is the subject of Marc Galanter

---

1. National Research and Development Corporation v. Commissioner of Patents, 102 CLR 252, 271 (1959).
2. Peter Weill & Michael R. Vitale, Place to Space: Migrating to business Models (Harvard Business School Press 2001).

and Thomas Palay's seminal book *Tournament of Lawyers: The Transformation of the Big Law Firm*);[3]

- partnership structure and related culture;
- pricing predominantly through time-based rates, i.e., billable hours; and
- an emphasis on technical perfection with scant regard for the relationship between resource allocation and risk.

The combination of these characteristics leads to challenges in governance and strategy. Because partner-owners behave as largely autonomous units and are involved in most decisions, and because no profit is retained, it is hard to execute strategies that involve behaving as "one firm" and investing in the future (as will be discussed in more detail in chapter 13). It is also hard to mandate change in a group of self-assured, successful, high-earning individuals. In addition, remuneration linked to personal exertion measured on time-based outcomes limits the incentive to manage profitability by becoming more efficient, as we will discuss in chapter 9.

The evolution of today's law firms can be traced back to Cravath Swaine & Moore LLP, founded in New York in 1819. The firm perfected a system of hiring, training, and promoting legal talent to provide legal work of consistently high standards through the leverage of junior lawyers. The system was in part designed to counteract the variable standards in legal education at the time.[4] The "Cravath system," and its pyramid structure, was very well suited to provide increasing numbers of high quality lawyers in times of economic and global expansion. Firms like Baker & McKenzie, which grew from its beginnings in the United States in 1949 to 2,000 lawyers around the globe in 1997, and more than 4,000 lawyers in 2015, attest to the enduring strength of the business model.[5]

LIMITATIONS OF THE BIGLAW BUSINESS MODEL

Edwin B. Reeser's article *Origins of the Modern Law Firm* sets out how the model has changed in some deleterious ways, including lateral hiring practices, multiple classes of partners, increasing use of debt for working capital and investment purposes, and overall firm size well beyond what benefits clients.[6] The BigLaw business model has attracted other widespread criticism questioning its sustainability in light of global and local hypercompetition, movement away from time-based

---

3. Marc Galanter & Thomas Palay, Tournament of Lawyers: The Transformation of the Big Law Firm (University of Chicago Press 1991).

4. The history of the firm and its people from 1819–1948 is chronicled in detail in 1–3 Robert T. Swaine, The Cravath Firm and Its Predecessors (The Lawbook Exchange 2007) (originally published in a slightly different edition in 1948).

5. Jon R. Bauman, Pioneering a Global Vision: The Story of Baker & McKenzie (Harcourt Professional Education Group 1999).

6. Edwin B. Reeser, *Origins of the Modern Law Firm*, S.F. Daily Journal, Jan. 29, 2015, at 1.

remuneration, downward pressure on price, demand for flexible work styles and services, increasing digitization, and decreasing information asymmetry about law.

The late professor Larry E. Ribstein of the University of Illinois College of Law wrote a cogent academic analysis of the traditional law firm business model in 2010; it has since become a landmark.[7] Ribstein argued that the traditional law firm model was doomed and not merely shaken by tough economic conditions, because in the absence of firm-specific property, law firms depended on certain conditions to hold them together. He argued the rise of competition from both clients, that is, in-house lawyers, and globalizing firms, and from new types of legal services providers, was now pulling large law firms apart. Following an in-depth analysis of the shortcomings of the traditional partnership-based model, illustrated with a number of case studies, Ribstein pointed to potential new business models, and new types of firms, as a way of the future.

Revisiting Ribstein's findings in 2013 with the benefit of another three years' worth of observations, William D. Henderson reached the conclusion that while not dead, the viability of the traditional model was finite, because insufficient demand in the market was failing to support the ongoing growth that the traditional business requires.[8] Henderson applied Clayton Christensen's concept of disruptive innovation[9] in the context of the competitive partnership dynamics within a law firm. Henderson also linked the state of the competition among firms based on the traditional model to the fictitious "Hunger Games,"[10] a different sort of tournament for sheer survival, rather than career advancement. Overall, he anticipated that this situation would lead to the emergence of more stable organizational forms delivering legal services with a focus on delivering services better, faster, and cheaper, and building sustainable reputational capital that way.[11] It should be noted that both Ribstein and Henderson use the term "Big Law" (two words) to refer to large law firms. We have coined the neologism "BigLaw" (one word) to connote the business model of large law firms— with the emphasis on the characteristics of the model described above. These characteristics, more than their size, are now causing the problems traditional firms are experiencing.

It would be far too simple to say that all the well-established and well-known U.S. law firms that have failed over the last 20 years simply did so because they operated based on an outdated business model. Their stories are more complex and worth looking at in detail, as for example David Parnell has done in his instructive book *The Failing Law Firm: Symptoms and Remedies*.[12] But the expansion-driven BigLaw business model has many characteristics that are simply not

---

7. Larry E. Ribstein, *The Death of Big Law*, 3 Wis. L. Rev. 749 (2010).

8. W.D. Henderson, *From Big Law to Lean Law*, 38 Int'l R. L. & Econ. Supplement 5–16 (2013).

9. As set out in Clayton M. Christensen, The Innovator's Dilemma: The Revolutionary Book That Will Change the Way You Do Business (Collins 2003).

10. *See* Suzanne Collins, The Hunger Games (Scholastic 2008).

11. Henderson, *supra* note 8.

12. David J. Parnell, The Failing Law Firm: Symptoms and Remedies (ABA Publishing 2014). The book contains an analysis of over 40 failed firms going back to the 1990s.

suited to meeting the challenges encountered in a mature industry. In response, a number of types of new legal services providers have evolved, usually structured as companies rather than partnerships, and with clear alternative value propositions. The following section provides an overview of these new legal services providers, and contrasts them with firms that use a traditional business model.

TAXONOMY OF TODAY'S LEGAL SERVICES PROVIDERS

In summarizing the different types of legal services providers in the market today, Figure 2.1 differentiates the business models of traditional law firms, termed BigLaw, from nontraditional entities, called NewLaw, based on the key differences in how work is won, how work is done, and how an entity is governed. This taxonomy is therefore different from one grouping firms by their strategic or client orientation, as for example Bruce McEwen has suggested.[13] Remade law firms are those that have reacted to client demands and anticipated changes in an increasingly mature market for legal services by changing aspects of how work is won and how work is done, while maintaining a partnership-based governance structure. Many of them have also built an innovation portfolio, by investing in NewLaw providers through either setting up captive entities or pure legal staffing providers, or by providing commoditized Internet-based services.

The legal services market has evolved far beyond the binary (in-house department or partnership-based law firm) options that existed throughout the 20th century. And given the trends in the industry described in this chapter, we anticipate that the competitive pressures on legal services providers will increase rather than decrease. The slow pace of many incumbent law firms in reacting to these challenges provides further opportunities for new legal services providers to enter and take market share.

THE MORE FOR LESS (AND NO LONGER NEW) NORMAL

In conducting the interviews for this book, we found a strong consensus that price-down pressure from the client side in the post–global financial crisis commercial world is here to stay, even though the views differed on the exact consequences that this paradigm shift would have for BigLaw. To allude to British poet, lawyer, and cleric John Donne, no law firm is an island, any more than any man is (*And therefore never send to know for whom the bell tolls . . .*). Cost pressures on commercial clients will continue to filter through to law firms, since law is a "mature industry," as described by Michael E. Porter (a more detailed exploration of the

---

13. Bruce MacEwen, A New Taxonomy: The Seven Law Firm Business Models (Adam Smith, Esq., LLC 2014).

FIGURE 2.1

Taxonomy of Legal Services Providers

Hallmarks	Types of Legal Services Providers				
	BigLaw Firms		NewLaw Providers		
	Traditional BigLaw Firms	Remade BigLaw Firms	NewLaw Firms	LSOs and LPOs	Legal Staffing Providers
A. Primary purpose	Practice law as outside counsel			Provide legal services to clients and firms	Provide contract lawyers
B. How work is won					
B1. Brand promoted	Mainly personal	Corporate and personal	Corporate		
B2. Business development	Mostly done by practicing lawyers	Some separation of lawyers from BD	Separation of practicing lawyers from BD		
B3. Pricing risk	Borne mainly by clients	Shared with clients	Borne mainly by provider		Not applicable
C. How work is done for clients					
C1. Staffing model	Fixed cost, predominantly full-time lawyers	Mixed cost with flexible work practices	Partly variable cost, matching their supply to client demand		Completely variable cost, matching their supply to client demand
C2. Value to clients	Legal excellence, hourly rates and some AFAs	Based on commercial relevance and price certainty with AFAs			Based on price competitiveness
C3. Technology	Support individual fee earners	Substitute for lawyers where feasible			Not applicable
C4. Processes		Support 'better, faster, cheaper' legal services			
D. How a firm is governed, and managed					
D1. Ownership structure	Restricted to equity partners		Includes non-lawyers and employees	Corporate, including pure investors	
D2. Compensation	Profit share		Salaries – Incentives – Dividends		
D3. Culture	Partner- and lawyer-centric	Multidisciplinary	Corporate style		

Types of Legal Services Providers

	BigLaw Firms		NewLaw Providers		
	Traditional BigLaw Firms	Remade BigLaw Firms	NewLaw Firms	LSOs and LPOs	Legal Staffing Providers
Hallmarks	Incumbents with traditional business models that provide legal services to in-house departments and companies without legal departments.	Incumbents with remade, i.e. changed, business models including re-engineered processes, captives, commoditized online services, ownership interests in legal staffing providers, and strong branding of the firm.	Provide legal services to companies without legal departments, but also in-house departments, some recognised as 'virtual' law firms.	Provide support to in-house departments, law firms, or both, often focused on commoditized work.	Mostly provide support to in-house legal departments.
Notes | Examples	Vast majority of incumbents, typified by AmLaw200 and equivalents in other countries	Also small break-aways from traditional BigLaw firms. — Allen & Overy Seyfarth Shaw Gowlings Marque Lawyers Valorem Law — Law firms associated with the Big Four diversified professional services firms	— Bespoke Conduit Law Cognition Potomac Law Radiant Law Riverview Law Temple Bright	— AdventBalance Axiom Law CPA Global Cognia Law Elevate Exigent Radiant Law Riverview Law Captives owned by BigLaw firms	— AdventBalance Axiom Law Cognition Elevate HireCounsel Virtual Law Captives (part) owned by BigLaw firms, e.g. Agile LOD Orbit Peerpoint Vario

concept follows). Michelle Mahoney, Director of Legal Logistics at King & Wood Mallesons, sums it up:

> The GC–law firm interaction is an ecosystem. Law firms are facing the brunt of the business pressures applied on the in-house legal departments as they are hand-balled the task to make consumption of legal services more efficient.[14]

Coming from a slightly different perspective, Leon Flavell, Global Legal Services Leader at PwC, agrees that these cost-down pressures are not simply a by-product of the past recession that will vanish with a rising economic tide. In his opinion, this is partly due to more sophisticated procurement for legal services in companies. He also sees legal services provided by multidisciplinary professional services firms as well suited to providing services that produce value in this new normal.[15] Many law firms are meeting these price-down pressures by discounting, and some are meeting them by changing the way that they produce and sell legal advice. Only the latter option is sustainable in the long-term.

There is also consensus that BigLaw firms share one common feature: they are big, and with size comes a loss of agility. Whether it is the metaphor of the super-tanker under "full steam," or the 787 Dreamliner in flight, or any other complex, moving structure, they are all apt to illustrate that if law firms foresee the need to change their course in the future, even if not in the immediate future, they should start to prepare *now* to be able to change course when the time comes. Legal services consultant Ron Friedmann deems that a slower, rather than faster, pace of change in the BigLaw business model will be best suited to the majority of client in-house departments anyway:

> We do not see firms in deep trouble for the most part. From the ones that have dissolved, it is hard to draw general conclusions. Most firms are managing to muddle through hard times. We see some change, but it is happening slowly, and probably sufficiently fast for their clients, who change equally slowly. The law departments that retain larger firms are themselves service providers to their internal clients. There is little evidence that the way they, as internal service providers, operate or provide legal advice are changing any faster than at law firms. And when you look at smaller companies that retain mid-sized law firms, my guess is that they are probably not demanding rapid change either. So I do not see a collapse, but I see a lot of adjustment.[16]

Across the Pacific, and with a global perspective, Andrew Grech, Group Managing Director of Slater and Gordon Ltd. (Australia's and the world's first incorporated

---

14. Interview by George Beaton, Eric Chin, and Imme Kaschner with Michelle Mahoney, Director of Legal Logistics, King & Wood Mallesons, in Melbourne, Australia (May 1, 2014).

15. Telephone interview by George Beaton with Leon Flavell, Global Legal Services Leader, PricewaterhouseCoopers (Aug. 4, 2014).

16. Telephone interview by George Beaton with Ron Friedmann, Consultant, Fireman & Company (Aug. 14, 2014).

and publicly listed law firm, which expanded into the United Kingdom in 2012), shares the cautious optimism, but with a caveat:

> Speaking to other CEOs and general counsel, my sense is that while a premium will continue to be paid by clients for highly value-added work, in future there will be less of it and a greater demand by consumers for choice and innovative pricing. For the legal profession this means a greater demand for more disciplined project management, a more collaborative approach, and strong budget management. The fact that activity levels have improved does not mean that fee volumes for corporate law firms will increase in a directly correlated way as they have historically tended to. There are now many more options available to corporate and individual clients, and there is a greater confidence in the effectiveness of those alternatives.[17]

In later chapters, this book will explore how some of those alternative providers are meeting corporate legal demands.

DO THE RIGHT LAW

One phrase that frequently comes up, and that was used by some interviewees, was "do less law" in response to clients' demand for decreased costs. The predictable response by many lawyers when faced with this demand is some variation of "Well, sure, if clients are willing to take the risk." Such a response assumes that risk is a black-and-white, you-or-me, with-us-or-against-us concept. But reality works in shades of gray. Quantitative, in addition to qualitative, risk analysis is necessary as a basis to make decisions about the best course of action in a specific set of circumstances. Risk analysis can result in a more sophisticated understanding and management of risk. As a profession, lawyers are used to the notion that they might be liable if things go wrong—they are, after all, human. If clients demand approaches that lawyers feel are more risky than established practices, then this might need to be addressed through changes to professional liability insurance, or perhaps through contractual arrangements. But to preclude any conversation about "doing less law"—in an appropriate context and with the increased risk disclosed—as we have seen many lawyers do, is to misunderstand legal processes as a goal unto themselves, rather than as a means to an end; that is, to serve client needs in accordance with the law. A one-dimensional way of looking at legal risk is hard to reconcile with a standard business approach that sees risks as a normal part of doing business, to be assessed, quantified, contextualized with expected returns, and managed.

But there is also the possibility of setting up processes in such a manner that there is simply less need to do the expensive, court-driven type of law that may be exciting for litigation specialists, but a headache for in-house departments, by simply increasing the likelihood that ADR will be employed instead. The in-house

---

17. E-mail from Andrew Grech, Group Managing Director of Slater and Gordon Ltd (Australia's first incorporated and publicly listed law firm) to George Beaton (July 17, 2014) (on file with authors).

team at FedEx Ground provides an example of how this can be done. By researching the basis on which ADR provisions were likely to be enforced in courts across different states, the team modified vendor agreements to bring arbitration clauses in line with their findings, resulting in a reduction in general litigation expenses of about a third.[18]

There is of course the possibility that clients are simply not ready for a more preventative, "do the right law" approach, as Toby Brown of law firm Akin Gump points out:

> My experience in offensive versus defensive is that there is very little offense going on. If I reach back to experience in a previous firm in a client conversation about a regulatory issue, the fee we had proposed was, say, $25,000. We were going to do something on offense which could potentially save them hundreds of thousands of dollars down the road. And their response was "I do not have a budget for the defensive projects; what you are asking is impossible. If I went to my boss, I would not get the money for this. I have been charged with spending less money on legal services, not to find new projects to fund. They are only going to give me money to react to the legal issues they know we have right now."
>
> I think clients really need to change. If they want firms to change, they need to start changing too. They need to take that more offensive approach because that will save them a ton of money. And in terms of the law department providing value to their internal client, this will have very high value. I know clients are frustrated right now, but one of the things I think they do not often see is that they've helped build this system. They think that law firms are not being efficient and maybe not being fair with them, but the clients helped build the system. My conversations with clients always start with, "Let us work together to change it." But their internal pressures are not on change, they are on cost savings.[19]

Real change always starts with a dialogue. Doing the right law, which means sometimes doing less, or sometimes doing more law as an investment for the future, partly based on quantitative analysis of past and anticipated legal problems, needs to proceed from an open dialogue. This opens opportunities to improve outcomes for both law firms and clients, while accommodating the cost pressures commercial clients are under.

GC INSIDE: BRINGING WORK IN-HOUSE

One consequence of the cost pressures on clients has been the increasing trend to bring work in-house. Ron Friedmann comments on the ubiquity of this change:

> In the early days when I worked for Integreon and I was talking to law firms about legal process outsourcing, I would ask the question, "How many of you have ever

---

18. See Jennifer J. Salopek, *How to Launch and Sustain a Value Initiative on Multiple Fronts*, ACC VALUE CHALLENGE, http://www.acc.com/valuechallenge/valuechamps/2015champ_profilefedex.cfm.

19. Telephone interview by Eric Chin with Toby Brown, Chief Practice Officer, Akin Gump (Aug. 8, 2014).

worked for an outsourcing company or an outsourcing provider?" Very few hands would go up. Then I said "Well, isn't it fair to say that a law firm is an outsourcing provider, because your clients, by and large, are large law departments and they have a make–buy decision to make?" What we have seen since I raised that question is that the answer is yes. There is definitely more change happening in companies now—they are hiring more lawyers. The make–buy equation has changed. In every survey I see, the direction is the same, that is, more work is moving in-house.[20]

Recent survey data confirms this ongoing trend, with 67 percent of respondents indicating that they are currently losing business to corporate legal departments in-sourcing work, and an additional 24 percent of respondents seeing that as a potential threat.[21] This trend will be discussed in more detail in chapter 4. On one view, this is an interesting move, given that companies in general follow a trend to outsource functions to external providers who can complete tasks better, faster, and cheaper based on specialization and economies of scale. Yet *traditional* legal services providers in many instances seem to have failed to convince clients that they are in a position to provide services in such a manner. Looking at what this might mean for ongoing developments in the U.S. legal services industry, other jurisdictions can provide interesting perspectives. Karl Chapman, CEO of U.K. NewLaw firm Riverview Law, analyzed this situation from the point of view of an experienced provider of outsourced services:

> One theme that never ceases to shock me—and it says a lot about the market in the U.K.—is the trend for GCs to grow the size of their in-house functions. When you ask them why they are doing this, their answer is simple—it is cheaper for them to employ lawyers than use law firms. What supply chain would create a situation where it is cheaper for the customers to do it themselves? I think that this is just a short-term, unsustainable, labor arbitrage. With a few exceptions (e.g. Cisco) it will be very hard for a GC to sustain the cost savings and quality. To do so requires a fundamental change in the culture and the way in-house functions work, plus significant investment in IT. So, while today GCs may be able to do it cheaper in-house, they will never be able do it cheaper and better in the short and medium term than a professional outsourcer with a business model that has talented people (a mix of lawyers and non-lawyers), supported by great IT, and heavy R&D spend, who are underpinned by a one team culture and business insight driven by comprehensive business intelligence and data analysis.[22]

Ultimately, the make versus buy decision needs to be made by companies and law firms based on their individual circumstances. But there can be no doubt that the very structure of the legal services industry (see chapter 3) is changing as a result of clients' increasing ability to compete with law firms for work that they used to outsource to those same firms in the past.

---

20. Friedmann, *supra* note 16.
21. Altman Weil, *2015 Law Firms in Transition*, 20 (2015), http://www.altmanweil.com/dir_docs/resource/1c789ef2-5cff-463a-863a-2248d23882a7_document.pdf.
22. Karl Chapman, *BigLaw's Challenges*, in George Beaton, NewLaw New Rules (Beaton Capital 2013).

BRAVE NEW WORLD: DIGITIZATION AND TECHNOLOGY

Another trend mentioned frequently by interviewees is the rapidly growing role of, and opportunities through, technology use and digitization in legal services. This affects lawyers as end users, law firms as organizations, and the legal profession at large, in part through increasing professional obligations.

There is a great deal of public interest in technology—in this context usually referred to as artificial intelligence (AI)—taking over the work that lawyers do. The International Legal Technology Association published their most recent 2014 report, collating extensive survey evidence on what technological innovations lawyers and law-affiliated technology professionals expect in the legal technology space in the near to intermediate future. The results emphasized not AI, but rather a plethora of gadget-type solutions, including implanted and wearable devices (possibly because of a selection bias in the tech-minded respondents?).[23] On the other hand, the progressively easier availability and decreasing price of extremely powerful processors with natural language capabilities will undoubtedly lead to new solutions. IBM's Watson for law is one highly publicized example, as will be discussed in chapter 12.

Beyond that, digitization will of course continue to shape the real and virtual spaces that lawyers practice in, possibly in ways that are hard to foresee right now. Innovations like cryptocurrencies (for example, bitcoin), enabled by powerful algorithms that preserve value transfers by documenting transactions in a decentralized way, are just one example of such potentially influential technologies.[24]

Beyond end-user focused hardware, the more influential trend for law firms today is the digitization of business activities in general, causing an impact on client expectations for smarter service delivery, avoiding duplication and non-value adding processes. MIT professor Peter Weill, author of many books on the impact of digitization and strategic technology use,[25] sums up what digitization means for professional services firms, including law firms, partly based on his own earlier work with these firms:

> We call this the movement from *"place to space."* Industries go in domino, with media going first, and now we are seeing education being massively disrupted; also retail and banking. You can imagine a whole train of industries moving—professional services are in there too.
>
> . . .
>
> The general impact that digitization has on any business, particularly on a professional services business, is that *it requires it to be much more cognizant of the*

---

23. International Legal Technology Association, *Future Horizons* (May 2014), http://www.iltanet.org/MainMenuCategory/Future-Horizons.

24. *See, e.g.*, Joe Dewey & Shawn Amuial, *Blockchain Technology Will Transform the Practice of Law* (June 25, 2015) Bloomberg BNA, https://bol.bna.com/blockchain-technology-will-transform-the-practice-of-law/.

25. *See, e.g.*, Weill & Vitale, *supra* note 2.

business goals and strategies of their individual clients, and much more of a plug and play business model in a broader ecosystem. If you want your services integrated with other people's services, then give an integrated experience. Those are two major effects we see in any business.

For law firms, this means not charging to do a precedent or a contract more than once. We hear over and over again in professional services that in a digital world, clients do not want to pay for the learning of your firm, the training of your people, the writing of a contract, the design of an offering. So because of the transparency of price and cost, law firms, like every other professional service, are having trouble charging for what they used to charge for. They need to be much, much more value relevant.

The third major trend with digitization is your *transparency*. It comes with digital. It is the ability to search your own internal data, and to prepare documents, and to have reporting. Those are general trends that we see in every industry experiencing digitization, and they are happening right now in the legal industry (emphasis added).[26]

So Peter sees the legal industry as experiencing digitization in the same manner that other industries are, and with similar consequences, specifically the need to become more client-centric, more focused on a convenient service experience for clients, and more data-driven.

For the legal profession at large, a look at the American Bar Association's Bar Rules, specifically paragraph [8] of the comment to rule 1.1, makes it clear that for a lawyer today, an understanding of what technology as part of legal services can offer is no less than a matter of professional competency:

> To maintain the requisite knowledge and skill, a lawyer should keep abreast of changes in the law and its practice, including the benefits and risks associated with relevant technology, engage in continuing study and education and comply with all continuing legal education requirements to which the lawyer is subject.[27]

Andrew Perlman, a professor at Suffolk University Law School and the Chief Reporter for the ABA Commission responsible for the amended comment above, sees it as one more piece adding to changes in the profession:

> The Commission that produced those changes amended many rules on many different subjects. That particular change seems to have received a good deal of attention, even though it was not a change to the Model Rules, but rather just a comment. I think lawyers are generally paying attention to the importance of technology and want to fulfill their ethical obligations. As a practical matter, I am not sure that this change is really going to cause people who are otherwise reluctant to change to suddenly step up and realize, "Oh, my goodness, now I need to use

---

26. Telephone interview by George Beaton and Eric Chin with Peter Weill, Chairman, MIT Sloan School of Management's Center for Information Systems Research (July 22, 2014).

27. MODEL RULES OF PROFESSIONAL CONDUCT R. 1.1 cmt, *available at* http://www.americanbar.org/groups /professional_responsibility/publications/model_rules_of_professional_conduct/rule_1_1_competence /comment_on_rule_1_1.html.

expert systems and automated document assembly and legal project management." I am somewhat skeptical that this amendment is going to drive real change
by itself, but I think the amendment reflects an increasingly prevalent mindset
about the importance of technological competence in a digital age.[28]

Technology will continue to enable more efficient work styles for individual lawyers, but also ways of commoditizing legal services and delivering them directly
from the producer to the commercial end user, in addition to enabling more direct
and efficient cooperation for legal teams for complex legal problems. Digitization
is likely to have the same effects on law as on other industries, namely an increasing pressure to be aware of and meet client needs, the expectation of a seamless
and ready-to-use "plug and play" delivery, the necessity to learn new internal processes, and the need to run a lean practice and organization.

The examples of innovative technology we have observed indicate the real
change that has occurred so far is through a mixture of people, processes, and
technology to provide efficient solutions to large-volume work that lends itself to
standardization. Technological advances make it easier and cheaper to cooperate
across large distances and break down knowledge barriers by facilitating the collection, collation, and distribution of information in very short time frames. Technology makes disintermediation possible by enabling do-it-yourself tools for end
users; think about the level of sophisticated services, including contract templates
or platforms to negotiate divorce settlements that are now available on the Internet with little need for human interaction beyond the initial setup. Real-time customer reactions; 24-hour news cycles; and the demand for customized, functional
service solutions in both business-to-consumer and business-to-business interactions are the result of both the Internet and the increasing affordability and functionality of personal devices. Branding and marketing are also on the rise to cut
through information overload and cope with faster cycle times. Lawyers sell services that provide contextualized legal information, and fundamental changes in
how information can be stored, accessed, and distributed are changing the custom
and practice in the industry.

Within law firms, technological solutions today are mostly used to support the
delivery of bespoke (or custom-made) legal advice. The metrics that are applied
to information technology often revolve around user time, since this is the unit of
production (the billable hour) that largely determines revenue. Therefore, system
outages that limit user access, or help desk resolution times for user problems, or
numbers of supported end-user devices, are common examples of metrics used to
measure law firm IT productivity. They reflect an understanding of IT as an operational cost center rather than a strategic asset.

---

28. Telephone interview by Eric Chin and Imme Kaschner with Andrew Perlman, Professor of Law,
Suffolk University Law School, and Vice-Chair, ABA Commission on the Future of Legal Services (Aug.
26, 2014).

Michelle Mahoney comments on a shift toward information technology that is better adapted to support the flexible, team-focused lawyers of today, and on the limits of technological innovations:

> Projects are no longer run by IT for IT's sake, but are related to the delivery of strategic objectives of the firm. With project cycles becoming shorter, the technology needs to be agile, rather than hardware-driven. However, the ability of firms in general to invest in information technology is limited by the "profit today" mentality that prevails in law firm partnerships. Adding to this, is the challenge of limited uptake of new technological solutions by lawyers as users.[29]

Gerard Neiditsch, previously CIO at several large law firms, anticipates law firms will increasingly move to cloud service providers and away from dedicated hardware, allowing for more such agile setups. He sees disintermediation as a trend that will significantly influence not only law firms, but also in-house legal departments:

> The long-term trend affecting everyone is the loss of the middlemen in everything that is happening. All of us can look at ourselves as middlemen, other than those who provide direct service to the end-customer. Law firms are a middleman, because at the end of the day, they provide only one aspect of a transaction, namely legal advice as part of a risk-management service to their clients. When legal services can come in a form that can be consumed directly by business unit heads of an organisation, the in-house legal departments will face the same disintermediation challenge as law firms, but this is a much longer-term trend.[30]

Gerard also anticipates that technology will significantly change the way the lawyers interact with one another:

> Immersive technology is at the beginning of the S-curve. We are at the phase similar to one or two years before the launch of the iPhone. There are two or three relevant technologies that will be consolidated and commoditized. These developments are enabled by demand and innovation stemming from online gaming communities. In two to five years, virtual work environments will be a reality, and you will be able to sit down anywhere in the world as if your collaborators were sitting next to you in a virtual office. This has the potential of reducing the need for physical office space—the second highest cost item for top tier law firms.
>
> The cost of establishing megafirms of the future, which will not be based on bricks and mortar, will drop dramatically. It will become easier to aggregate lawyer networks at much lower costs. The barriers to entry for the high-end legal market will be dramatically reduced, and smaller firms with well-established brands will be able to expand and leverage those. Once the enabling technologies, which will be better than traditional video conferencing and Skype, are created and adopted, it will have profound implications on the physical work environment.[31]

---

29. Mahoney, *supra* note 14.
30. Telephone interview by Eric Chin and Imme Kaschner with Gerard Neiditsch, then CIO, Allens Linklaters (July 16, 2014).
31. *Id.*

Gerard anticipates that technology will not just change what individual lawyers do, but will rather open up the possibility of new and better ways of cooperative working, with much lower set-up and maintenance costs.

THE TALENT CHALLENGE

Many interviewees referred to the continuing challenge of recruiting talent, both lawyers as well as professionals, for related fields such as information technology, business development, and project management. Gender equity and representation, and advancement of minority groups among staff to promote equal opportunity and social justice overall, remain significant aspirations for most law firms. The challenge to persuade legal practitioners to make use of new and more efficient ways to do work was also frequently mentioned, as was the need to define more closely what work is best done by qualified lawyers as opposed to staff with other law-related qualifications. Recruiting and on-boarding staff, and in some cases even agreeing on and setting up educational courses leading to new law-related qualifications, are other aspects of the talent task faced by firms.

Developments such as the Washington State Supreme Court adopting the Limited License Legal Technician (LLLT) rule in 2012, opening the option of licensed and regulated professionals that are not lawyers eventually providing legal advice in certain areas,[32] and including the possibility of fee sharing and joint ownership of partnerships between LLLTs and lawyers[33] indicate that the regulatory framework that reserved the provision of advice, and the receipts of fees, to lawyers is beginning to soften. Such developments are likely to have an influence on how law firms will recruit and retain their talent pool, remuneration, and leadership structures.

Flexible work arrangements, with their challenges and opportunities, are also here to stay. In the same way clients want more than a one-size-fits-all service, employees will seek out opportunities to work in ways that are a good fit for their personal situations, be that caregiver responsibilities, other commitments outside of work, or simply interests that are not commensurate with an expectation of (near) unlimited physical presence at a workplace. A strong law firm brand necessitates a component of being known as an employer of choice. Information technology allowing access to relevant information, and the ability to communicate regardless of physical location, leads to both an ability and a demand from employee and employer alike for work to be done in a flexible, task-appropriate manner. At the same time, virtual work arrangements create new challenges

---

32. See, e.g., the Washington State Bar Association, http://www.wsba.org/licensing-and-lawyer-conduct/limited-licenses/legal-technicians.

33. WASHINGTON RULES OF PROFESSIONAL CONDUCT R. 5.9 (Business Structures Involving LLLT and Lawyer Ownership). *See also* Robert Ambrogi, *Washington OKs Fee Sharing and Joint Ownership Between Lawyers and LLLTs*, LAWSITES (Apr. 3, 2015), http://www.lawsitesblog.com/2015/04/washington-oks-fee-sharing-and-joint-ownership-between-lawyers-and-lllts.html.

because of a loss of unstructured interactions (think water cooler, hallway, or cafeteria conversations) that promote a shared culture, learning, peer support, and open-ended communication (think "now that I see you, did we ever figure out . . ." conversations) in high performing teams.

Beyond flexibility in full-time or part-time employment, new ways of doing legal work often rely on a reduction in fixed costs through only paying for work on an as-needed basis, necessitating changes in financial planning and life planning for freelance legal professionals. Law firms also face significant emotional and financial cost in restructuring internal processes in ways that cause the loss of jobs held by long-term employees.

Significant lateral mobility among law firm partners, and law firm strategies that seek growth through lateral hiring, continue to pose significant economic and cultural challenges for law firms, not the least because they erode a long-term focus and partners' willingness to invest in a firm, thereby limiting resources that are available for strategic innovation initiatives. In a service profession where the most significant asset, in spite of increasing commoditization, is still individuals' intellectual capital, recruiting, developing, and leveraging that asset will continue to be a significant challenge.

GLOBALIZATION

Leon Flavell comments that "globalization has seen a call by clients for legal services in multiple, often smaller countries, and law firms have responded to this by expanding off-shore."[34] The growing geographic spread of business activities is increasing complexity directly and through the greater number of jurisdictions that have to be considered for legal advice. In addition, it seems the amount of laws and regulations in developed countries only ever increases. This also applies to corporate compliance obligations, and should be contrasted with the pressure to reduce, or at least not increase, corporate legal spend to meet these obligations. Stephen Allen, Head of Marketing Strategies at DLA Piper, points out this dichotomy:

> Almost as a counter-factor to this downward pressure on costs, at the very same time we are seeing an unprecedented burgeoning and unstoppable increase in the level and complexity of regulations. The obligations to comply are more onerous, both in terms of the penalties and the requirements. Regulation happens more quickly, and therefore the responses of major corporations have to be much quicker. The quality of regulation and legislation is perhaps less than it used to be, because it is done within shorter time frames, making things even more difficult.[35]

---

34. Flavell, *supra* note 15.
35. Telephone interview by George Beaton with Stephen Allen, Head of Marketing Strategies, DLA Piper (July 29, 2014).

Increasing digitization, which allows for more efficient processing and distribution of information, and decreases the need to mirror clients' geographic footprints in law firms' physical locations, can to some extent counteract the challenges arising from globalization and increasing regulation. However, the complexity and challenge of multijurisdictional work will continue to increase.

OUTLOOK: ALTERNATIVE LAW FIRM BUSINESS STRUCTURES

The question of law firm ownership by natural or juristic persons other than lawyers has been the subject of deliberation for quite some time, most recently being debated by the American Bar Association's Commission on Ethics 20/20, with the commission declining to further develop a proposal in relation to non-lawyer ownership and relevant changes to the *ABA Model Rules of Professional Conduct* for the consideration of the House of Delegates in 2012.

Far from being resolved, however, the topic of alternative business structures is now being looked at as part of the ABA's Commission on the Future of Legal Services by the Regulatory Opportunities Working Group. The group has the specific mandate to study existing regulation innovations in the United States and abroad (notably, the United Kingdom and Australia) including alternative business structures for the delivery of legal services, as well as related developments including potential regulatory changes in Canada. This will provide a basis for recommending regulatory innovations that ultimately will improve access to "competent and affordable" legal services.[36]

Both the United Kingdom and Australia have allowed non-lawyer ownership of law firms, including incorporation, for a number of years. The following sections will provide some considerations as well as a brief overview of the overseas experiences, to provide some pointers on what a deregulated future may look like in the United States.

POSSIBLE CONFLICTS WITH CORPORATE LAW FIRM OWNERSHIP

Andrew Perlman succinctly summarizes the potential conflicts with publicly traded incorporated law firms:

> Let us take the most extreme version first and say publicly traded law firms, like Slater and Gordon. One potential concern is that lawyers might treat their clients as secondary to the interests of shareholders. I think you can overcome this potential conflict, but it is a fair question to raise: Where do your loyalties lie when you

---

36. ABA Commission on the Future of Legal Services, *Issues Paper on the Future of Legal Services*, http://www.americanbar.org/content/dam/aba/images/office_president/issues_paper.pdf.

are delivering legal services through a publicly traded corporation and have obligations to shareholders?

Issue number two is confidentiality: To what extent do your confidentiality obligations to your clients clash with public reporting requirements that come along with being a publicly traded company? You would have to manage that.

There are also related issues of attorney-client privilege: To what extent can you maintain that privilege within a publicly traded company, given that you will have non-lawyers who are also part of that corporation at a managerial level? Again, I think these issues can be addressed through appropriate regulation, but they are issues that a publicly traded company [delivering legal services] would need to resolve.

If you are talking about a publicly traded corporation that is involved in more than just the delivery of legal services, a multidisciplinary practice, then that raises other ethics issues, such as whether the non-lawyer side of the entity might try to influence the legal side. The boogeyman that you hear people raise in this context is the Arthur Andersen fiasco and Enron. The claim was that the consulting side of the practice was adversely affecting the objectivity of the accounting side of the practice. People say that if you put too many services under the same roof, then that will happen with law firms as well. If we are talking about the incorporation of law firms, and if by that we mean multidisciplinary practices, then you would have this additional layer of concern. Once again, I think you can address this through proper regulation, but it is an issue that would need to be addressed.[37]

The question of conflicting duties to the client and the shareholder arises in a slightly different manner in Australia, as the primary duty of the legal practitioner is to the court. Steve Mark AM, former Legal Services Commissioner of the Australian state of New South Wales, illustrates this potential dilemma:

> For example, where an incorporated legal practice decides to settle a major piece of litigation because they decide it is in the best interest of the client to do so, the practices shareholders may suffer the loss of a potential profit. Under the Corporations Act, the shareholder could sue the directors for such a decision. The challenge for regulators of the legal profession is to ensure, to the extent possible, that a lawyer's primary duty to the Court or the client will prevail in any clash with a director's duty to the corporation and shareholders.[38]

Steve further comments on the different approaches in Australia and the United Kingdom in avoiding conflicts between legal professional obligations and obligations under corporations law:

> This goes to the core principles of the legal profession. One of the small distinction, albeit a consequential one, is the way in which the English and the Australian models differ on the alternative business structure, even though we do not even

---

37. Perlman, *supra* note 28.

38. Steve Mark, *A Short Paper and Notes on the Issue of Listing of Law Firms in New South Wales*, at 10, http://www.olsc.nsw.gov.au/Documents/notes_for_joint_nobc_aprl_aba_panel.pdf.

use that term in Australia. One of the things we do here is to allow law firms to be incorporated, multidisciplinary, or otherwise.

What the English do is they look at the external ownership of law firms. And so the two jurisdictions approached this from two different philosophical perspectives. The English view of external ownership means the focus is on due diligence and the "fit and proper" test, applied to whoever will own the shares. The process in Australia is that this does not matter, we apply the legal ethics of the lawyers to everyone in the firm, whether they are lawyers or not, under the "proper management system" approach. That is why it is not material in Australia who owns the shares, because they do not have a controlling interest in telling lawyers what to do—*the primary duty for everyone is to the Court.* That is why this primary duty is so important. We worked with Slater and Gordon on their constituent documents before they listed, and the hierarchy of duty has been taken to England with them. In a sense, we have turned the corporation law on its head, because the primary duty is to the Court, and not shareholders or the entity (emphasis added).[39]

Steve's comments highlight that there is a possibility that legal professional obligations and obligations of an officer of a company under the Australian Corporations Act 2001 (Cth) might conflict. A lawyer's choices in such a situation might later be open to scrutiny from all sides, and could give rise to professional liability claims. At this point, though, we are not aware of any matter having arisen in this regard in Australia.

DEREGULATION: EXPERIENCE IN AUSTRALIA

Australia and the United Kingdom are in the vanguard for legal services deregulation. Both jurisdictions provided new answers to the question of how the delivery of legal services may be structured beyond traditional partnerships of lawyers. Increasing competition in a market is mostly regarded as beneficial for individual and corporate consumers, and the market for legal services is no exception. Lowering barriers to entry by deregulation can be an effective tool to increase market competition. Deregulation's two main effects on law firms in those two jurisdictions are to provide the option of a corporate structure and to allow non-lawyer ownership. It has provided a proof of principle that it can be done without the sky falling in, prompting consideration and assessment of this option in other jurisdictions. It also provides an opportunity for law firms to consider the potential benefits of incorporation and access to external capital, and how firms might be able to achieve similar benefits through parallel entities in jurisdictions that do not (currently) allow incorporation.

In 2001, the Australian state of New South Wales (N.S.W.) became the world's first common law jurisdiction to allow law firms to pursue alternative business

---

39. Telephone interview by George Beaton and Eric Chin with Steve Mark and Tahlia Gordon (Aug. 20, 2014).

structures as multidisciplinary or incorporated practices.[40] The provisions allowing full incorporation of legal services were slowly adopted in other states and territories, following the N.S.W. example.

The principal legislation in N.S.W. was the Legal Profession Act 2004 (LPA-NSW) and the dependent Legal Profession Regulations 2005. The Act permitted a legal service provider to incorporate and provide legal services either alone or alongside other legal service providers who may or may not be legal practitioners.[41] Similar provisions in other states and territories of Australia were enacted first by Victoria (as an amendment to the now superseded Legal Profession Act 2004),[42] followed by the Australian Capital Territory (Legal Profession Act 2006) and the Northern Territory (Legal Practitioners Act 2006).[43] Queensland (Legal Profession Act 2007)[44] and Tasmania (Legal Profession Act 2007)[45] joined the deregulation stream soon afterwards, followed by Western Australia (amending the Legal Practice Act 2003)[46] and South Australia (amending the Legal Practitioners Act 1981).[47] Uniform laws relating to the legal profession came into force in 2015 in the states of Victoria and N.S.W., covering about 70 percent of practicing Australian lawyers. The Legal Profession Uniform Law unequivocally states that legal services may be provided under any business structure (subject to the act), and that the legal and professional obligations of legal practitioners and law practices are not influenced by the chosen business structure.[48]

The LPA-NSW gave legal service providers the ability to register as a company with the Australian Securities and Investments Commission (ASIC), which oversees compliance with the Corporations Act 2001 (Cth).[49] For the first time in Australian legal history, law firms could incorporate, share receipts, and provide legal services, either alone or with other service providers who may or may not be lawyers. An incorporated law firm still had to appoint at least one lawyer as director, responsible for both managing legal services and ensuring that those services complied with the professional obligations of lawyers under the LPA-NSW, regulated by the Office of the Legal Services Commissioner.

---

40. The population estimate of N.S.W. was 7.2 million in 2012 compared to 23.6 million of Australia overall in 2014. See the World Population Review at http://worldpopulationreview.com/countries /australia-population/.

41. *Legal Profession Act 2004* (NSW) pt 2.6, ss 135–164 (Austl.).

42. *Legal Profession Act 2004* (Vic) pt 2.7.4–2.7.35 (Austl.).

43. *Legal Profession Act 2006* (ACT) pt 2.6 (Austl.); *Legal Practitioners Act 2006* (NT) pt 2.6 (Austl.) (commenced 31/03/07, replacing *Legal Practitioners Amendment (Incorporated Legal Practices & Multidisciplinary Partnerships) Act 2003* (NT) (Austl.), commenced Jan. 5, 2004).

44. *Legal Profession Act 2007* (Qld) pt 2.7 (Austl.) (provisions were originally inserted in 2003 but only came into effect when the 2007 Act commenced on Jan. 7, 2007).

45. *Legal Profession Act 2007* (Tas) pt 2.5 (Austl.).

46. *Legal Practice Act 2003* (WA) ss 45–74 (Austl.).

47. *Legal Practitioners Act 1981* (SA), s 24 and sch 1 (Austl.).

48. *Legal Profession Uniform Law* ss 32, 33 (Austl.) (enacted in Victoria under the *Legal Profession Uniform Law Application Act 2014* (Vic) (Austl.), and in N.S.W. under the *Legal Profession Uniform Law Application Act 2014* (NSW) (Austl.)).

49. *Corporations Act 2001* (Cth) (Austl.), *available at* http://www.austlii.edu.au/au/legis/cth/consol_act /ca2001172/.

During the past ten years, the number of ILPs has grown steadily in N.S.W.[50] Steve Mark, N.S.W. Legal Services Commissioner from 1994 until 2013, describes the early days of deregulation:

> As soon as incorporation was allowed in Australia, 300 small law practices became incorporated within the first six months. We went around with Law Cover [provider of professional indemnity cover for lawyers in N.S.W.], and ran seminars for the new solicitor directors. The issue was that most of them became incorporated for the wrong reasons. Once these solicitor directors received really good accountancy and actuarial advice, and understood the duties of a solicitor director, they realised it was not all that useful. The big firms, however, were looking at it from a business perspective. Most of the firms were doing just fine, not needing a capital injection from the public.[51]

In 2004, the LPA-NSW was changed again to permit non-lawyer equity investment in law firms.[52] The solicitor-director was assigned several additional duties, one of which was the requirement that the solicitor-director ensure that the incorporated legal practice has appropriate management systems for compliance in place.[53] Failure to comply can amount to professional misconduct for the lawyers.[54] According to an empirical assessment of deregulation in N.S.W.,[55] the management systems have proven to be very helpful for incorporated legal practices in N.S.W. Declining complaint rates by clients and self-assessment ratings completed by the incorporated legal practices are the basis for this conclusion.

DEREGULATION: THE U.K. EXPERIENCE

The Legal Services Act 2007 (U.K.) (LSA) changed the market for legal services in the United Kingdom. It enabled new forms of legal practices to develop in the form of legal disciplinary practices (LDPs) that could involve different kinds of lawyers and up to 25 percent non-lawyers, but were only allowed to provide legal services; and in the form of alternative business structures (ABS) that enabled external ownership of legal businesses and multidisciplinary practices.[56] From October 2011 onward, firms were able to apply for a licence to become an alternative business structure firm, although the Solicitors Regulation Authority (SRA) did not start to accept applications until January 2012. The main effect was that U.K. firms

---

50. Office of the Legal Services Commissioner, LSC, *2012–13 Annual Report, see* http://www.olsc.nsw.gov.au/Pages/lsc_publications/lsc_annualreports.aspx.

51. Mark and Gordon, *supra* note 39.

52. Justin D. Petzold, *Firm Offers: Are Publicly Traded Law Firms Abroad Indicative of the Future of the United States Legal Sector?*, 1 Wɪs. L. Rᴇᴠ. 67, 69 (2009).

53. *Legal Profession Act 2004* (NSW) s 140(3) (Austl.).

54. *Id.*

55. Christine Parker, Tahlia Ruth Gordon & Steve A. Mark, *Regulating Law Firms Ethics Management: An Empirical Assessment of the Regulation of Incorporated Legal Practices in New South Wales*, 37(3) J. L. & Soc. 466 (2010).

56. The City UK, *Professional Services Series: Legal Services*, 4 (Jan. 2014), *available at* http://www.thecityuk.com/research/our-work/reports-list/legal-services-2014/.

were able to seek investment from third parties, including corporations. This has opened up the option of external ownership of law firms, and the delivery of legal services by businesses that are not traditional law firms.

The LSA has (not necessarily disparagingly) been referred to as "Tesco Law," referring to a large U.K. supermarket chain. The idea that legal services would be as widely and easily available as groceries, and possibly in similar locations and from the same providers, holds some appeal, certainly for consumers. Tesco has not sought an ABS licence, but the Co-Operative Group supermarket chain has, and its application was approved in March 2012.

The number of incorporated law firms in the United Kingdom has grown steadily since 2007. By June 2014, 32 percent of legal practices functioned as limited companies.[57] According to figures published by the SRA, as of June 2014, 3,424 of the 10,571 U.K. law firms were incorporated, compared to 3,064 a year before. In comparison, the number of limited liability partnerships (LLPs) has remained roughly the same during the same period—1,552 (14 percent) in June 2013 and 1,589 (15 percent) in June 2014. The numbers of traditional partnerships and sole practitioners both fell by nearly 10 percent, to 2,508 from 2,941, respectively.[58] This trend is likely to continue, according to a survey conducted by Deloitte and Winmark in 2012, which indicated that almost half of the respondents anticipated using the ABS regime in the coming years.[59] While these trends have yet to affect the "big end of town" among corporate and commercial law firms, there can be little doubt that a "trickle-up" effect will bring changes made possible by deregulation, as clients drive change and firms learn new ways.

Overall, the experiences with incorporation of law firms in Australia and the United Kingdom are positive. There is a need to consider how the professional duties of a lawyer will be reconciled with other obligations under new regulatory frameworks, but, so far, potential conflicts have been shown to be manageable. We anticipate the number of jurisdictions opening up the options of multidisciplinary practices and external law firm ownership through corporate structures will continue to increase. The Canadian Bar Association's June 2013 paper, *The Future of Legal Services in Canada: Trends and Issues*, for example, was intended as a starting point for discussion on how to best respond to a number of forces driving change in the legal marketplace.[60] The report acknowledges that the global trends of deregulation of legal firm ownership could "migrate to Canada as markets become more closely connected and competition increases." It further states that

---

57. See the monthly updated Solicitors Regulation Authority figures at http://www.sra.org.uk/sra/how-we-work/reports/data/solicitor_firms.page.

58. *Id.*

59. The City UK, *supra* note 58, at 5.

60. The Canadian Bar Association, *The Future of Legal Services in Canada: Trends and Issues* (June 2013), *available at* http://www.cbafutures.org/cba/media/mediafiles/pdf/reports/trends-isssues-eng.pdf?ext=.pdf.

[l]iberalization of law firm ownership may spread to other countries despite being rejected recently in the American Bar Association's Commission on Ethics 20/20. From a regulatory standpoint there will likely be a need to seriously consider permitting non-lawyer ownership of legal practices, as well as finding ways to require lawyers to adhere to their code when working in non-traditional areas. With publicly traded companies such as Slater and Gordon in Australia already in existence, this will require thoughtful assessment of the impact of non-lawyer ownership on competence, conflicts of interest, confidentiality, independence, fidelity to law and other issues.[61]

BENEFITS OF INCORPORATION FOR LAW FIRMS

At this point, direct incorporation with its access to external equity capital and possibility of instituting corporate governance is not an option for law firms in most jurisdictions. But some of the benefits of incorporation can accrue to law firms through buying stakes in other entities or setting up captive service providers, and are therefore worth considering. Andrew Grech, lawyer and Group Managing Director of Slater and Gordon is in a unique position to answer the question what the benefits of incorporation for law firms are:

> *The better question is—what is the strategy of the firm concerned?* Structure should follow that. A decade on from our own corporatization, I can say that it has provided us with the organizational decision making and capital agility required to achieve our evolving strategic goals. I doubt we would have been as successful as an organization and therefore been able to accelerate the journey we are on to achieve our mission—to provide people with easier access to world class legal services, had we not incorporated and listed.
>
> It is not my experience that incorporation itself makes it harder to either formulate or execute strategy. On the contrary, my experience has been that it makes it easier.
>
> Structure follows strategy. Be open to *all* the options that may enable your organization to achieve its purpose. Be careful not to confuse the career aspirations and personal preferences of the current incumbent owners with the mission of the organization. That is not strategy—it is career planning at best, and a bunch of lawyers simply sharing overheads disguised as an enterprise with purpose at worst. Whilst I think to some extent it is true that there is very little (beyond raising capital from the public and tax effectively reinvesting earnings) that you can do as a company that you cannot do as a partnership, in my experience, corporatization tends to encourage higher standards of governance, a greater sense of strategic discipline, and greater decision making agility, and therefore effective execution.
>
> . . .

---

61. *Id*, at 36.

> There really are not too many incorporated firms who publish sufficient information to make an informed judgment, but there is published data which suggests that incorporated firms have a lower incidence of client complaints than unincorporated firms—which is a step in the right direction for the profession overall. I have seen many examples of firms incorporated and unincorporated which stand out in both the U.K. and Australia. In all cases, the key differentiator was a clearly articulated strategy based on strongly held and lived and shared professional and business values.[62]

In Andrew's experience, the benefits of incorporation depend on a clear strategy and values. Incorporation facilitated this, partly through the availability of external investment capital for the firm's expansion and partly through transparent accountability. Law firms with an innovation agenda can similarly consider setting up external corporations that attract external investment, for example for online law-related services that do not constitute the giving of legal advice.

CONCLUSION

The legal services industry today shows all the characteristics of being mature, and incumbent law firms are under pressure from each other, new entrants, a variety of new types of legal services providers, clients, and suppliers. Industry growth at a level to which the traditional law firm business model was well adapted is unlikely to return. Pervasive trends of price-down and cost pressures, technology use and digitization, talent challenges, globalization, and deregulation will continue to shape the market for decades to come. Firms that are trying to adapt need to make significant changes in their business model. There is little to add to *ABA Legal Journal* "Rebel" Jeff Carr's comment:

> The organized bar and many lawyers can catch the train, miss the train, or get hit by the train. But make no mistake, the train is driven by today's legal consumer—the customer—and it has left the station. The time is now, the choice is ours.[63]

---

62. Email from Andrew Grech, *supra* note 17.
63. Jeff Carr, *The Profession Is Doomed*, 3 Geeks and a Law Blog (Feb. 12, 2015), http://www.geeklaw blog.com/2015/02/the-profession-is-doomed.html.

Chapter 3

Porter's Five Forces and Maister Maxed Out

Key Points

- Application of Michael E. Porter's five forces framework shows incumbent traditional law firms under unrelenting pressures from hypercompetition with each other, backward integrating clients, NewLaw substitutes, lawyers who have more power in supplying their talent, and the entry of new firms. The industry is now truly and irreversibly mature, which has profound, mainly adverse, consequences for BigLaw firms that do not respond and remake their business models.
- A case study illustrates why strategies that rely on pulling the levers in David Maister's formula for law firm profitability are no longer a sustainable way forward.

INTRODUCTION

The previous chapter provided an overview of the origin and limitations of the BigLaw business model, a taxonomy of BigLaw firms and NewLaw providers, and a discussion of the ongoing industry trends of

- a demand for more for less;
- a need to "do the right law," that is, adjust resource allocation based on looking not only at the single matter, but also at the underlying system, and possibly invest in prevention;
  - an increasing role for information technology, and digitization, in the practice of law;
  - the talent challenge, that is, the need to attract and retain a diversity of human resources, frequently accommodating the demand for flexible work practices, while reducing fixed labor costs;
  - globalization; and
- deregulation.

We now bring these different facets together by providing a conceptual summary of the legal services industry today, based on Michael E. Porter's five forces framework.

THE FRAMEWORK

Renowned business theorist and Harvard Business School professor Michael E. Porter formulated an enduring framework for analysis of the forces driving competition in an industry in 1980.[1] Stephen Mayson applied this framework to the legal services industry in 1997. He considered that industry competitors (that is, other law firms) were threatened to some degree by both potential entrants and substitutes, and were subject to the bargaining power of buyers (the clients) and suppliers (the lawyers who produce the legal services that a law firm sells), but, overall, these forces were not particularly adverse.[2]

At that time, Mayson considered that the threat from new entrants, among which he listed multinational firms and multidisciplinary practices arising from accounting firms, was limited, mainly due to "barriers to mobility" that prevented firms from switching between different segments of the market. Examples of such segments are litigation and transactions, client industries, or areas of law on which boutique firms focus. Today, the ongoing threat of new entrants is an important factor limiting incumbent firms, as many law firms operate on a truly international scale, and the Big Four accounting firms are increasing their diversification and building substantial legal groups with capabilities that rival many traditional, large law firms.

Mayson enumerated some potential substitute products for traditional legal services, namely "do-it-yourself wills and conveyancing products," and technology, specifically expert systems and litigation support systems, though he did not provide any specific examples. His choice of potential substitute products makes it clear that the focus at the time was on consumer legal needs. Mayson pointed out that substitution would limit the profits that can be derived from the work that is potentially subject to substitution. Today, a large variety of sophisticated substitute legal services for in-house legal departments and corporations without legal departments has evolved. These substitute services now constitute a significant threat to BigLaw firms.

Mayson pointed to clients' size and sophistication as relevant factors contributing to the growing bargaining power of buyers. Clients' ability to generate services themselves, so-called backward integration, also increases their bargaining

---

1. Michael E. Porter, Competitive Strategy: Techniques for Analyzing Industries and Competitors 3–5 (The Free Press 1980).
2. Stephen Mayson, Making Sense of Law Firms 62–67 (Blackstone Press 1997). *See also* the brief pieces by Patrick Fuller, *Porter's Five Forces Applied to the Legal Industry* (2015), http://www.elite.com/article/bd/porter-five-forces; and Frank Strong, *Porter's Five Forces for the Legal Industry*, http://businessoflawblog.com/2014/05/porter-five-forces/.

power, since it limits the price that they are willing to pay for a service to one that is lower than their own cost in producing such a service. Today, a pervasive trend of bringing work in-house (see chapter 2) makes it clear that backward-integrated clients now possess huge bargaining power.

On the other side of the bargaining equation, Mayson listed qualified lawyers as the most important suppliers. The heated competition for star lateral hires among large commercial firms and the sums and risks involved in recruiting them are indicators of the bargaining power these "suppliers" wield. The advent of other legal services suppliers (see chapter 10) could decrease bargaining power for providers of a different segment of law firm supply—that is, lower-complexity work often done by junior associates. But in order to take advantage of that, law firms have to be willing to forego the profits that accrue to the firm through the work these junior trainees do that is charged to clients. Starting salaries for legal graduates are high compared to, for example, similarly demanding professions with high workloads for junior trainees, such as medicine. In numbers, first-year medical doctors in the United States earned about $51,000 in 2014.[3] Participants in the first legal residency program for legal graduates, jointly launched by four U.S. law schools and legal outsourcer UnitedLex Corp, earned between $55,000 and $70,000 depending on where they worked.[4] Graduates at top-tier law firms, on the other hand, can start out at salaries of $160,000.[5] Law firms are likely to say that even though the supply of graduate lawyers far exceeds their demand, they are only able to recruit the absolute top talent that their standard of work demands by paying these salaries. An alternative view is that because the rates that law firms charge for the work of their junior and senior associates per time are multiples of their salaries, paying higher salaries from the start makes business sense. If this is correct, then law firms cannot simply decrease cost pressure by paying their junior talent less or sourcing that work elsewhere at market rates. They can only increase profits through sourcing cheaper supplies from alternative legal services providers if they change their pricing model from time based to results based (see chapter 9).

In summary, applying Porter's five forces model to the legal industry today clearly shows that the incumbent law firms are facing a perfect storm of pressures from new entrants, substitutes, clients, suppliers, and competing peers.

---

3. Medscape, *Residents Salary & Debt Report 2014*, http://www.medscape.com/features/slideshow /public/residents-salary-and-debt-report#4.

4. Erin E. Harrison, *Four U.S. Law Schools and UnitedLex Launch Legal Residency Program*, LEGALTECH NEWS (May 28, 2015), http://www.legaltechnews.com/id=1202727711964/Four-US-Law-Schools-and-UnitedLex -Launch-Legal-Residency-Program?mcode=0&curindex=0&curpage=ALL&slreturn=20150517214828.

5. Susan Adams, *Law Schools Whose Grads Make the Highest Starting Salaries*, FORBES BLOG (Mar. 28, 2014), http://www.forbes.com/sites/susanadams/2014/03/28/law-schools-whose-grads-make-the-highest -starting-salaries/.

LAW IS A MATURE INDUSTRY

In addition to his enduring framework for setting out the forces that shape an industry, Porter also described predictable stages in the life cycle of an industry. In 1980 he published his hypothesis that any industry passes through the defined stages of introduction, growth, maturity, and decline. The hallmark of a good hypothesis in a scientific sense is that it can be empirically tested. Porter's depiction of the dynamic processes that occur in a mature industry is an accurate description of what is happening in the legal industry today in regard to service commoditization, excess capacity, buyer sophistication, and price-focused competition.[6] Our own Beaton Benchmarks data based on annual large-scale surveys of corporate clients of professional services firms in Australia indicates that buyers' perception of the price level of legal services has been steadily declining from 2008 to 2014 (see Figure 3.1). Lest these year-on-year declines appear small to the reader's eye, we note that most are statistically significant and the trend is in one direction.

Falling prices are a hallmark of a mature industry. The consequences of competing in a mature industry for law firms are manifold. As Porter wrote:

> When it occurs, the transition to maturity is nearly always a critical period for companies in an industry. It is a period during which fundamental changes often take place in companies' competitive environment, requiring difficult strategic responses. Firms sometimes have trouble perceiving these environmental changes

FIGURE 3.1

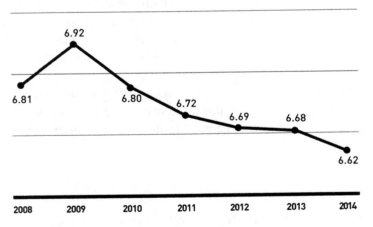

Clients' Perceptions of Fees Charged

6.92

6.81   6.80
        6.72
            6.69   6.68
                        6.62

2008   2009   2010   2011   2012   2013   2014

Q. "How would you rate the fees charged by [Firm] over the last 12 months, where 0 = 'extremely low fees' and 10 = 'extremely high fees'

---

6. *See* PORTER, *supra* note 1, 156–188, 237–253. *See also* Stephen Mayson's application of Porter's model to the legal services industry in the 1990s: MAYSON, *supra* note 2, at 82–86.

clearly: even when they are perceived, responding to them can require changes in strategy that firms balk at making. Moreover, the impact of transition to maturity extends beyond strategic considerations, holding implications for the organizational structure of the firm and the role of its leadership. These administrative implications are at the heart of some of the difficulties in making the required strategic adjustments.[7]

Written more than 30 years ago, these words are directed to today's generation of BigLaw firm leaders. Better fasten your seatbelts, because in a mature industry, you are in for a bumpy ride. The following case study illustrates how the pressures at industry level manifest for a typical law firm. Industry trends shape the foreseeable future of this firm that emerged from the 2008–2009 financial crisis well ahead of its peers. By relying on David Maister's equation for driving profitability, the firm has reached the end of the road, and must be remade to sustain its performance and relevance.

CASE STUDY: MAISTER MAXED OUT

This case study illustrates the challenges that traditional business model law firms face today. In 1993, David Maister published his influential book *Managing the Professional Services Firm.*[8] Chapter 3 is entitled *Profitability: Health and Hygiene,* and in it Maister sets out a formula to calculate the profit of a professional services firm. This formula has been extremely influential in shaping law firms' profitability strategies:

$$PPP = \frac{(EP\,(1+L) \times U{\times}R \times BBR) - TE}{EP}$$

- Utilization (U) is the number of hours per fee-earner per year charged and recovered from clients. In the formula, U is multiplied by Recovery (R), as not all recorded hours are fully recovered at the firm's budgeted rate. U is commonly reported as the recovered utilization, reflecting discounts, write-offs, and write-ons of recorded time; thus R is not reported separately. Total utilization (TU) is the total number of hours per year charged and recovered by all fee-earners.

- Total expenses (TE) are all the costs incurred in generating the firm's income. The largest expenses are salaries, premises, information technology, and professional indemnity insurance.

- Leverage (L) is the number of FTE fee-earners, which may include chargeable paralegals, for each FTE equity partner of the firm. Depending on the nature of a firm's clients and services, leverage may range from zero in a solo practice to over ten with high volume, repetitive work.

---

7. PORTER, *supra* note 1, at 237–238.
8. DAVID H. MAISTER, MANAGING THE PROFESSIONAL SERVICES FIRM (Simon & Schuster 1993).

- Blended billing rate (BBR) is calculated by dividing the firm's annual fee income by the total recovered utilization, in other words, all hours recovered in a year by all fee-earners.

- Equity points (EP) on issue are the total number of profit units owned by the current (equity) partners. Income (i.e., nonequity, salaried, or general) partners are employees and are counted in TE.

Maister classified U and TE as hygiene factors. "Hygiene" was applied to U and TE because these are short-run profit drivers, readily responsive to being managed (hence "today's business") to reach their natural respective upper and lower bounds.

L and BBR were described as "health" factors because these are long-run profit drivers. Increases in L and BBR require substantial behavioral changes, especially by partners, in their practice leadership, staff supervision, specialization, and marketing. Profit, calculated by subtracting total expenses (i.e., TE) from revenue (i.e., EP (1 + L) $\times$ U $\times$ R $\times$ BBR), is distributed to the equity partners (EP) in proportion to their share of the equity points, giving rise to a profit per partner (PPP) average.

Guided by Maister, BigLaw firm leaders have long relied on these five levers—leverage, utilization, blended billing rate, total expenses, and equity on issue—to manage performance, pricing of their services, and allocation of resources. Getting the mix of these levers—or factors—right remains the mainstay of producing and distributing profit in BigLaw firms. Figure 3.2 describes a very well managed, traditional mid-sized law firm. Maister's profit levers have been analyzed for the 11 years 2004–2014. To avoid the global financial crisis (GFC) and year-on-year fluctuations distorting the results, two averaged four-year periods before and after the GFC were used.

As happened in many firms, the GFC caused a major reexamination of how the firm was managed. In 2009 leadership adopted a "squeeze the lemon" strategy, meaning that they intended to drive every Maister lever as hard as possible, including reducing the number of equity partners.

By 2011 profitability had been restored and was sustained for the next three years, evidenced in the following comparison of the 2011–2014 averages with 2004–2007 averages:

- On the top line revenue was up 10 percent and revenue per lawyer (RPL) up 11 percent;

- In spite of the 10 percent increase in revenue, FTE was down by 15 percent;

- L was up 20 percent, achieved by holding lawyer FTE constant and deequitizing;

- U went up by 9 percent;

- BBR was steady, that is, the firm had managed to avoid discounting its fees;

- TE was down 2 percent, thanks to a reduction in occupancy cost (by reducing floor area per lawyer by 34 percent) and cutbacks in shared services staff. Lawyer salaries were almost unchanged.

"Squeezing the lemon" resulted in a 52 percent increase in PPP by 2014, lifting the firm well into the top decile of its peer group. The remaining equity partners understandably felt they had cause for celebration, and in many ways they did. But at the same time, the results of their diligence and sacrifice marked the end of an era.

FIGURE 3.2

Profit Levers Analysis

		2004-2007 average	2011-2014 average	% change	2015+ trend
Revenue (Fees/Year $)	Rev	87,250,000	96,066,500	10%	Little or no growth
Total lawyers (FTE)	TL	233	232	0%	No growth
Revenue per lawyer (= Rev ÷ TL $)	RPL	374,843	414,538	11%	Little or no growth
Total equity partners (FTE)	EP	39.5	33.7	-15%	Steady or small declines
Leverage (= [TL - EP]/EP)	L	4.9	5.9	20%	No change
Utilization (Hours recovered/ lawyer/year)	U	1,479	1,618	9%	Little or no growth
Blended billing rate (Realized revenue/ hour = Rev/TU $)	BBR	253	254	0%	Steady declines
Total expenses $	TE	54,007,500	52,923,893	-2%	Little or no reduction
Profit per equity partner $	PPP	843,430	1,281,703	52%	Steady declines from peak

For the first meeting of 2015, prompted by Aric Press's article *Big Law's Reality Check*,[9] the firm's Executive Committee produced what is shown in Figure 3.3, with the added "2015 + trend" column on the right side of the table.

Aric's 2014 analysis showed that only 10 percent of firms in the AmLaw 200 firms had improved their performance since 2008, and the firm here fell into that group. But extrapolating the dynamic in the Maister levers in accordance with the predicted trends (see Figure 3.3), the partners also saw that they had maxed out on each lever. PPP was at record levels, and yet the future did not look promising.

BBR would start to fall, driven down by hypercompetition and client pressures, causing PPP to fall in parallel, all other levers being held constant. Further EP reductions might delay that day, but just how few owners did a firm turning over nearly $100 million need? What about partner cover during holidays, let alone questions of succession and continuity? Some partners already viewed L as dangerously high from quality

---

9. Aric Press, *Big Law's Reality Check*, THE AMERICAN LAWYER BLOG (Oct. 29, 2014).

FIGURE 3.3

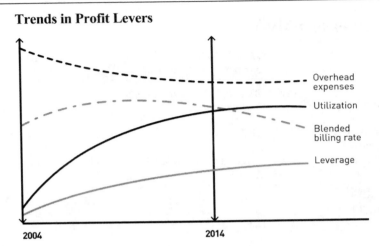

Trends in Profit Levers

- Overhead expenses
- Utilization
- Blended billing rate
- Leverage

2004   2014

and professional indemnity perspectives. A little more U would also delay the decline. Or maybe a few more shared services staff could be cut—did the firm really need all those HR and marketing people?

Ultimately, their own analysis led the partners to conclude that the only way forward was to address what is missing in Maister's formula—*the value provided to clients*. This changed approach provided a basis to reassess how work was attracted, produced, and priced by the firm. This reorientation marked the start on the path to sustainable future profitability: the remaking of this law firm's business model.

CONCLUSION

The legal services industry today shows all the characteristics of being mature, and incumbent law firms are under pressure from each other, new entrants, a variety of new types of legal services providers, clients, and suppliers. Industry growth at a level to which the traditional law firm business model was well adapted is unlikely to return. Pervasive trends of price-down and cost pressures, technology use and digitization, talent challenges, globalization, and deregulation will continue to shape the market for decades to come. Maister's traditional formula for determining law firm profitability, suggesting that profit can be increased at any point by driving any of the levers harder, is simply maxed out. Firms that are trying to adapt instead need to make significant changes in their business models.

Chapter 4

Clients of the Future

Key Points

- The role of the in-house corporate lawyer today is increasingly that of a strategic business advisor. The community of in-house lawyers is becoming more diverse, and is developing an increasingly trans-jurisdictional focus.
- Clients are more discerning and seek value beyond mere price reductions; drivers of client behavior are not always intuitive. Where relevant, clients expect a uniform international experience from their outside counsel.
- The growth of in-house departments parallels a reduction in external legal expenditure with the allocation of the remaining spend depending on the nature of the work and on internal and market data analytics. Spending is more consolidated through panels and other means to maximize clients' buying power and the benefits of long-term co-operation between clients and their external providers. Procurement professionals are increasingly involved in selecting outside counsel.
- Client companies without in-house legal departments offer growth opportunities for law firms. Rapidly scaling start-up companies are a subset of these that need legal services that meet their needs over the company lifecycle.

INTRODUCTION

Today's BigLaw firms mainly sell their services to corporate commercial clients who may or may not have internal legal departments. Company legal departments are far from uniform. Companies in certain industries, financial services for example, tend to have comparatively large in-house departments. Approximately half the members of the Association of Corporate Counsel (ACC) are lawyers from legal departments with five or fewer lawyers.[1] This reflects the typical size of corporate

---

1. Michael Roster, *ACC Value Challenge: Facing Up to the Challenge—The Transition* (Association of Corporate Counsel 2013) 3, https://www.acc.com/advocacy/valuechallenge/loader.cfm?csModule =security/getfile&pageid=1365193&page=/valuechallenge/index.cfm&qstring=&title=ACC%20Value%20 Challenge%3A%20Facing%20Up%20to%20the%20Challenge%20-%20Law%20Firm%20Metrics.

law departments, although that doesn't mean the companies themselves are small entities. Many have revenues or sales exceeding a billion dollars, but they have chosen to have a limited number of in-house lawyers, or their legal problems are in fact well contained. Company size and revenue partly determine the size of legal departments; HBR Consulting recently found a median number of 3.6 in-house lawyers (and 6.8 total legal staff) in large corporations per billion dollars of revenue.[2]

The Australian Corporate Lawyers Association (ACLA) in its 2012 CLO Survey, which it considered representative, found that the turnover of organizations with in-house lawyers started at AU$1 million.[3] It also found that 17 percent of organizations in the sample only had one lawyer, 42 percent had two to four, and 26 percent had five to ten,[4] not dissimilar to U.S. numbers.

Looking at our own Beaton Benchmarks data from Australia, we have seen companies with lawyers on staff that are much smaller than a AU$1 million turnover. These lawyers might of course provide services to the company that are not of a strictly legal nature, such as those of the company secretary and risk management, or might simply not act for the company in a legal capacity.

Many large companies have a constant need for legal expertise to do business. Their in-house departments deal with legal work of varying complexity and volume, and today's legal ecosystem offers them a variety of resources to utilize in serving their internal clients. There are clear trends of in-house departments seeking to reduce their external spend, while bringing the work in-house and growing in size to achieve this.[5] These combined trends alone suffice to call into question any law firm strategy that is simply built on the premise of continuous growth, at least without growth in the broader economy, which may or may not happen. It is worth noting that the U.S. economy has grown under 2 percent on average over the past ten years.[6] Without accessing new markets and clients, an organic growth strategy will not be feasible for the majority of firms because of a lack of demand growth. Based on Thomson Reuters Peer Monitor data, demand growth in the U.S. legal industry since 2010 has been hovering between 1 percent and occasionally even turning negative, with a moderate 0.5 percent for 2014.[7]

---

2. BusinessWire, *Total Legal Spending Up by 2 Percent Worldwide According to HBR Consulting's 2014 Law Department Survey* (Oct. 1, 2014), http://www.businesswire.com/news/home/20141001005951/en /Total-Legal-Spending-2-Percent-Worldwide-HBR#.VNrTXPmUfK0.

3. Australian Corporate Lawyers' Association/Corporate Lawyers' Association of New Zealand, In-house Counsel Report: Benchmarks and Leading Practices (2012) 8.

4. *Id.* at 8–9.

5. Oxera, *The Role of In-House Solicitors* (Feb. 2014) 11–17, *available at* http://www.oxera.com/getmedia /b1458656-c019-49cd-9611-142d6032f158/The-role-of-in-house-solicitors.pdf.aspx?ext=.pdf.

6. These numbers obviously vary greatly between different jurisdictions, with developing countries frequently growing at a much higher rate. Based on World Bank data, average GDP growth from 2004–13 in the United States was 1.71 percent. See http://data.worldbank.org/indicator/NY.GDP.MKTP.KD.ZG (last visited Jan. 7, 2015).

7. Georgetown Law Center for the Study of the Legal Profession and Peer Monitor, *2015 Report on the State of the Legal Market* (2015), at 3, *available at* http://www.law.georgetown.edu/academics/centers-institutes /legal-profession/upload/FINAL-Report-1-7-15.pdf.

This chapter sets out the most important developments in the changing in-house landscape, and highlights what the clients of the future seek from their external providers. This applies to both in-house departments and, to a smaller extent (because they have less expertise as discerning buyers of legal services), corporations with no internal specialized legal expertise. Susan Hackett, former senior vice-president and general counsel of the ACC, opines:

> The trending issue right now is whether clients will increasingly in-source or right-source work that used to be done exclusively by their larger outside firms. As clients have applied theories of process management (such as Lean Six Sigma) to work so as to unbundle legal services into more manageable stages, and to look at solving problems with greater efficiency and with technologies and workers specifically trained for the task, they have become less enamored of law firms doing all that work at a much higher price and with greater inefficiency. And the work that is done by firms is therefore changing—both in terms of scope and pricing, but also in terms of collaborative teaming, knowledge management, and project management.
>
> Question: Who is the top competition for these traditional law firms? Answer: Their clients, who are more and more capable of doing it with contractors or specialized LPOs or consultants, as well as their own trained staff. This does not mean they do not hire law firms anymore. Rather, what they want to partner with firms for and what they want to do without firms is very, very different from what it was even five years ago, let alone 20.
>
> I have spent my entire career working with in-house departments—this is the first time that I have truly seen an absolute increase in the size of staff and budgets in legal departments, rather than just a growing number of legal departments.[8]

CHANGING IN-HOUSE COUNSEL

The diverse roles of in-house counsel continuously evolve along with the companies that employ them. Professor John Flood concludes a review of the literature relating to in-house counsel by pointing to the shift in the role from a compliance focus to a more complex one, with the giving of strategic business advice as an essential component. He sees this trend spreading from the United States to the United Kingdom and other parts of the world, including emerging economies.[9] The increasing shift of work from outside to in-house counsel goes along with the latter now being better positioned to take on more complex challenges that had previously been dealt with by external firms.[10] In-house counsel as proportion of

---

8. Telephone interview by Eric Chin and Imme Kaschner with Susan Hackett, former Senior Vice-President and General Counsel of the Association of Corporate Counsel (Sept. 4, 2014).

9. Oxera, *supra* note 5, at 8.

10. For a review of the academic literature relating to the changing role of in-house counsel prepared by John Flood, Professor of Law and Sociology at Westminster University, U.K., see *id.* at 11–17.

all practicing lawyers overall is rising.[11] And as David Perla, co-founder of legal services outsourcer Pangea3 and now president of Bloomberg BNA Legal, makes clear:

> There is no way you are going to persuade your client to leave work at the law firm if your client rightly believes it can be done in-house and they have the capacity and desire to do it, whether it is for example securities, regulatory, or compliance work. In-house, today, is too established to be held back by a law firm to persuade a client not to do it.[12]

The demographics of in-house counsel are also changing. The gender balance depends on the jurisdiction, the seniority, and the type of entity (public or private company, government, not-for-profit). In the United States, women make up far less than half of the members of the legal profession (34 percent based on data from the American Bar Association); while 21 percent of general counsel of Fortune 500 companies are female.[13] This is in the same zone as the percentage of female equity partners at U.S. law firms, at 17 percent.[14] In the United Kingdom, in contrast, women are overrepresented in the overall in-house community, 56 percent compared to 46 percent in the legal profession as a whole, including government and not-for-profits. In Australia, 42 percent of in-house legal department leadership positions are occupied by women, while the number of equity partners in firms, though rising, is only about 17 percent.[15]

Representation of ethnic and other minorities in law firms varies. These numbers are important because diversity in companies is often achieved through considerable effort in deliberate recruitment and promotion. Companies are well aware of their options to promote their diversity goals beyond their own backyard, for example by instructing law firms that demonstrate a commitment to similar goals.[16] When considering allocation of external legal spend, clients may prefer firms that have demonstrated an alignment of interests through successful programs to increase minority representation in senior positions. This is one example of a point to highlight in response to the dreaded "Is there anything else that you would like us to know?" question in a request for proposal.

---

11. *E.g.*, in the United Kingdom from about 15 percent of all solicitors holding a practicing certificate in 2004 to about 18 percent in 2012 (*id.* at 7); in the Australian state of New South Wales from 13 percent in 2002 to 18.8 percent in 2012, Urbis, *2012 Profile of the Solicitors of NSW: Final Report* (2013), *available at* http://www.lawsociety.com.au/cs/groups/public/documents/internetcontent/687930.pdf.

12. Telephone interview by George Beaton with David Perla, President, Bloomberg BNA Legal Division/Bloomberg Law (Aug. 14, 2014).

13. American Bar Association—Commission on Women in the Profession, *A Current Glance at Women in the Law: July 2014* 2–3, *available at* http://www.americanbar.org/content/dam/aba/marketing /women/current_glance_statistics_july2014.authcheckdam.pdf.

14. *Id.*

15. Chris Merritt, *More Women Take Up Leadership Roles in In-House Legal Departments*, The Australian, Dec. 19, 2014, at 25.

16. *See, e.g.*, American Bar Association Task Force on Gender Equality and the Commission on Women in the Profession, *Power of the Purse: How General Counsel Can Impact Pay Equity for Women Lawyers* (2013), *available at* http://www.americanbar.org/content/dam/aba/administrative/women /power_of_purse.authcheckdam.pdf.

GLOBAL IN-HOUSE BUSINESS LAWYERS

The traditional career of an in-house lawyer started, and mostly still starts, with a stint at a commercial law firm, lasting anywhere between a few years to the time it takes to make partner or even longer. Most in-house legal departments currently do not feel they have the resources to train lawyers straight out of law school because of the cost of providing training through a mix of hands-on work and further courses for graduates, as law firms traditionally do. BigLaw associates gain a solid skill set that enables them to acquire the necessary additional competencies and business-specific knowledge required of a competent in-house lawyer after their move; at least that is the traditional view. They are well positioned to be the intermediaries who package the company's business problems to hand over to an external firm, and translate the results back into company speak as necessary. But if in-house departments increasingly keep complex matters in house, and require a strategic understanding of the legal aspects of business transactions, and a global business perspective that takes more than a few years to acquire, it makes sense for them to start training their own lawyers.

Hewlett-Packard is one company that is well known for its innovative approach to training its own legal staff from the ground up. Thomas Thoppil, vice-president and deputy general counsel, Hewlett-Packard Asia Pacific, comments on the rationale behind this:

> There is going to be more demand for lawyers with strong business acumen, who can deliver solutions, who can align and easily understand what business is looking for . . . and what the inherent problems are. I see legal departments becoming more "talent makers," and we are one department that is really going in that direction.
>
> The way it used to work for someone joining in-house was that the person came in with several years of experience—usually obtained at a firm—and remained in that role for the next 10 to 15 years. Today there is no place for that. The dynamic company, the company undergoing change, wants lawyers who are willing to evolve with changing times and developments in technology. . . . We want to be a department that can really bring in people at a younger stage and then train them up and move them around within the company and make it dynamic, and in that way be more of a "talent maker" than a "talent taker." These concepts assume relevance as legal departments get into more data-driven productivity analysis and decision making. They realize the inherent strength that is available in the department, and the ability to create better business lawyers—much better than a law firm. I think there will be more and more focus on providing that training which traditionally legal departments did not touch.
>
> Legal departments are much more international than most law firms. A company like HP has operations in 180 different countries, and its legal department plays a role supporting the business worldwide. We had our country legal counsel meeting recently; there were 90 lawyers from different countries and nationalities at that summit. We have 1,000 plus in-house lawyers in the department. There is

now a major focus on building a fully international legal team, which I think most legal departments can do much more effectively than law firms.[17]

Whether international companies will increasingly train their own lawyers from a junior stage, or focus on building global business competencies in their lateral-hire staff, it can be expected that as clients, these global business lawyers will expect a comparable international and collaborative approach from their outside counsel.

GLOBALIZATION AND FOOTPRINT

Today's multinational corporations want legal services that match the multinational expertise and uniformity of service experience that those corporations offer to their clients or customers. This is not necessarily a matter of having a physical presence in a multitude of jurisdictions. Susan Hackett, former long-term senior vice-president and general counsel of the ACC, comments:

> Many law firms think that globalization means having a physical footprint in 116 markets, as opposed to changing the way that they operate to adopt a "borderless" viewpoint or practice, where teams cooperate based on expertise, not location. This means they have to understand how laws interrelate in multijurisdictional practices, not just how each jurisdiction is different. It is not about having a partner in Belgium and a partner in Singapore whom they can call; rather, it is about how they view and deliver client service to global businesses.
>
> For example, if you are doing business such as selling goods and services through the Internet, you have to understand the impact of your work in every market in which your company's goods and services can be accessed. You are not going to hire law firms who have offices in a 100 jurisdictions to advise you on general commercial law in each of those jurisdictions. You are going to hire an Internet law expert who can coordinate with the in-house legal IP team and the business web experts to advise them on how to operate in all of those jurisdictions. *Clients need their firms to see their issues in a global work and business context, as opposed to seeing the single jurisdictional requirements of each location—companies cannot, and will not, have 100 different standards for doing business—they need advice that creates a consistent and irreproachable standard in all markets.*
>
> From the corporate perspective, other than litigation, business is borderless. But many American firms fundamentally misunderstand globalization: It is the way you practice law for a company that needs to be represented across borders, not a long list of international addresses that house local experts (emphasis added).[18]

Mike Roster, a former senior in-house lawyer at and co-chair of the steering committee of the ACC Value Challenge, similarly points to a misconception about the benefits of a large global footprint:

---

17. Telephone interview by Eric Chin and Imme Kaschner with Thomas Thoppil, Vice-President and Deputy General Counsel, Hewlett-Packard Asia Pacific Pty. Ltd. (Sept. 14, 2014).

18. Hackett, *supra* note 8.

[W]ithout exception, every one of the general counsels and deputies I've spoken with say, with respect to the mega firms with 3,000 or more lawyers in many, many countries, "Absent a truly unique global matter, we do not need them. We do not even know who is telling these firms that we do [need them], even though we hear their chairmen saying, 'Oh, but our clients are demanding it.'" Every one of the general counsel or deputies says, "If they've got the right talent and are in the right place, we use them despite their size and the conflicts that arise from that size, but mostly we're using the mid-sized regional firms in the United States and their counterparts in other countries." The mega firms might get chosen *notwithstanding* their size, cost, and conflicts (emphasis added).[19]

Thomas Thoppil of Hewlett-Packard confirms shortfalls in legal services delivered in an international context:

In the Asia-Pacific and Japan region we struggle with getting the same level of services in different markets. Firms tend to be national. Invariably, consistently high standards across different markets, even within firms, are not that great. HP is a company that operates in 180 countries. There are a lot of cultural differences, but we are all fully aligned as an organization in our approach to the customer.

Can you expect a similar service level from a law firm? I do not think so; law firms have simply not evolved to that level. The reason is that legal services tend to be local and national. In some areas like mergers and acquisitions there are international lawyers. But beyond that, if you deep-dive into different areas of law, law firms retain more of a national than an international character. Law firms need to evolve much, much more.[20]

One way that law firms have sought to meet the demands of global clients is of course through international alliances, not just in general, but dedicated to meeting the specific needs of one client. The advantage can be that members of the alliance sign up agreeing on specific service standards, and sometimes fixed fees, that are provided to the client. If needs arise that necessitate additional expertise because of the jurisdiction or area of law involved, additional alliance members committing to the standards can be selected. The recent Nike Alliance of 21 European law firms is one example, and it will be telling to see how similar arrangements succeed and evolve in the future.[21]

IN-HOUSE DEPARTMENT GROWTH PARALLELS EXTERNAL SPEND REDUCTION

There is clear evidence that in-house departments are under continuous pressure to reduce external spend, and that they are doing so by bringing work in-house and

---

19. Telephone interview with Michael Roster, Co-Chair of the Steering Committee of the ACC Value Challenge (Oct. 14, 2014).

20. Thoppil, *supra* note 17.

21. Joanne Harris, *Why the Nike Alliance Is a Legal Trendsetter,* THE LAWYER BLOG (Mar. 10, 2014), http://www.thelawyer.com/why-the-nike-alliance-is-a-legal-trendsetter/3017277.article.

growing their departments as a result. A 2014 survey by HBR Consulting quantified the increase in worldwide legal expenses in 2013 as 2 percent, with inside legal spending rising 5 percent, while outside legal spend decreased by 2 percent. For the United States, overall legal spend increased by 1 percent in the same period, with a 4 percent increase in internal spend offset by a 1 percent decrease in out-side counsel spending, similar to the decrease in demand as cited previously.[22] BTI Consulting Group quantified the sum shifted from external to internal legal spend at US$ 5.8 billion in 2013 and an additional US$ 1.1 billion in 2014.[23] Altman Weil found an ongoing trend for in-house departments to plan to increase size through hiring lawyers, paralegals, and affiliated staff.[24] This was coupled with plans to keep the use of outside counsel the same (56.8 percent) or decrease it (26.2 per-cent), but rarely increase it (only 14.2 percent).[25] These developments indicate that the pie of external legal spend that commercial law firms are competing for is shrinking—and the clients who allocate it are clearly in a position to pick and choose what services best meet their needs. As David Morley, Senior Partner at Allen & Overy, dryly put it, "Clients want more choice of service delivery at lower cost but at no reduction in quality. In other words, they want to have the cake, eat it, and lose weight."[26] But, as the Weight Watchers group of companies demon-strates, such a situation still provides "ample" business opportunities.

TIERS OF WORK

Law firms frequently like to maintain that, given the size and risks of a large-scale litigation or transaction, the legal costs they charge are so small in relation to the potential gains that they are simply considered the necessary cost of doing busi-ness for the client. This is the classical concept of lawyers adding value as trans-action cost engineers.[27] No doubt this holds true for some, perhaps many, matters. But from the perspective of in-house lawyers, those high-risk transactions are not all that common. These clients are developing a clear understanding of different tiers of work, and are sourcing work accordingly.

Mike Roster explains what he calls the "85/15 rule":

Everyone knows the 80/20 rule. This is a different one. In recent months, I have been in a number of conferences with general counsels and deputy general counsels

---

22. BusinessWire, *Total Legal Spending Up by 2 Percent Worldwide According to HBR Consulting's 2014 Law Department Survey* (Oct. 1, 2014), http://www.businesswire.com/news/home/20141001005951/en/Total-Legal-Spending-2-Percent-Worldwide-HBR#.VKyu8cbldSU.

23. BTI Consulting, *Corporate Counsel Shift Another $1.1 Billion In-House* (Sept. 15, 2014), http://www.btibuzz.com/buzz/2014/9/15/corporate-counsel-shift-another-11-billion-in-house.html.

24. Altman Weil, *2014 Chief Legal Officer Survey* (2014) 1, 3, *available at* http://www.altmanweil.com/CLO2014/.

25. *Id.* at 4.

26. Telephone interview by George Beaton and Eric Chin with David Morley (July 10, 2014).

27. Ronald J. Gilson, *Value Creation by Business Lawyers: Legal Skills and Asset Pricing,* 94 YALE L.J. Vol. 94 no. 2 at 239 (1984); *Lawyers as Transaction Cost Engineers* (Aug. 1997), abstract *available at* http://ssrn.com/abstract=11418.

from very well-known companies. Many of them are among the largest multinationals and may have 400 or more in-house lawyers who are front-line lawyers, and some companies are smaller in size but with brands readily recognized throughout the United States and even worldwide. In other words, these are sophisticated and well-known companies.

They all suddenly were saying the same thing. For 15 percent of their legal spend (and that is total legal spend, not total number of matters), the price does not matter one iota. It is the kind of matter—litigation, corporate transaction or something similar—where the general counsel does not care about the cost. And the CEO and the board do not care. It is a very important matter and cost is not the issue.

But for the remaining 85 percent of their legal spend, they say "Yeah, cost is determinative." There are typically 10, 20, or more law firms and practice groups who can handle the work superbly, not just okay, but superbly. So in light of that market reality, the legal work is going to go to whoever is most competitive on cost. That doesn't mean the work will always go to the absolutely cheapest firm. Corporate counsel typically know if a firm has underbid or doesn't understand the matter, and if that's the case, the firm won't get the work. But the firms that have the right expertise and clearly understand what is at stake are going to be in the running and will be selected on the basis of cost.

One company has gone so far as to put one, two, three, or four dollar signs on the computer listing next to each law firm they use. The firms have been ranked according to their historic costs to the company. At the moment this turns on hourly rates, but over time, that likely will be changed to measure the true cost of each firm's legal services. If the company has a bet-the-company matter, firms that have been ranked with three or four dollar signs might be in contention. But those firms are not even going to be considered for most of the company's work. Notwithstanding that many of these firms have 50 or more people in their marketing departments and everyone is talking about value selling, the reality is, they are not even in contention. They have been identified as a high cost firm and now won't be considered for what they often have pejoratively called commodity work even though they are bidding on that work. The result is that the firm has marketed itself out of getting the vast majority of the work it wants, or at least certain of its practice groups want.[28]

Mike's comments indicate that while in-house counsel appreciate the value that more expensive firms may bring, they clearly differentiate between outside work that necessitates this added value—and that which does not. Silvia Hodges Silverstein, an expert on how legal services are bought, predicts that "[w]e will see a more segmented market as clients are increasingly scrutinizing appointment processes and introducing procurement panels."[29]

Steven Walker, associate general counsel at Hewlett-Packard, echoes the need for traditional law firms to recognize tiers of work. He comments on beginnings

---

28. Roster, *supra* note 19.
29. Telephone interview by George Beaton with Silvia Hodges Silverstein, Executive Director, Buying Legal Counsel (Aug. 20, 2014).

and current developments in the legal outsourcing space, and the important questions that these developments raise for law firms:

Every in-house department has a segment of its portfolio characterized by repetitive work of low/moderate risk and value, mid/high volume (which is reasonably predictable), and yet which is resource-intensive and requires a fast turnaround. These workloads are susceptible to commoditization.

Generally speaking, law firms did not invest in the commodity market opportunity as it evolved. Those that did experimented with alternative fee and service models—such as fixed fee "all you can eat" arrangements—which adjusted some elements of delivery and pricing, but did not fundamentally depart from time-honored law firm practices. Success for both firms and clients was modest. In contrast, first generation LPOs assaulted this segment with solution-specific offerings which: (a) took advantage of more agile business models and low cost locations, decoupling time input considerations from price; and (b) deliberately re-engineered the People, Process and Technology trinity from the ground up. Their success is a matter of record. Some law firms are now revisiting these opportunities by means of LPO-style solutions through low cost or best shore captives or partner LPOs.

Yet, other than for the most repetitive tasks at the bottom of the value stack (such as discovery or due diligence), first generation LPO business cases and customer/supplier relationships encountered difficulties. Just as early ITO and BPO customers expected to be passive recipients of a cost-effective, high quality outsourced service, legal departments buying first generation LPO neglected to model, in their business cases, the cost of resources and effort associated with service management and internal process transformation. Additionally, for services higher up the value stack, which require the application of commercial judgment, in-house teams became disenchanted with LPOs who specifically disclaimed the practice of law and risk judgment for their clients.

The original LPOs and an emerging breed of "legal service outsourcing" (LSO) suppliers are embracing this challenge, and are developing repeatable methods to apply risk-adjusted legal/commercial judgment for their customers in fully-managed, legal services higher up the value stack. This will be a key battleground in the next generation of legal outsourcing. Somewhat ironically, in a market defined by LPO, this new battleground presents significant opportunity for law firms, who have long been comfortable operating at the blurred intersection of legal advice and commercial judgment, and have the domain expertise to offer a differentiated value proposition. *But if neither LPO/LSOs nor law firms find the secret sauce quickly, I expect some multinational corporations—with scale to leverage—may respond by constructing their own in-house captives for end-to-end control over QA and commercial decision processes.*

So, it is interesting to me that most large law firms already have most—if not all—of the ingredients needed to offer comparable or even superior next generation commodity offerings to LPO/LSOs, if they wish to do so. They face two strategic questions. First, whether to play in the commoditized space at all (and if they do, will that cannibalize any of their own current revenue), or to concede it to LPO-style solutions from outsourced suppliers or in-house captives. Second, whether they play or not, how do they: (a) continue to differentiate themselves for bespoke consulting services; and (b) manage the gradual but inevitable erosion of that market, as alternative sourcing models for the commodity segment mature and gain acceptance, such that suppliers set their sights ever higher on commoditizing elements of the bespoke market? (emphasis added).[30]

So the clients of the future expect their trusted advisors to understand that it is not a sole-source world anymore, and to facilitate clients receiving commoditized legal work from competitively priced sources, whether those are linked to law firms or independent.

CLIENT INITIATIVE: THE ACC VALUE CHALLENGE

The ACC has been promoting active buyer behavior and process improvement among its members through its "ACC Value Challenge" since 2008. The initiative aims to "help improve alignment of law department and law firm relationships and to help reconnect cost and value of legal services,"[31] through the provision of educational resources and relevant seminars, as well as through the recognition of "ACC Value Champions" and publication of their "case studies." Mike Roster, one of the steering committee members, remembers the early days:

> When we launched the Value Challenge all those years ago, we said to ourselves, "If we get everyone talking about value, we've succeeded." We never dreamt we would get as far as we did in just the first six months. A year into it, all the firm websites were talking about value. All the marketing departments were focusing on value. We created a benchmark, if nothing else, that everyone wants value. More recently, we identified and have posted what we think are the three targets, that is, to define what value means over time.[32]

Value is measured in three dimensions in the ACC Value Challenge; these can be applied independently or jointly:

- Reducing legal cost by a significant amount year-on-year or based on relevant industry benchmarks.
- Providing (near-complete) predictability in cost and processes.
- Significantly improving outcomes assessed through appropriate metrics (these can be as diverse as average settlement costs or jury verdicts in product liabilities cases, significantly reducing the number of cases that arise in specific areas, turn-around times of certain tasks for the internal client, etc.).[33]

---

30. Telephone interview by Eric Chin and Imme Kaschner with Steven Walker, Associate General Counsel and Region Counsel South Pacific, Hewlett-Packard (Sept. 4, 2014).

31. Association of Corporate Counsel, *Association of Corporate Counsel's GC Value Insights: What Multinational General Counsel Value Most* (2012), at 2, http://www.accvaluechallenge-digital.com /accvaluechallenge/2012gc#pg1.

32. Roster, *supra* note 19.

33. Roster, *supra* note 1, at 2.

While cost reduction is one element of value in this context, it is clearly not the only one, and many of the (freely available) case studies detailing the "stories" of the value champions highlight the collaborative nature of the process involving both outside counsel and in-house law departments.[34] It is beyond the ambit of this book to detail all the strategies used by the recognized champions. Nominations may mention law firms and legal departments working jointly. There is an emphasis on the value-adding initiatives, with structures or resources being applicable and reproducible beyond the originator. Being recognized as a law firm that is involved in a cooperation that is celebrated by the ACC as a value champion clearly results in a large amount of positive publicity for those firms.

As part of giving a voice to the clients, the ACC has also published an extensive resource on what it is that general counsel of multinational companies expect from their law firms, *Association of Corporate Counsel's GC Value Insights: What Multinational General Counsel Value Most.* The publication includes material from the law departments of 17 well-known companies regarding types of AFAs that they use for certain areas and matters, estimated savings, and other best practices and suggestions.[35]

The impact of the ACC initiative goes beyond the United States. Value champions included the giant British Telecommunications plc. in 2012, and Catherine J. Moynihan of the ACC points out that ACLA has a focus on improving outside counsel management that is very similar to that of the ACC.[36] Recent 2015 ACC value champions include the Australian Bendigo and Adelaide Bank, a fairly unique bank with a strong community focus through both services aimed at local businesses and charitable initiatives. Since 2014, the bank no longer has hourly rates as part of its terms of engagement for institutional panel work.[37]

Beyond individual progressive client corporations, the expectation of being able to negotiate fees and services in a comprehensive manner has become widely entrenched in the in-house community. The initiative has also served to highlight the multitude of ways in which value can be generated through long-term cooperation between clients and law firms that are not driven by push and counter-push around time-based billing and hourly rates.

---

34. Association of Corporate Counsel, *Meet the 2014 ACC Value Champions*, http://www.acc.com /valuechallenge/valuechamps/avc_valuechampions_2014.cfm (last visited Jan. 12, 2015).

35. Association of Corporate Counsel, *supra* note 31.

36. Catherine J. Moynihan, *True Leaders Employ Key Value Management Principles,* Aust. Corp. Lawyer, June 2013, at 20, 20–21, *available at* https://www.acc.com/advocacy/valuechallenge/toolkit /loader.cfm?csModule=security/getfile&pageid=1351417&page=/valuechallenge/index.cfm&qstring=&title =True%20Leaders%20Employ%20Key%20Value%20Management%20Principles.

37. Jennifer J. Salopek, *Make It So: An Australian Bank Banished Hourly Fees*, ACC Value Challenge, http:// www.acc.com/valuechallenge/valuechamps/2015champ_profilebendigo-and-adelaide-bank-limited.cfm.

DATA MASTERS

In-house legal departments of varying sizes increasingly make use of their own and others' granular data on outside legal spend to identify opportunities for decreasing external spend, in addition to using these methods to monitor and improve the efficiency of their own processes. The hours billed, rates, matter types, and time frames might be less than perfect proxies for the value and the quality of legal services received, but they do allow for easy benchmarking in comparing external providers on a range of criteria including cost. HBR Consulting recently found that 50 percent of respondents from in-house departments used data analytics to select and support their stance in negotiations with outside counsel.[38] This indicates that firms should be ready to comment on the price of their own offers relative to comparable ones in the market, and to use engagement metrics as basis for improvements for future cooperation with clients.

On the simplest level, an in-house department reviewing its external spend might find that there are avoidable costs that arise from simply working with the wrong type of firm. A simple example: FedEx Ground in Pittsburgh realized that they spent a lot of unnecessary travel costs by briefing local firms to do West Coast litigation. Having identified this, they conducted a request for proposal for preferred West Coast firms, and negotiated value-based fees instead of hourly rates with the much-reduced number of panel firms, resulting in very positive vendor relationships.[39]

Mike Roster cites an example of a company which, instead of putting out a request for proposal, simply filled in the desired information about firms they had worked with from their own analytics systems, and awarded the work based on this—much to the surprise of the successful law firm.[40] Law department analysis of external spend also often provides the basis for discussions about alternative fee arrangements, for example where a law firm is offered a portfolio of all work that arises in one area (relating to human resources, for example) over a given period of time, in return for a fixed fee. To negotiate engagements like this profitably, firms need to comprehend such data, and relate it to the costs that they expect to incur in delivering the services.

It is important to realize that, for the in-house client, the value of data analytics goes to their very core, far beyond reducing external spend on a matter-by-matter or even portfolio basis. Data analytics enables legal departments to run lean operations while providing excellent services to their internal clients. Companies do not run on stories about great cases, they run on numbers. Appropriate metrics allow law departments to demonstrate both their utility, and increases in performance, to their internal clients. When asked to describe the best practices in-house legal

---

38. BusinessWire, *supra* note 2.

39. *See* Jennifer J Salopek, *How to Launch and Sustain a Value Initiative on Multiple Fronts*, ACC VALUE CHALLENGE, http://www.acc.com/valuechallenge/valuechamps/2015champ_profilefedex.cfm.

40. Roster, *supra* note 3.

department in five years' time, Steven Walker of Hewlett-Packard pointed to the large role for analytics:

Historically, in-house departments operated without much data on how they deliver services, except for information around headcount and internal/external spend, relying instead on the experience and judgment of seasoned managers to guide strategy and decision-making. This impeded departments in adopting modern, professional, data-based management methodologies and in articulating the value of the legal function to CEOs and CFOs.

HP's legal department comprises some 1,200 lawyers and legal professionals covering the 180 countries in which the company conducts business. A department of that scale requires sophisticated tooling and instrumentation—ideally generating real-time data—and managers who understand how to use the data and manage to their key metrics.

At HP, we wanted smart technology solutions to assist us: (a) in developing a granular understanding of our workload and services; (b) in managing our services; and (c) in enabling data analytics around how/where the department is spending its time, and how/where it should or shouldn't be spending its time, what suppliers and law firms we have engaged to do what, how the activity is progressing. Our General Counsel regards the enabling information systems and software as of strategic importance to the department and to HP, whether for litigation management, electronic billing and reporting, IP portfolio management, digital signatures, document review, or many other applications. As we continue to collect data, the prospects for mining and big data analytics become ever more compelling. We are harnessing insights which illuminate adjustments we may make in order to deliver the highest possible levels of service for our clients.

As an example, in 2013 we deployed a cutting-edge cloud-based workflow and contract management solution to revolutionize how the legal department supports HP's large supply transactions. It interfaces with the business's CRM tool and updates automatically, so that the legal professional allocated to support a sales opportunity accesses the same information as the sales team. He or she can access the tool from a PC or mobile device, and use it to manage the transaction end to end, capturing key data around the transaction lifecycle, including total negotiation time and time spent in HP or customer review.

Each legal manager has a dashboard displaying the workload for his or her team, the mix of business, how responsive his or her department is being to business requests for legal support, critical deadlines, and incoming work. Via the tool, managers can dynamically allocate and reallocate the workflow, communicate with sales teams, and view draft documents and associated governance materials. Analysis of the transaction data is helping us to continuously improve the services we provide for our internal clients and HP's customers, and to turn contracting at HP into a competitive advantage.

The best-performing legal departments of the future will be run by professional legal managers (as distinct from just good lawyers), who are acclimated to managing by the use of dashboards, instrumentation, key metrics, and data analytics. A company's legal resources are precious assets, which must be applied deliberately, selectively, and in a manner properly scaled and proportionate to the risk/

Developing scenarios is both a creative and analytical process, adapted to the particular circumstances to which it is being applied; it is not a precise science. During the process of scenario preparation it is paramount to acknowledge uncertainty, but not become lost in endless alternative futures, combinations, and permutations of numerous factors. Our business strategy experience and extensive research in the legal services industry in many parts of the world position us to prepare a credible scenario, and explain the strategic consequences and options it poses for law firms, their clients, and new forms of providers in the industry.

SCOPE AND STAKEHOLDERS

The following scenario is designed to help stakeholders in the legal services industry explore what the industry might look in 2025. Those stakeholders include corporate clients who might or might not be lawyers themselves, decision makers in law firms with the traditional business model, NewLaw providers,[5] lawyers in their individual capacities, the judiciary, regulators, legal educators, law students, and professional societies. They also include publishers and legal software vendors, as well as lenders to and investors in the sector.

In our view, the scenario we have developed for this book is fit to serve the planning purposes of client organizations and all forms of legal services provider. While those using this book should necessarily form their own view of the future—and how they should respond to it—the work involved in starting ab initio to build one or more scenarios is unlikely to be cost-beneficial for the majority of firms and clients.

TRENDS AND DRIVERS

The starting point for generating the 2025 Kaleidoscope scenario was the identification of changing trends, potentially disruptive events, and innovations in the corporate legal services industry. Over the course of two years, we gathered and tested input by discussion, observation, surveys, and publications across 17 countries.[6] Our sources included clients of law firms, corporate counsel associations, traditional law firm leaders, NewLaw leaders, and consultants to law firms. Our view of the current state of the legal services industry is summed up in chapter 2.

The material was reviewed and grouped, and trends and factors of lesser importance were discarded. Themes were identified and uncertainties assessed in detail. Interdependencies, consequences, and likely responses were assessed. In keeping with scenario building best practice,[7] this process of narrowing down and

---

5. GEORGE BEATON, NEWLAW NEW RULES—A CONVERSATION ABOUT THE FUTURE OF THE LEGAL SERVICES INDUSTRY (Beaton Capital 2013).

6. Australia, Canada, China, Hong Kong, Indonesia, India, Japan, Malaysia, New Zealand, Singapore, South Korea, Spain, Taiwan, Thailand, United Kingdom, United States, Vietnam.

7. *See, e.g.*, GILL RINGLAND, SCENARIO PLANNING: MANAGING FOR THE FUTURE 1–27 (John Wiley & Sons 1998).

grouping was not entirely objective; it was shaped by personal experience, opinion, and canvassing with others. It was conducted by our multidisciplinary team and tested with law firms, clients, and in conference settings in the United States, the United Kingdom, and Australia.

SCENARIO GENERATION

In the final step, the information was crafted into a coherent and evocative narrative to describe a possible future. The ultimate goal of the scenario is clarity and credibility to allow firms to explore what course they would take if the scenario materialized, and what strategic actions now would position the firm favorably in that future.

To achieve this goal, a common way to create scenarios proceeds from the identification of two relevant and mutually independent trends. By scaling the trends, for example, high/low, four combinations result, which form the basis of four scenarios. Specific details are added to yield internally consistent narratives for each scenario.

An example of scenario building in the legal context is the Law Society of England and Wales' *The Legal Services Market in 2025: Scenario Planning for the Future.*[8] This scenario is based on proposed key drivers of increasingly or decreasingly connected laws in a global context and active or passive buyers of legal services, which include commercial clients of all sizes as well as private individuals. The scenarios describe a 2025 environment for individual private clients, corporate and commercial clients, and their service providers. In our opinion, it is unlikely that the chosen factors would have the same relevance for and similar effects on both individual consumers and corporations as clients. The effect is that the resulting scenarios fail to persuade because they lack coherence and internal consistency, a key criterion expounded by Michael Porter as discussed above.

The Law Society's report illustrates the problem caused by generating a two-by-two matrix of four scenarios based on two key drivers, resulting in what is a largely arbitrary delineation of supposedly distinct possible futures. Also, unlike the Law Society's scenarios, the scenario analysis in this chapter focuses solely on corporate and commercial law firms, and does not stretch to consumers as clients and the law firms exclusively serving consumers and smaller businesses. Particularly with complex and heterogeneous groups of stakeholders in an industry, the futures they face are likely to be many and varied. Or as Richard Susskind noted in the words of William Gibson, the future is not going to be "evenly distributed."[9] For the legal marketplace, this means in client–supplier transactions and relation-

---

8. The Law Society of England and Wales, *The Legal Services Market in 2025:—Scenario Planning Scenario Overviews* (2012), http://www.lawsociety.org.uk/policy-campaigns/research-trends/market -assessment-2012-13/ (last visited Nov. 14, 2015).

9. Richard Susskind, The End of Lawyers? Rethinking the Nature of Legal Services 21 (Oxford University Press 2010).

ships, there will almost certainly be many variations within one all-encompassing scenario.

The future of the legal market will be multifaceted, with a wide range of offerings to meet clients' legal and related needs delivered through a variety of mostly unbundled services. The service providers will range from traditional law firms (themselves varying greatly) through externally owned new forms of firm to client-owned backwards-integrated providers. This is visualized as a "kaleidoscopic" future.

While many of the building blocks of these services will not be all that different from what they are today—like written documents containing advice, for example—they will be generated and assembled in different ways, by standardized processes, adding technology, and by in-, co-, and outsourcing each process in the most cost-effective combinations and manner.

LIMITATION

While certain trends such as, for example, globalization, increasing connectedness, digitization, and more flexible workforces informed our kaleidoscope scenario, economic cycles are unlikely to influence the projected future beyond speeding up or slowing down progress toward it. The global economic crisis of 2008–2009 did not vastly damage traditional law firms, nor has the recovery ended the rise of NewLaw providers or slowed the advance of structural changes in the industry. The outcome of the structural trend is a progressive reduction in external corporate legal spending with traditional law firms; it continues regardless of the stage of the economic cycle.[10]

A SINGLE SCENARIO

In our view of the legal services industry, there are two key drivers that will determine the structure of the future industry.[11] The *first* is the rate of change in the way corporate and commercial clients define and meet their legal needs, including the way and extent to which they procure outside legal counsel and other services. The *second* is the rate at which traditional law firms, currently still by far the main provider of external legal services to clients, adapt and remake their business models, and therefore maintain their relevance to these clients.

As set out in chapter 3 (*Porter's Five Forces Analysis for Law*), the structure of an industry is largely shaped by rivalry among the incumbents, the bargaining power of major inputs, that is, attorneys, and the buying power of clients. Also to

---

10. We acknowledge there are law firm leaders who disagree that the causes of the pressures on the BigLaw business model are structural. One such leader is Peter Kalis, Chairman and Global Managing Partner of K&L Gates. He forcibly argues the depth and extended nature of the recession that started in 2008 is the primary cause.

11. Industry structure is used in the sense described by Porter, see *supra* note 1, at 1–11.

be factored in are the impacts of substitute services and of new entrants to the market as additional forces.

Partners, employee lawyers, and other types of skilled talent are the key input factor to law firms. Being abundant, the supply of talent will not be a particularly powerful force in shaping the future industry. There are, however, circumstances, such as many partners leaving a firm at the same time, where talent can determine the success or failure of an individual firm.[12]

Substitutes will become increasingly important as new types of provider, that is, NewLaw, create very competitive offerings of certain types of legal services. The services of NewLaw providers for corporate end-clients are becoming increasingly sophisticated, and in some cases are already part of corporate supply chains, along with traditional law firms.

The future structure of the legal services industry will depend on the degree to which traditional law firms will be able to adapt and meet changing client demands, including by incorporating novel elements into their supply chain and by offering additional services. This will determine how much demand there will be for legal services from alternative providers who, in turn, will progressively expand and diversify their offerings.

We propose that it is arbitrary to generate four separate scenarios around low/high rates of change in the way clients satisfy their needs, and law firms adapt their business models. The four scenarios seemed artificial and too neat, based as they were on supposedly uniform and independent developments across such a large and diverse number of enterprises.

Based on our analysis, the corporate legal services industry in 2025 is not best envisaged as a series of mutually exclusive scenarios. Rather, it will be the outcome of changed client demand giving rise to a vastly evolved range of services offered by traditional law firms that have been "remade" to varying degrees; a large, diverse, and growing group of NewLaw providers; and clients' own self-sufficient solutions. This scenario is the result of the manner and power of client demand changing faster than most traditional commercial law firms can adapt. This prediction is based on our observations, analysis and modeling,[13] and is supported by others.[14]

---

12. See, e.g., DAVID PARNELL, THE FAILING FIRM: SYMPTOMS AND REMEDIES 261–96 (ABA Publishing, 2014), for a number of case studies illustrating instances where partner exodus was associated with law firm failure.

13. See, e.g., Eric Chin's modeling of possible revenue growth comparing an expanding NewLaw firm (Axiom) and a traditional law firm (DLA Piper) in Beaton, *supra* note 5.

14. *See, e.g.,* Allen & Overy, *Unbundling a Market: The Appetite for New Legal Services Models* (May 2014), http://www.allenovery.com/SiteCollectionDocuments/Unbundling_a_market.PDF (last visited December 17, 2014).

KALEIDOSCOPE: THE LEGAL SERVICES INDUSTRY IN 2025

Overview

Bundled and unbundled services are procured and provided in a variety of ways in the legal services industry. In addition to traditional law firms, a wide variety of other providers leverage talent, technologies, and processes—and in many cases external capital—to provide final or intermediate legal services.

Legal services providers are subject to the same relentless market pressures as their corporate clients. A strong demand for flexible, integrated, and cost-effective services has fueled the entry and expansion of diverse legal service providers into the market, enabled by deregulation in many jurisdictions, following the example of the United Kingdom and Australia. These providers differ in terms of their business models and their services, but they all leverage information technology, offer highly specialized services to meet legal needs, and often provide services on a global scale. Document generation systems have increased the efficiency of legal work and made a lot of human talent redundant by providing sophisticated, very close to final document drafts.

The relatively simple constellation of previous decades comprising corporate clients and largely homogeneous law firm providers has given way to an ecosystem where law firms widely use NewLaw providers and even their clients' captive legal centers as part of their supply chains. Self-sufficient, in-house legal departments offer services to other companies. Many entities in the market are both providers and consumers of legal services. The billable hour as the predominant way of pricing legal services is a distant memory—legal services are priced in fixed ways based on their value to the client.

Multidisciplinary teams of project managers, knowledge managers, business analysts, and IT specialists work alongside attorneys to provide complex legal services, particularly for large transactions. Quantitative assessments of the cost and risk of proposed solutions for the legal aspects of business problems are now considered a necessary part of any commercial legal advice.

Clients

Clients have acquired considerable expertise in legal process management. They analyze and unbundle their legal needs, segmenting these along the lines of "commodity," "run-the-company," and "mission-critical" legal needs. Client organizations source services internally or externally or combine the two to deliver the best value. This is done using professional procurement methods with a mixture of in-, co-, and outsourcing.

The widespread adoption of fixed, task-, and outcomes-based fees by legal services providers has resulted in a highly transparent and hypercompetitive market for legal services. Corporate legal departments source unbundled services from the most efficient provider, assessed on price, quality, risk, and speed. Clients are used to trusting NewLaw firms with more complex work, since NewLaw entities have built a track record of handling complex transactions and partly assuming liability for the legal services that they deliver. Clients regularly use different types of providers simultaneously for different tiers of work, for example, a BigLaw firm combined with a NewLaw legal services provider, and an LPO. This is an example of the now widespread phenomenon of "co-opetition." All forms of legal services providers regularly both compete and collaborate with each other, as occurs in many other industries.

When buying bundled legal solutions from law firms with specific expertise, clients demand executable advice that seamlessly integrates with business operations, delivered directly to the company's internal data management systems, rather than advice that needs an additional layer of adaptation by the corporate legal team.

Corporate legal departments have become proficient in managing legal risk proactively through information technology, by embedding legal information and checklists in the software and processes used by their businesses. Business information triggers flag the need for managers to review legal information, or to seek advice from the in-house team, with the data simultaneously being used to create a briefing memorandum through document generation software. Legal process specialists with deep industry knowledge, who manage both flexible taskforces and electronic decision-support resources, staff corporate legal departments.

Many of those corporations that choose to retain their own legal departments instead of outsourcing them entirely have turned them into profit centers, to provide legal and related services to other companies. The complex captives offer legal services, for example, related to occupational health and safety, high-volume small claims management, and legal logistics.

Traditional Law Firms

Incumbent law firms are subject to hypercompetitive forces exerted by traditional and new forms of providers. Commercial law firms have shrunk because other providers are now the preferred choice of clients for lower-complexity work, and because technology has decreased the number of lawyers required for a given task. The surviving law firms have positioned themselves on high levels of specialized legal expertise and strong brands, combined with highly efficient processes. This includes extensive LPO and LSO use, and services beyond individualized advice. One example is artificial intelligence-supported expert systems leveraging firm expertise that deliver individual advice in response to specific questions. The systems draw on a variety of sources, including information from client relationship management systems.

Many law firms have gone through a stage of owning captive outsourcing centers in areas of lower labor and facilities costs to decrease fixed costs. By now, these captive centers have mostly fallen by the wayside, since traditional firms find it more efficient to source such services as needed from alternative legal providers. Specialized NewLaw firms provide the same service at lower cost, leveraging economies of scale combined with large investments in innovative technological solutions and project management capabilities. High-volume legal support services are viewed as commodities on par with payroll or janitorial services, and are outsourced in a similar manner.

Some law firms have successfully differentiated themselves by offering integrated solutions, that is, combined legal and nonlegal advice, for clients in certain sectors, frequently entering into partnerships and joint ventures with other professional services firms to do this. In some instances, they have become part of the now truly giant and diversified "Big Four" professional services firms, which were only accountants in a long-gone era. With some success, newcomers are challenging the Big Four for membership of this very powerful strategic group.

Incorporation is allowed in many jurisdictions and has allowed firms to implement more efficient governance structures and to benefit from diverse expertise beyond that of lawyers. In addition, firms use external capital to invest in multidisciplinary and technology-enabled service models, either through external investment or through parallel vehicles in jurisdictions where external investment is not yet permitted.

A small number of firms with high relationship capital serve corporate clients who still buy bundled legal services, but this niche market is shrinking, and is therefore extremely competitive. These clients are willing to accept slightly above-market prices for low-complexity work in return for convenience. These services are delivered as fixed-price package deals.

NewLaw Firms

NewLaw firms continue to increase their market share by meeting the demand for competitively priced legal services, and have lifted the quality and complexity of their offerings by using the "attacker's advantage."[15] The collapse of some NewLaw pioneers like Clearspire in 2014 did not slow this trend, and is viewed as a necessary side effect of innovation in the industry. NewLaw start-ups are the dot-coms of the roaring twenty-twenties.

Many of these NewLaw firms cooperate closely and efficiently with BigLaw firms, offering them competitively priced solutions enabled by investment in innovative technologies and process efficiencies.

Beyond low-complexity work, alliances of independent legal practitioners, project managers, and IT, financial, and other supporting professionals, assembled by legal services agencies, now commonly handle complex transactions. Lawyers joke about BigLaw firms having gone the way of the Hollywood studios of old.

---

15. *See* Richard N. Foster, Innovation: The Attacker's Advantage (Summit Books 1986).

(Remember when studios actually *employed* actors, producers, and other talent needed to make movies on long-term contracts?) The value proposition of NewLaw firms assembling these teams is the management of legal and other talent, using platforms to integrate knowledge, project, and financial management with risk management. The benefit of this "task force" approach is the ability to assemble expertise and capacity exactly as and when needed for a project. These transactions are awarded through tenders and covered by adapted forms of professional indemnity insurance.

For mid-sized businesses with relatively small legal needs, or those that do not wish to invest in legal departments, full-service corporations that provide integrated legal and other professional services have mostly replaced traditional law firms. In the main, lawyers do not manage these professional services firms, and the legal services for clients are generated in standardized ways. The extensive use of legal and professional knowledge management technology allows for high-quality services to be provided with lower labor costs.

SYNTHESIS

In the scenario, we described how clients group their legal requirements in the three categories of "commodity," "run-the-company," and "mission-critical" needs. Figure 5.1 maps these three segments of need against ways of meeting them through insourcing, cosourcing, or outsourcing.

The figure shows the many types of legal services providers that are part of the 2025 kaleidoscope. These range from senior general counsel who have long-held advice-giving and decision-making roles related to mission-critical corporate needs (top left) to completely outsourced, commoditized services providers that include artificial intelligence, document suppliers, traditional BigLaw firms that transformed themselves into very efficient "factories," and online legal marketplaces that now also serve corporations, not just consumer legal needs (bottom right).

The smallest changes have occurred in the top row where mission-critical work is still done much as it was a decade ago, save for the now prospering elite NewLaw firms. Across the bottom row a great deal has changed and new types of services providers are flourishing alongside traditional firms that had the foresight to remake their business models. The new breed of services providers includes vendors of artificial intelligence and documents, and online legal marketplaces.

CONCLUSION

Scenario planning is a useful tool for managing strategically in the face of high uncertainty, including disruption. A credible scenario enables a firm to explore strategies that preserve flexibility, and to build capacity to deal with changes in the structure of its industry.

Section C

The statements in section C relate to the way a law firm produces services for clients. The questions cover the general areas of strategic organization, alternative sourcing (including insourcing through temporary staff and outsourcing to captives or third parties), more efficient resource use with increased predictability through project management and process improvement, and application of technology. A lack of active initiatives in this area, indicated by a score of less than 24, means a firm is locking in high costs by not taking advantage of feasible and established methods of creating better, faster, cheaper services in a predictable and standardized manner. Ultimately, this makes a firm less competitive than others that actively manage and progressively lower their cost structure. Underlying causes of this may be general (again, lack of awareness with a low score in section A and lack of change readiness with a low score in section D) or specific, if the firm has not turned its mind to these areas. Sourcing, project management and process improvement, and use of technology are considered in chapters 10, 11, and 12, respectively.

Section D

Section D relates to change management and innovation in a law firm. A lack of a vision, limited change readiness, a lack of willingness to commit adequate resources, and unwillingness to experiment with small-scale innovation, indicated by a score of less than 24, mean that a firm will not be able to execute successfully the strategic changes in the various areas covered in chapters 8 through 12. Change readiness and change management are core competencies that underlie the winning execution of any new strategy. Chapter 13 describes change management and innovation strategies in general, and how these can be applied in the notoriously risk-averse setting of a law firm partnership.

CONCLUSION

The self-assessment tool in this chapter provides a starting point for law firms that are considering remaking their traditional business model to a significant degree as well as for readers seeking to focus their use of this book. By enabling leaders to identify their firms' specific strengths and weaknesses, the self-assessment tool helps them to choose on which sections of *Remaking Law Firms* they wish to focus, as well as considering on which areas their firms need to concentrate in remaking themselves.

PART II

How

Chapter 7

Designing the Business Model

Key Points

- A business model sums up how a firm works, and how it makes money. The use of the word "model" refers to the ability to describe mathematically the performance of a business. A good business model is based on a solid understanding of the "job to be done" from the perspective of the client as customer.
- The business model of a law firm needs to articulate how work is won, how work is done, and how the enterprise is led and governed. Each of these dimensions can be further broken down into specific hallmarks. The business models of BigLaw and New-Law firms are quite different in regard to each of those hallmarks. Each firm lies on a continuum somewhere between BigLaw and NewLaw for a given hallmark. Remaking a firm means designing its business model to move toward the more client-centric, more efficient, and more agile hallmarks of the NewLaw business model.
- A larger firm can consist of two or more different business models, for example through an ownership stake in captives or legal start-ups, through sourcing from NewLaw providers, by providing on-demand legal talent agencies, and/or by offering commoditized online services. Chapters 8 through 13 cover how specific aspects of the law firm business model can be remade.

INTRODUCTION

The previous chapters of this book demonstrate why law firms need to remake their long-established business model. Chapters 8 through 13 address different aspects of the traditional law firm business model, and show how they can be remade. In each of these chapters, key principles are illustrated with practical examples of what pioneering law firms, in-house departments, NewLaw providers, or other professional services firms are doing. This chapter provides a keystone, linking the *why* and the *how* parts of the book. It explains the business model concept in some detail and applies it first in the context of the traditional law firm described in chapter 2, and second, in the context of the quite different remade or newly designed business models, often within NewLaw entities.

THE BUSINESS MODEL CONCEPT

Chapter 2 made a number of references to the "business model" of traditional law firms. A useful definition of the term "business model," along with pertinent insights, was published by Joan Magretta in 2002:

> [Business models] are at heart stories—stories that explain how enterprises work. A good business model answers Peter Drucker's age-old questions:[1] Who is the customer? And what does the customer value? It also answers the fundamental questions every manager must ask: How do we make money in this business? What is the underlying economic logic that explains how we can deliver value to customers at an appropriate cost?[2]

A firm's business model is distinct from its business strategy. This book does not address the many aspects of business strategy for law firms, as many others do.[3] Magretta explains the difference:

> Business models describe, as a system, how the pieces of a business fit together. But they don't factor in one critical dimension of performance: competition. Sooner or later—and it is usually sooner—every enterprise runs into competitors. . . . A competitive strategy explains how you will do better than your rivals. And doing better, by definition, means being different. Organizations achieve superior performance when they are unique, when they do something no other business does in ways that no other business can duplicate.[4]

But back to the two conceptual components of a business model. The first is the narrative of what is at the heart of how the enterprise makes or intends to make a profit. Magretta offers the example of the business model of American Express traveller's checks in the early 20th century. Traveller's checks offered customers a risk-free way of taking cash abroad (because the checks were insured against loss and theft, and were far superior to letters of credit that depended on businesses abroad knowing and trusting the issuing bank), and also offered business establishments a low-risk way of doing business with the travelers (because the checks were backed by the American Express brand and corporation). The crucial underlying economic logic was that there was no business risk beyond initial setup costs, because customers always paid cash for the checks, giving American

---

1. Leading management theorist Peter F. Drucker, author of numerous books including Management: Tasks, Responsibilities, Practices (Harper & Row 1973) and The Essential Drucker (Harper Business 2001).

2. Joan Magretta, *Why Business Models Matter*, Harv. Bus. Rev. May 2002, at 3.

3. *E.g.*, Jordan Furlong, Evolutionary Road: A Strategic Guide to Your Law Firm's Future (Attorney at Work 2013); Stephen Mayson, Law Firm Strategy: Competitive Advantage and Valuation (Oxford University Press 2007); Law Firm Strategy for the 21st Century: Strategies for Success (Christoph H. Vaagt ed., Globe Business Publishing 2013).

4. Magretta, *supra* note 2.

Express interest-free loans and an assured cash flow. For law firms, the traditional business model of selling legal advice priced on the basis of the production cost (reflected in the billable hour), as described in chapter 2, has been a compelling narrative for a long time. This is no longer the case.

The second component is "modeling," which goes back to the advent of electronic spreadsheets in the 1960s and 1970s.[5] Physical spreadsheets used in business accounting have been around since Dickens' time (remember poor Bob Cratchit slaving over the ledger in *A Christmas Carol*?), but the advent of computer programs where data could be manipulated based on preset formulas and linked to other data, allowed for the rapid calculation and visualization of business outcomes with different inputs. Magretta points out the significance of this development:

> The spreadsheet ushered in a more analytic approach to planning because every major line item could be pulled apart, its components and subcomponents analyzed and tested. You could ask what-if questions about the critical assumptions on which your business depended—*for example, what if customers are more price-sensitive than we thought?*—and with a few keystrokes, you could see how any change would play out on every aspect of the whole. In other words, you could model the behavior of a business (emphasis added).[6]

So the second aspect of a "business model" is the quantitative analysis of how the business makes money, based on stated assumptions about customer behavior and other factors, for example, changes in regulation that affect demand. As Magretta acknowledges, there have been business models (as in "stories that explain how enterprises work") that were vastly successful without any detailed modeling being done prior to launching the business—any successful business prior to the commercial availability of spreadsheet applications, and a good many after that, in fact. But today, designing a business model should include quantitative analysis supporting the "underlying economic logic."

The strength of such a comprehensive business model concept is that it necessitates not just a sound idea, but also a clear delineation of assumptions, the correctness of which will determine if a business is likely to succeed. The concept makes it clear that if the assumptions that are the basis of a successful business model cease to be correct, the model is unlikely to continue to be successful. Examples of relevant assumptions for the legal services industry include assumptions about clients' willingness to pay a certain level of fees, about clients' acceptance of time-based billing structures, and about the level of future demand. The case study "Maister Maxed Out" in chapter 3 illustrates how the profits of a particular firm operating on a traditional law firm business model, expressed in Maister's

---

5. *See, e.g.*, Richard Mattessich, *Spreadsheet: Its First Computerization (1961–1964)*, http://www.j-walk .com/ss/history/spreadsh.htm, and D. J. Power, *A Brief History of Spreadsheets*, http://www.dssresources.com /history/sshistory.html, Museum of User Interfaces, Computer Science Department of the University of Maryland.

6. Magretta, *supra* note 2.

profitability formula, were predicted to drop because the assumptions that hourly rates or utilization or leverage could be increased year on year did no longer hold.

Beyond the ability to model outcomes of a business plan, Magretta's business model concept underscores the opportunity to modify aspects of a business model to maintain profitability even in the face of changed circumstances:

> When managers operate consciously from a model of how the entire business system will work, every decision, initiative, and measurement provides valuable feedback. Profits are important not only for their own sake but also because they tell you whether your model is working. If you fail to achieve the results you expected, you re-examine your model . . . . Business modeling is, in this sense, the managerial equivalent of the scientific method—you start with a hypothesis, which you then test in action and revise when necessary.[7]

In summary, a rigorous business model consists of a compelling narrative of what the business will offer that is preferable to what is already available in the market, combined with a quantitative assessment setting out why the business will be profitable. Such a model provides the opportunity to remake it, based on data that is fed into the model. A successful business model has to meet customer demands in a demonstrable way. This necessitates a clear understanding of what the potential customer considers to be the "job to be done," as opposed to the job that the business would like to do, a phrase coined by Clayton Christensen.

THE JOB TO BE DONE

Christensen discussed the concept of the "job to be done" in his book *The Innovator's Solution* published in 2003, using the example of "the job that customers hired a milkshake to do."[8] This not necessarily intuitive example is from a case study detailing why customers buy milkshakes, specifically, what they want to achieve with their purchase. This leads to an assessment of competing offerings in the market that might otherwise have been overlooked (because they were not in the milkshake/drinks category, but customers nevertheless turned to them to "do the same job," for example bagels). The insights into the customers' desires ultimately allowed the fast food company to tweak its milkshake offerings, and to increase sales as a result. Defining the "job to be done" means that instead of approaching a potential business model from the perspective of the business and the wares or services it would like to sell, the design starts from the customers' desire or need

---

7. *Id.*

8. Clayton M. Christensen & Michael E. Raynor, The Innovator's Solution: Creating and Sustaining Successful Growth 74–78 (Harvard Business School Press 2003).

situations where personal relationships are not sufficient, namely when partners leave a firm, and when a firm seeks to develop relationships with new clients. Professional services firms for example have developed company-centric ways of maintaining client relationships, including mandatory rotations. David Perla, President of Bloomberg BNA Legal Division (and previously founder and co-CEO of Pangea3), comments on this difference between law firms and professional services firms:

> If law firms wanted to go that route . . . , they could; you could simply say all clients belong to the firm. One of the fascinating things about working in a public company is the difference between how their accounting firms interface and how their law firms interface.
>
> With the law firm you have your law firm partner and that person is your contact and that could go on for years and years between that partner and the legal department, and usually the finance department has a good relationship with that partner too. At the accounting firm, the assigned partner rotates and usually there is also a manager, and the manager rotates, and eventually the manager becomes partner. You cannot say to one of these professional services firms "we want this person to be our partner contact forever." They don't do that, partly also for compliance reasons. It is a fascinating model, . . . you won't ever own the client, but it also means the client won't walk out of the door unless the firm fails the client as a whole.[13]

David Perla's views on the merits of the different styles of relationship management in law and Big Four accounting firms is backed by some evidence that clients stay with law firms longer when multiple partners are identified as liaison contact for a client. Client-sourced research by Beaton Research + Consulting shows a few large Australian law firms have "stickier" relationships with clients than do the majority of their peers. These firms are known to have been early movers in instituting sophisticated "velcro" style client relationship management, whereby several partners and practitioners are tasked with and measured on fostering the client relationship, not simply doing the legal work.

Obviously, handing over clients between key partners poses a risk of expertise and relevant client-specific knowledge getting lost. But whether or not this risk materializes largely depends on the processes a firm has in place for capturing, storing, and retrieving client-related information in a structured way. Similar arguments about unacceptable loss of relevant information have been raised in the medical profession to justify doctors working prolonged on-call periods over many days, until the clear risks to patients due to fatigued doctors prompted change. Now medical providers use structured handover protocols that allow for multiple doctors and nurses to rotate at regular intervals, without loss of crucial information.

---

13. Telephone interview by George Beaton with David Perla, President of Bloomberg BNA Legal Division (and previously founder and co-CEO of Pangea3) (Aug. 13, 2014).

As an aside, having robust structured and transparent documentation in place is also beneficial in teams that are partly comprised of members who work part-time. Emphasizing the firm over the individual partner is likely to improve clients' confidence, knowing they are being taken care of by a strong team, with members who can be replaced if necessary. Given the commercial success of the Big Four global accounting firms in meeting the challenges of increased footprints, globalization, and growth through diversification—remember, each of the Big Four is more than ten times the size of the world's largest law firm by revenue—their approach to strengthening client ties to the firm at the expense of individual relationships is an aspect of building a strong brand that is worth noting. This concept is of course a tough sell in law firms with cultures heavily influenced by remuneration based on bringing in work through client "ownership," and lateral hires being recruited based on their expected "books of business."

BUILDING A BRAND: DIFFERENTIATION AND DIVERSIFICATION

So what characterizes a strong law firm brand in a mature market? Differentiation in this context is connected to the meaning of brand as set out above, and is often lacking with even strong law firm brands (defined by top-of-mind recollection). A differentiated firm has a positive utility (What does working with Firm A do for me/us?) and feel (What does working with Firm A say about me/us?) for the client that others do not have, and the brand purpose expresses these comparative advantages and communicates them to current and prospective clients, and current and prospective staff.

A contemporary example of differentiation is advice in one of the firm's specific areas of expertise that is provided through subscription-based self-service portals instead of as a customized one-off service—think of the convenience of a 24/7 ATM on the corner versus having to find an open bank.[14] Such commoditized services provide a convenient, efficient, and innovative (at least for some time) brand experience. Another example is diversification through consultancy services delivered by law firms to large in-house departments providing implementation advice for project management and process improvement drawing on the firm's own experience and expertise.[15] Such an offering can position the branded law firm as thought leader for complex, cutting-edge projects.

Yet another example of combined differentiation and diversification is the provision of comprehensive integrated compliance and legal risk management solutions, including implementation. In this example, the focus is shifted from dealing

---

14. *See, e.g.*, Allen & Overy's aosphere online services relating to capital markets and derivatives, http://www.aosphere.com (last viewed Jan. 30, 2015).

15. *See, e.g.*, SeyfarthLean® Consulting, http://www.seyfarth.com/Subsidiaries (last viewed Jan. 30, 2015).

with legal issues as they occur to preventing costly problems from arising in the first place, with backup insurance as an added bonus. Mike Roster gives an example of a company, not a law firm, providing such a service. In reading this, consider that promoting weight loss and smoking cessation has not put doctors out of business, nor has health insurance; quite the contrary. A law firm could equally well provide comprehensive prevention-based solutions and be uniquely positioned as a result. Mike Roster comments:

> I was talking to an owner of one of the largest food processors in Europe. I asked, "How are legal services working for you?" His answer was, "Wonderful—we don't use lawyers anymore." He went on to say that 95 percent of his company's legal issues were work force-related and health and safety-related and that there happens to be a service provider, not a law firm, that handles all of this. They come in, they write his manuals, they train his people, and they do compliance audits. They have a large stable of clients that need HR and health and safety management, just like his company.
>
> This service provider is like a law firm of old, seeing trends happening. But unlike a law firm of old, they modify the manuals as soon as they see need for changes. They say, "Look; there is a problem. The so-and-so regulatory agency has said such-and-such. We'll change page 43 of the manual to comply." And they change it straight away. They are very good at keeping their client companies out of trouble.
>
> The owner went on to say, "We have almost no disputes anymore." The owner also said, "Oh yeah, and in the rare instances when we might get sued, they have lawyers to handle it." He said this almost as an after-thought. And by the way, this service provider now also has an insurance arm. If a client wants, it can buy an insurance policy to cover the off-chance that a dispute results in some amount of liability. Thus, the cost for an entire set of operations (HR and health and safety) is fixed, and if something happens that is out of the ordinary, it's insured. This alternative service provider is brilliant at keeping its clients out of trouble. How many law firms think like this?[16]

Such offerings would provide a brand experience characterized by a long-term focus on collaboration, innovation, and quantifiably improved client outcomes. Roster notes this is how his fixed-price portfolios worked when he was general counsel at Stanford University and Stanford Medical Center. Firms had whole portfolios (HR, environmental, real estate, IP, etc.) including both counseling and litigation. The better the firms provided high-quality corporate work and counseling and likewise identified defects in operations that created legal exposures, the more profitable the firms became. The concept was based on Roster's experience as a managing partner and practice group head at Morrison & Foerster: If they could harness a firm's expertise, not hours, both they and the firm would benefit in very substantial ways.

16. Telephone interview by George Beaton with Michael Roster, member of the ACC Value Challenge Steering Committee (Oct. 14, 2014).

IT STARTS WITH THE CLIENTS

The starting point for defining differentiated, and possibly diversified, offerings is not the firm. As Alastair Morrison, head of client strategy at U.K.-based firm Pinsent Masons points out,

> [l]aw firms need to start to think about the job to be done from the clients' perspective, not from the lawyers' perspective. . . . For law firms to get an understanding of the job to be done for their clients' businesses, so that they can then facilitate the outcome, the clients need to be generous enough to let them in first—providing access to a collaborative environment where both parties can scope out the job.[17]

This concept of the "job to be done" was set out in more detail in chapter 7. As Alastair points out, being able to design client-centric offerings needs a dialogue with the clients who, in turn, need to let law firms in the door and under the bonnet to understand what really drives them.

While ad hoc personal conversations between partners and key client contacts are valuable, they are not sufficient to capture a comprehensive matrix of clients' and prospective clients' challenges and drivers over time to continuously develop and modify law firm strategy. Mel Anderson, former director of benchmarks at Beaton Research + Consulting and now head of information & insights at Grant Thornton Australia, highlights some issues with law firms obtaining client feedback and information:

> I am not saying large law firms are not client-centric. The problem, in my opinion, is the mechanisms they have in place for listening to, collecting, collating, analyzing, and acting on the insights from clients are at best rudimentary. Not to be dismissive of the good work some firms are doing, but there is still a long way to go. In the changing dynamic of client relationships, even what we recommend today is not going to be sufficient in ten years. Technology is evolving. Topics change. The issues clients face change, and you need to make sure you ask the questions that relate to clients' changing needs.[18]

This is, of course, yet another Catch-22, but the only way to address it is to start to gather relevant client-derived information in a structured and iterative way. The strategy for capturing actionable business intelligence from and in regard to clients' needs is to use a variety of methods, such as open-ended conversations, structured interviews, and surveys, gathered at planned intervals and from diverse relevant sources. Philip Kotler and Paul N. Bloom also point to the importance of understanding client behavior, in addition to the drivers.[19] These different inputs together provide a solid basis to develop key offerings for a brand, and to monitor their success on an ongoing basis. Looking into the future, firms might choose to

---

17. Interview by George Beaton with Alastair Morrison, Head of Client Strategy at Pinsent Masons (Aug. 7, 2014).

18. Interview by George Beaton with Mel Anderson, Head of Information and Insights, Grant Thornton Australia, Melbourne (Jan 12, 2015).

19. Philip Kotler & Paul N. Bloom, Marketing Professional Services 65–90 (Prentice-Hall 1984).

become more client-centric by relying more on client-derived data to assess partner and staff performance, by mandating positive client feedback as condition for advancement.

SECOND STEP: PLAY TO YOUR STRENGTHS

The second step in building brand purpose is to assess how client needs fit with the capabilities of the firm, as Stuart Fuller puts it,

> [t]here is no point doing work that you think your clients need, but at which you are not all that good, because you are at risk of disappointing the client. We need to make sure we can do work we are good at, not just do work that we need to do to keep the client. . . . The business model will evolve to a slightly broader model. I do not think the lawyers will follow the accountants. The evolution of the model will be driven by clients' needs rather than firms' needs to diversify their portfolio.
>
> One of the challenges in the law firm model is moving from delivering what it thinks the client needs to delivering what the clients actually want.[20]

This is part of a general position assessment that should underpin strategic planning in a law firm. Peter Doyle offers an excellent summary on strategic position assessment in the context of marketing for companies in his book *Valued-Based Marketing*.[21] The analysis of both client needs and firm strengths might uncover service areas that are not likely to be profitable for the firm, and therefore need to be divested. Firms have to find other ways to ensure that those client needs are met at an appropriate price point. Mark Rigotti of Herbert Smith Freehills proposes a cut-off:

> You have got to be able to do, say, 80 percent of clients' work types. . . . This is not precisely the right number, but if you broke it down and unbundled what we sell into 20 products, that would be about right over time. Some of these products will become commoditized, and our business model will not allow us to serve clients who want products 18, 19, and 20, unless we change our model or it is an investment decision for relationship purposes.[22]

Sourcing options are covered in more detail in chapter 10, but we would add the caveat that any such "investment decision" must be clearly calculated with a predicted return on the investment, and predefined criteria that will result in termination of the product if the returns at product or client level are not achieved.

---

20. Telephone interview by George Beaton with Stuart Fuller, Global Managing Partner, King & Wood Mallesons (Sept. 8, 2014).

21. Peter Doyle, Valued-Based Marketing: Marketing Strategies for Corporate Growth and Shareholder Value 151–88 (John Wiley & Sons, 2nd ed. 2008).

22. Telephone interview by George Beaton with Mark Rigotti, Joint CEO of Herbert Smith Freehills, (Aug 8, 2014).

It is a misconception that the commoditized services are necessarily those that a firm should get out of in the long-term. Mark Tamminga of Canadian firm Gowlings jokingly talks about his (very lucrative) "burger flipping" practice:

> Gowlings is really an amalgam of a number of law firms. . . . The little piece that I came from specialized in retail banking and from my earliest days I worked in the scrappy world of mortgage enforcement. In that early time I was responsible for developing what amounted to the first automated portfolio management system in a law firm that I knew of anywhere. At this point, I still work in that practice with about nine lawyers.
>
> Gowlings now has the largest mortgage remedies practice in Canada. That acquainted us with the whole concept of portfolio management. The ability to do a high velocity, fungible set of files in a restricted domain using database and document assembly technology with the rule set built into the machine. We have since taken these tools into small business debt collections and commercial loan placement. These practices have now become a *very* significant source of revenue for the firm. . . . And it is quite profitable. Historically, there was still a bit of disdain for the substance of the work; it is viewed as a burger flipper practice. But that is 15-year-old news. There is now a great deal of respect for the operational cleverness we have brought to what is, in effect, a commodity practice, as well as the underlying technology, which is first rate.[23]

Going back to branding, the summary of effective branding is executing a brand purpose based on differentiated and diversified offerings. This necessitates starting from the client's point of view and then matching the proven current and future client business needs with the firm's own areas of strength in designing, delivering, and communicating about its services and products. The brand encapsulates the unique way the firm meets client needs that makes them preferable to others.

Brand purpose identifies and captures the differentiating synergy between the following three fundamental elements of a firm:

- Culture—What the firm stands for, how it behaves internally and externally, what it values;
- Reputation—What the firm is known for, the respect it attracts in the market, what problems it is asked to solve; and
- Relationships—Who is the "company" the firm keeps, for example, its clients and advocates, and into which circles is it invited, for example, agents of influence, knowledge, and power.[24]

Brand purpose is the organizing principle that directs everything a firm does. It is fundamental to differentiation and establishes the relationship between "what a firm stands for" (internally) and "what a firm is known for" (externally).

---

23. Interview by George Beaton with Mark Tamminga, Leader, Innovation Initiatives, and Rick Kathuria, National Director, Project Management and Legal Logistics, Gowling Lafleur Henderson LLP, in Toronto, Can. (Sept. 14, 2014).

24. Riddell, Beaton & Welsh, *supra* note 12.

BRAND PERMISSION

A strong brand is in some ways a double-edged sword. There is no such thing as a free lunch, and there is no such thing as a brand that gives you unlimited opportunities, because, let's face it, deciding to be really good in one area means that you have fewer resources to be equally good in other areas. Having a strong brand purpose means your clients will punish you if you do not live up to it. Consumers expect companies to have a clear purpose that includes aspects such as community engagement, environmental sustainability, and generally doing the right thing in a worldwide arena, and they are ready to take their business elsewhere if companies violate these fairly high standards. Remember the outcry when upscale yoga-gear manufacturer Lululemon's CEO Chip Wilson went on the record as being happy to use child labor in third-world countries to make the garments that aid Western devotees on their journey to enlightenment?[25] Bad karma! Law firms should be aware of dangers to their reputation if they do not uphold a high standard even beyond their legal work into, for example, community engagement, building staff diversity, and environmental sustainability.

Brand permission "defines the limits of customers' willingness to accept a familiar brand name in new marketplace situations."[26] It is what your brand can get away with in extending beyond the confines of the brand image that you have carefully built and nurtured. The notion of brand permission is important in considering diversification beyond the legal services that a firm has traditionally offered, because even if there is a client need for a service, it is not a given that they will be willing to buy it from a branded provider that they associate with other things. A vivid illustration set out elsewhere[27] is the imagined provision of adult entertainment movies through a member of the Disney group of companies . . . enough said.

The Big Four professional services firms provide one example of slowly and successfully extending the brand permission given by clients. Peter Williams of Deloitte comments "[i]f 20 years ago somebody had said you go to your accountant to get a top-end website, I would have said 'What?' Now that happens all the time. I think it is about how we define ourselves."[28] But as Warren Riddell of Beaton Capital points out, even acquisitions in the professional services sector provide plenty of examples where the attempted absorption of the acquired brand into the "mother ship" failed in a commercial sense because brand permission did not simply transfer to the acquiring brand, and therefore the goodwill attached to the initial brand was lost.[29] Overall, the Big Four have a track record of successful

---

25. *See, e.g.*, Scott Deveau, *Yoga Mogul Has Critics in a Knot,* THE TYEE BLOG (Feb. 17, 2005), http://thetyee.ca/News/2005/02/17/LuluCritics/.

26. Yale School of Management Center for Customer Insights, *Brand Permission: When No Means No* INSIGHTS REVIEW BLOG (Dec. 12, 2011), http://som.yale.edu/brand-permission-when-no-means-no.

27. *Id.*

28. Telephone interview by George Beaton with Peter Williams, Chief Edge Officer at the Centre for the Edge, Deloitte Australia (Sept. 3, 2014).

29. Warren Riddell, *Professions, Acquisitions and Brand Permission*, BIGGER.BETTER.BOTH? BLOG (Oct. 22, 2012), http://www.beatoncapital.com/2012/10/professions-acquisitions-and-brand-permission/.

diversification that may well project into the future. Alastair Morrison considers that "the Big Four have a brand that is elastic across different services, industries, and geographies. . . . The Big Four will attack the risk, compliance, and regulatory area like they have successfully done in the tax market."[30]

The question remains, how can brand permission be assessed, particularly before deciding to embark on a strategy of diversification, and how can it be extended if desired? The first part is relatively easy. Clients and prospective clients can be surveyed independently to test for awareness and attitudes to see if they associate the brand with the services in question. If they do, hurrah, you are off to the races, since your brand is elastic enough to accommodate the expansion.

If there is insufficient brand permission as indicated by market research, it becomes necessary to invest in shifting the opinion of the relevant audience. This can be achieved by focused campaigns highlighting relevant expertise, resources, and appropriate emotional appeals: effectively, a rebranding exercise. Names that express such a branding facelift, though arguably not straying too far from the core, are SeyfarthLean or Gowlings Practical, branded initiatives changing how the work is done within the firm—and signaling that these firms are willing to change the very fabric of their core brand. There is of course always the risk that a failure of the new service or product will damage the brand, and this is probably the reason why law firms like Berwin Leighton Paisner, Allen & Overy, and Pinsent Masons (all hailing from the United Kingdom) are using newly created brands to market flexible workforce offerings that go beyond their traditional services.[31]

HOW CLIENTS BUY LEGAL SERVICES

Based on the extensive Beaton Research + Consulting research on how clients buy professional and specifically legal services, there are distinct stages in the decision-making process by client organizations, as set out in Figure 8.1. These are consideration, shortlisting, and final decision in the buying process—akin to a funnel, and then a period of assessment of the services that can result in client loyalty or, even better, client actions that provide positive word-of-mouth, in other words, referrals. Or, if the product falls short of the mark, clients will be switching to other services and start the process again, but likely without consideration being given to the "failed" service.

Each of these stages constitutes an increasingly narrow part of a funnel leading to a final purchasing decision by the client. And each offers opportunities to influence client decision making in favor of a specific law firm through appropriately targeted business development and marketing. The specific drivers of client

---

30. Morrison, *supra* note 17.
31. For example, three U.K. firms offering flexible legal staff as needed: Lawyers on Demand (founded with support from Berwin Leighton Paisner), Allen & Overy's Peerpoint, and Pinsent Masons' Vario.

FIGURE 8.1

Clients' Decision-Making Process

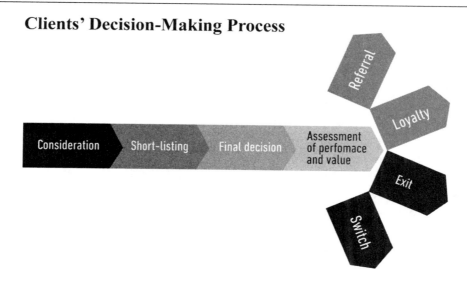

behavior for each stage are discussed in more detail elsewhere.[32] An in-depth analysis of client feedback on previous purchases or decisions not to purchase can aid a firm in fine-tuning its marketing strategy to appropriately address possible shortcomings in "funneling" client decisions along.

LAW FIRM MARKETING

The examples of the purple coke commercial and Jeremy Szwider's comments on comprehensive branding illustrate that marketing today has evolved far beyond static presentation of brochures and webpages to a comprehensive two-way communication around all aspects of goods or services, using a variety of channels to communicate the brand purpose. Peter Doyle posited that marketing is "the management process that seeks to maximize returns to shareholders by developing relationships with valued customers and creating a competitive advantage,"[33] highlighting the link between marketing and long-term value and strategy, as opposed to short-term profits. This comprehensive concept links marketing to value generation. It makes it clear that marketing costs are an investment in the future of the brand. The applicability of this concept also holds for professional services partnerships, including law firms. Client relationship management, in comparison, is the consolidated handling of relationships with current and prospective clients

---

32. George Beaton, Eric Chin & Tristan Forrester, *Research on the Procurement of Legal Services*, in BUYING LEGAL: PROCUREMENT INSIGHTS AND PRACTICE 1–7 (Silvia Hodges ed., Ark Group 2012).

33. PETER DOYLE, VALUED-BASED MARKETING: MARKETING STRATEGIES FOR CORPORATE GROWTH AND SHAREHOLDER VALUE 30 (John Wiley & Sons, 2nd ed. 2008).

commensurate with strategic goals, and leveraging information technology, to achieve this competitive advantage.

"Inbound marketing" is an increasingly utilized effective marketing approach. Instead of confronting clients and potential clients with marketing content in which they possibly have very little interest (equivalent to interrupting a movie with a commercial, or a newspaper article with an advertisement), it is a much more cost-effective starting point to offer them an interaction that has value for them, at a time and in a manner of their choosing. This can be, for example, well-researched information on a webpage, or a useful mobile phone application, or an interesting computer game, all resulting in a willingness by the addressee to eventually become a client through additional nudging following the first contact. Law firms usually provide a good deal of high-quality general legal information through their webpages and blogs, but forego the opportunity to link this in an integrated manner and more directly to the services that they are selling. Such information promotes the brand in a general way, but does not build on specific positive inter-actions to convert these into sales. A better option is to offer valuable information for free, but side-by-side with premium content that is only available on a sub-scription basis or other strings-attached basis. This places the client figuratively at the point of sale and in control, with a mindset of appreciating the quality of similar offerings, and therefore primed to make a purchasing decision.

For a law firm, a large part of their marketing activities will be directed toward specific addressees in chosen target client organizations. These activities should be tailored toward specific client drivers as much as possible. Mark Rigotti comments on different types of client relationships:

> On the one hand you have a type of client who is just ruthlessly commercializing the relationship, and you need to be able to deal with it on economic rationaliza-tion terms; and I do not know how many partners are well equipped to do that. One idea is "You want us to deal with procurement, well here is our procurement team."
>
> On the other hand, I was with . . . [company] the other day, where we have an incredible relationship with them; so far away from the first type of relationship I described. It is not metric-driven; it is very qualitative, very dialogue-driven.
>
> So we have professionalization of the internal procurement function going on and two types of clients emerging, a big generalization of course: Ones that are driven by economic rationalisms, and ones that expect exceptional service and relationships. This says to law firms that not one size fits all, and there are proba-bly 50 variations between those two ends of the range. So you need a very flexible and adaptable client relationship model if you are going to cover the field.[34]

Mark has clearly identified a major client driver, the need to customize marketing to each of the types, or segments, of clients. Alternatively, a firm could decide to

---

34. Rigotti, *supra* note 22.

position itself by specializing and limiting its offerings to better serve just one or two segments, a simpler task that more easily allows focused branding.

CLIENT-FACING RESEARCH IN CLIENT RELATIONSHIP MANAGEMENT

Ultimately, the goal of any branding and marketing, including client relationship management (CRM), is to grow the amount of the right kind of work coming into the firm, not to individual partners.

In too many firms it is not possible to reach consensus and firm-wide action on investing resources in CRM because each partner is first and foremost concerned about their personal brand and share of the pie. Experience shows any attempt at focusing and centralizing CRM in these firms, and thereby strengthening client relationships, is likely to be doomed.

On the other hand, CRM-driven growth of work from existing clients can turn into a positive feedback loop. Lisa Damon of Seyfarth Shaw shares some experiences:

> One of the things we were able to show very early on through data is that if we did right by our clients, whether that was lowering the cost, or making it more efficient, or reducing the cycle time, our clients would return that to us with more and better work in a very real, concrete way. As our people began to realize this, things just accelerated dramatically. As partners experienced it, they came to understand the benefits of their investment in time and working differently with their clients to drive efficiency while maintaining superb quality. The investment came back to the firm and partners in better, tighter, stronger relationships that are resulting in more work.
>
> Instead of approaching the world of change by putting a fence around it and saying I have got to hang on to what I have, we were able to turn around early on and show our partners that if we focused on the client and gave the client what the client needed, we would reach the same and better results in a way that was client focused.[35]

Lisa highlighted the importance of client feedback and satisfaction both for internal process improvements as well as for strategy. But without robust processes to collect client feedback, analyze it, and feed it back into an operations management strategy setting, these positive feedback loops are unlikely to occur. ALM Legal Intelligence has published survey data[36] indicating that only slightly more than half of respondents from law firms (56 percent) had a plan to track client loyalty and satisfaction, and out of those, 45 percent collected feedback annually and 47 percent episodically, that is, in an ad hoc manner. Such a piecemeal approach to data

---

35. Telephone interview by George Beaton with Lisa Damon, National Chair, Labor & Employment Department, Seyfarth Shaw LLP (Aug. 21, 2014).
36. ALM Legal Intelligence, *Thinking Like Your Client-Strategic Planning in Law Firms* 14 (2012).

collection will probably not yield actionable business intelligence. Instead, client engagement and data collection from clients needs to cover prospective and retrospective aspects (that is, feedback on past engagements) from a variety of sources in a comprehensive way.

In addition, when asked about their own assessment of their firm's expertise about the business drivers of their top 20 clients, only 22 percent of respondents rated their firm as "extremely knowledgeable."[37] Mel Anderson is familiar with such shortfalls:

> There have been a number of instances we have encountered in the work we have done with firms over the last ten years of firms setting client plans without ever having had a conversation with the client about their outlook for the year. Such as asking clients "What are your challenges? What is keeping you up at night, and how can we help you with that?" The number of firms who do not talk with clients in this way is more than a little surprising. And when we suggest it, they say "Oh yeah, that seems like a good idea!" It is not through lack of care. It is just not top of mind.[38]

All law firms highlight their business knowledge about industries and their clients' businesses. If these activities are intended to make a credible contribution to their brand, they should be regularly assessing their clients' performance, challenges, and future plans, and using this information in strategy formulation.

THE PERSONAL TOUCH: PROFESSIONAL SALES STAFF

The quantity and sophistication of firms' marketing and business development activities are on the rise, in part to keep up with clients' increasingly professional procurement practices. In this environment, it makes sense to build professional sales competency in a firm. Lawyers are not educated and trained to be effective marketers and sellers, though no doubt some are. "Effective" here is once again judged from a client's perspective, and this includes being a client advocate within the firm. David Worley of PwC (see the following case study) sums up what it takes to be effective as a marketer and business development practitioner:

> I don't know any clients who want to be sold to. Most clients want to have somebody who will work with them to help identify and resolve the issues that challenge them and do this in the most expeditious manner, with the best-qualified expertise they can provide. Then follow up. I mean relentlessly follow up, to be sure all of the issues are mitigated and you have done exactly what you said you were going to do and more, so you can exceed the client's expectations.
>
> I tell our salespeople, our business is not that hard. You will never understand everything we do as a firm, because we do so many things in so many different

---

37. *Id.*
38. Anderson, *supra* note 18.

areas of the client's business, but if you enjoy the basics of business and how all the pieces come together to make commerce work, then you will enjoy this job. You just have to understand what it is your client does to make money, what is the problem keeping them from making money, and then position our team so we can collaborate with the client to solve their problem.[39]

A novel (for law firms), more embedded marketing role like this necessitates a different kind of expertise than is found in law firms. The role can be cost-efficiently staffed by people with marketing and sales, not legal, backgrounds. Mark Rigotti considers the significant potential for separating selling and producing legal services in large firms as a logical next step:

> In the front office, sooner or later we are going to have to look at the role of the partner. You actually need to consider separating sales and execution, or have something of a sliding scale, rather than everybody trying to do everything. The role of the partner might change over time. When you look at the accounting firms, there is a clear differentiation between sales and execution.[40]

Such a separation has of course far-reaching implications for the internal structures of a firm, where performance on business development is usually tied to remuneration and is combined with the production of legal services. This obviously limits the willingness of law firm partners to invest in building a separate professional sales force, apart from a still-present cultural reluctance to "peddle" one's intellectual wares. But, as Mark points out, other professions have long since moved toward separate sales forces. And the sky did not fall in, as the following case study illustrates.

CASE STUDY: THE EVOLUTION OF A PROFESSIONAL SALES FORCE AT PwC U.S.

David Worley, currently West Region Business Development Leader and former U.S. Sales and Business Development Leader at PricewaterhouseCoopers U.S.A., has seen and shaped the growth and evolution of the professional sales force at PwC since 2002. His background is in sales management and operations, and he worked for Xerox in various capacities for 15 years prior to joining PwC.

Today the sales and BD team at PwC comprises about 170 people, compared to some 3,000 partners and 40,000 staff overall. The sales team directly secures about 10 percent of annual revenue, with additional account management responsibilities for another 20 percent. The team performs both direct sales functions as well as teaching PwC practitioners to sell and manage relationships. The value of the sales function for the parent has been regularly assessed, primarily by measuring return on investment.

---

39. Telephone interview by George Beaton with David Worley, West Region Business Development Leader and former U.S. Sales and Business Development Leader at PricewaterhouseCoopers U.S.A. (Oct. 28, 2014).

40. Rigotti, *supra* note 22.

David pointed out the similarities between challenges in changes in the sales function for professional services firms and what is happening in law firms today:

> I see the legal community embracing how we have positioned marketing and business development and being challenged with some of the same obstacles we've experienced. There are similarities in the partnership arrangement, for example, the challenge of separating sales and production, as well as the cultural fit of a sales organization within a professional services firm. To make it work, you need a commitment from leadership and you have to be able to navigate the various personalities and cultural challenges inherent in a professional services firm. Regardless, it comes down to knowing your client and their business and having strong relationships with them.
>
> . . .
>
> When I joined the firm, there were many challenges in having salespeople coexist with partners. Some partners and staff were averse to using sales professionals for business development. Shortly after the program started, the results began to speak for themselves. Partners began to see the benefits of working with sales professionals: They now had another way to leverage their time, be more consistent in managing and improving client relationships, and win work. Partners' perspectives started to change. What was originally "Why do we have these guys?" became "Why do we not have more of them?" Now the challenge is to make sure we have the appropriate business case to support the need for a salesperson, that all parties agree with the need, and that we are getting the proper ROI.[41]

David traced the development of the function within the firm from its early beginnings to its eventual consolidation with marketing in a way that is closely aligned with overall strategy:

> The genesis was probably in the mid-1990s when a leader in our tax line of service realized this dichotomy: As experts in their field, they have great technical minds and are brilliant with tax solutions and services. But, for the most part, they often struggled at selling services and creating an "easy to do business with" type of relationship between trusted advisor and client. They also didn't have time to cultivate new relationships and new opportunities.
>
> . . .
>
> We hired somewhere between 25 to 50 business development people at that time. Through that effort, we were able to foster new opportunities and relationships, and formalize those relations, often at a deeper level than we had been able to in the past. We saw improvements in our ability to serve our clients more broadly, and, in some cases, better understand their business issues and develop better solutions. With more salespeople working with clients, we created more leverage for the partners, which in turn created more opportunities and eventually helped to increase revenues.
>
> . . .

---

41. Worley, *supra* note 39.

> If you look at the evolution of the program from when I started to where it is today, we were very practice-oriented as a professional sales group. But this created a bit of a disconnect. There wasn't much of a sales structure other than the tax line of service, and our other lines of service were hiring sales professionals for their individual practice needs. Four or five years later, we knew we needed a common marketing and sales platform for the firm. At that time, there was a marketing group and a sales group and a sales support group. We integrated these groups into a single marketing and sales organization to support our priority non-audit clients and aligned the goals of the organization with the firm's overall direction and strategies. The organization is now led by two partners, one of them is a vice-chairman of the firm and the other is the lead partner over the sales organization. They now have full responsibility for this very large and important organization.[42]

Looking toward the future, David anticipates the need for additional specialization and integration with a sharp client focus, as well as a reliance on social media:

> It is now a question of how we leverage the sales and marketing team better for the future and where we want to be strategically as an organization. We continually seek to become an organization that creates strategic value for our constituents internally and externally. We know we need sales professionals with more industry expertise and better understanding of our clients' businesses, and how we can help those clients solve their toughest issues. We want our salespeople to hold the initial conversations with the client to assess the issue, surmise what actions need to be taken, collaborate with the client, and start developing opportunities to solve the issues together. After that initial contact, the salespeople bring in the experts to help the client solve the issue. This creates better leverage and creates more value for the client and the firm.
>
> Social media is now an expected standard. How we connect with the market and our clients will continue to evolve as technology evolves. With clients making decisions based on what they are finding through social media, marketing has to be very timely. A key to marketing through social media is knowing which channels potential clients are using to understand their issues and to identify who can help them solve their problems. Why? Because 60 or more percent of the time a client is looking on the Internet for the answer to their problem before they even contact a service provider.
>
> We invest a good deal of time in how we can develop channels that will connect us with our clients, and these channels include social media. But we also want to have the deeper relationships with our sales professionals personally connecting with clients so we have it covered on both ends.[43]

So in David's experience with the professional sales team at a large firm, PwC partners were initially reluctant to work with sales professionals targeting their clients, but over time have come to appreciate the qualitative addition to their ability to understand and address client issues, as well as the positive return on the investment in the sales force.

---

42. *Id.*
43. *Id.*

The function has been integrated with marketing, and moved up the reporting chain in the firm to ensure it is fully aligned with strategy. In the future, opportunities will arise through their deepened industry knowledge that will allow sales professionals to become even more solution-focused, and through client interaction using social media supplementing and complementing personal contact.

CONCLUSION

Firm brands are becoming increasingly important as services become more commoditized, as law firms diversify, and as partners with strong personal brands become even more mobile, often acting as free agents. The Big Four professional services firms have successfully moved to firm-centered ways of managing their brands and client relationships. Law firms need to invest in strengthening their brand purpose through credible focus and differentiation of their value proposition based on solid market- and client-derived insights. Successful diversification needs brand permission, which can be gauged by research. In marketing their services, firms need to influence client decision making at all stages of the funnel. Firms should consider at least partly separating production from selling legal services. Professional sales personnel add value for professional services firms by allowing for deep and ongoing engagement with clients beyond the less disciplined efforts of the practitioners, as the case study of building a professional sales and marketing force at PwC illustrates.

Chapter 9

Pricing and Fee Arrangements

Key Points

- The billable hour has long shaped the culture of traditional law firms, but in the interests of clients, firms must move away from it as the dominant form of pricing.
- Alternative fee arrangements (AFAs) can be profitably employed, particularly if offered proactively to clients. AFAs have the potential to increase realization rates, and demonstrate better alignment with clients' needs.
- Pricing strategy has implications for the entire firm. It needs to address how pricing fits into its overall strategy, who is responsible, and how pricing is measured and executed. Pricing needs involvement and data input from all parts of the firm, not just supervising partners, the CFO, or a pricing manager. Sustainable, that is, profitable in the long term, pricing decisions need to be based on internal and external data.
- Demonstrated cost consciousness is a stronger driver of clients' perceptions of value than is low price. Indeed, when price is too low from a client's perspective, it diminishes the client's perception of value.
- Communication with clients about price needs to focus on assessing client- and matter-specific factors, and client needs. This leads to pricing that aligns with the client's goals, and away from a one-size-fits-all approach.
- Fee arrangements that demonstrate alignment include fixed fees; bonus or holdback components around client-defined metrics; and outcomes-related fees, retainers, and contingency fees.

INTRODUCTION

Other chapters deal with various ways to promote, find the right buyers for, and ultimately sell a firm's legal services (see chapter 8) and to source or produce work more efficiently (see chapter 10). Pricing strategies bring it all together, since client demands today go beyond billable hours with a bit of a discount thrown in. The deregulated common law jurisdictions and Canada seem to be fertile ground for pricing innovation, even though pricing strategies are obviously not tied to specific law firm structures. Given the reliance of traditional law firms on time-based billing that pervades their entire reward system, starting from scratch with a corporate structure may just be more conducive to realizing the benefits of alternative pricing approaches. In this context, examples from abroad can offer insights that can lead to first mover advantages on home turf. "Me, too" strategies on the other hand might enable firms to keep up, but will rarely let them pull away from the pack.

But where did the billable hour come from in the first place? Private practice and in-house veteran Mike Roster traces the origins of time-based billing:

> The biggest challenge for many of the firms, certainly in the United States (but I note we exported this craziness to the world) is a reliance on billable hours. I think people forget that until 35 years ago, not a single bill went out the door in the United States (or anywhere, for that matter) solely based on billable hours. It happened because of the arrival of computers. Instead of hand-written time diaries, we started putting our time into the computer. The first generation of in-house lawyers a few years later knew we were using computers to keep track of our time and said "We want to see the computer printout." Firms resisted mightily at first but finally yielded and let the in-house lawyers see the computer printouts. The in-house lawyers said "That must be the value, then. We're only paying what the computer says, not what you say is the value." And so then the firms started making a science out of it. David Maister wrote a wonderful book and series of articles about professional services based on billing hours in law.[1] Firms thus built the use of hours into everything we did: producing the bill to the client, valuing a partner's book of business, evaluating the profitability of an office, calculating the business generation of a practice group, etc. And it is the main reason law firms are now struggling. They aren't sure how to run their firms and evaluate people and work other than on hours.[2]

As Mike Roster succinctly sets out and as the case study in chapter 3 illustrates, the problem is that in a traditional law firm, hours are used as both a main unit of measurement of practitioners' productivity—and as a major driver of profitability. Hours are therefore the unit that simultaneously drives the two diametrically opposed goals of efficiency and profitability.[3]

To become more efficient, a firm should use the fewest units of production, that is, hours, to be maximally efficient and still aim to turn out a high-quality product. But on the profitability side, the primary interest of a firm is to increase the number of hours billed, and to maximize the cost of those hours. Likewise,

---

1. *See* DAVID H. MAISTER, MANAGING THE PROFESSIONAL SERVICE FIRM 31–39 (The Free Press 1993). See also the case study "Maister Maxed Out" in chapter 3, illustrating the problem that a firm relying on Maister's concept faces today.

2. Telephone interview by George Beaton with Michael Roster, member of the ACC Value Challenge Steering Committee (Oct. 14, 2014).

3. Michael Roster, *ACC Value Challenge: Facing Up to the Challenge* (Association of Corporate Counsel 2013).

firms use the number of hours billed for internal measurement purposes leading to rewards, and even leadership legitimacy is heavily based on this paradigm. And there is an element of reluctance to change a running system on the part of the clients as well. Andrew Perlman, vice-chair of the American Bar Association Commission on the Future of Legal Services, sums this up:

> For in-house counsel, it is not their own money going out of the door. They feel like it will ensure that all of the bases are covered if there are billable hours, and they feel like the firm might cut corners with an AFA. The slowness of movement towards AFAs cannot be attributed entirely to law firm culture.[4]

Yet time-based pricing means a one-sided risk allocation and lack of predictability for clients that no longer works in what is generally acknowledged to be a buyer's market for legal services.

With increasing competition, the response to more-for-less requests from clients has mostly been met through discounts on hourly rates—demonstrating that if all you have is a hammer, the world tends to look like a nail. Such a view can even carry through into fixed-fee arrangements, with problematic effects, as Mike Roster points out:

> In those firms that are running on the Maister formula, their primary if not only means of maintaining profitability is to keep raising their rates and demanding more hours from their lawyers.
>
> As these firms move to fixed pricing, they totally misunderstand profitability because they keep saying, "Well, we would have made so-and-so much had we been able to put on twenty lawyers at these higher rates, and here we are only able to put on five lawyers at these fixed prices. We are losing money." They are making catastrophically wrong decisions for the future. *The initial challenge is moving a firm away from its entire dependence on the billable hour for everything the firms does* (emphasis added).[5]

If the value proposition that you are selling to a client is an unpredictable volume of bulk hours at a somewhat negotiable rate, you have set the stage for discount-bound negotiations. You also have aligned performance measurement to feed into an hours-based internal reward system. But since there is always some firm willing to do it cheaper, you eventually end up with nowhere to go. One joke among Western law firms operating in China today is that when competing for a job, in the first round, you slash your wrists and whoever is still standing makes it to the second round . . . at which point you slash your throat . . .

---

4. Telephone interview by Eric Chin and Imme Kaschner with Andrew Perlman, Professor of Law, Suffolk University Law School, and Vice Chair, ABA Commission on the Future of Legal Services (Aug. 26, 2014).

5. Roster, *supra* note 1.

CASE STUDY: PRICING AND STRUCTURAL EVOLUTION AT KENT COUNTY LEGAL, U.K.

It is hard to look beyond the status quo, in this case the billable hour, in a situation where this has been the almost exclusive way of valuing and pricing legal services for a long time. The following longitudinal case study is useful because it illustrates the advantages and disadvantages of hourly billing in the context of the changing structure of a specific type of legal services provider, namely a government in-house legal department. The following description is taken from an interview with Geoff Wild, Director of Governance and Law at Kent County Council in the United Kingdom, who enjoys an international reputation and many accolades for being a legal innovator par excellence, and not only in government legal services. Geoff describes the state of Kent County Legal Services when he took over the department in 1997 as being similar to many in-house legal teams at the time:

> The traditional local government in-house legal service is often poorly staffed and poorly managed. There is no performance management, there are no standards of quality, there is no idea of customer care, there is no idea of cost-efficiency or cost-effectiveness or value or, indeed, accountability. . . . You are given a sum of money, at the beginning of each year; it is called a budget. You are given this pot of money and told "There you are. Go ahead and spend it." And the only measure of your performance is by how much you meet that budget by the end of the year. But that pot of money is given to you by somebody who has no idea of demand or the output or the value of the legal service that you are going to deliver as an in-house team. It is simply calculated on some formula that bears no relation to reality.
>
> So the lawyers invariably have too little money to deliver the service which is being demanded of them, and that is because the clients who are receiving that legal service do not pay for it. They can basically ask for whatever they want; it is a free good. They can load the legal department with any number of requests, jobs and burdens, most of which are not legal work, anyway, they are just something people find too difficult to deal with, so they decide "Hey, we will just give it to the lawyers." The lawyers are struggling under this weight of work. The clients are complaining because they are not getting a good service. The funding is not sufficient to recruit any more lawyers; it is a vicious circle. It is a downward spiral resulting in demotivated and under-performing staff, poor quality work, and dissatisfied clients. It is just awful.[6]

The situation that Geoff sketches is one with a skewed allocation of cost responsibility and risk working against the legal service provider. There is no or very little meaningful dialogue between lawyer and client about needs, priorities, and potential for more efficient resource allocation. And it does not work well for either side.

The radical solution that was implemented at the time under Geoff's leadership was to reorganize the department, by giving the budgeted amount of money to the

---

6. Interview by David Goener, Eric Chin, and Imme Kaschner with Geoff Wild, Director of Governance and Law at Kent County Council, in Maidstone, U.K. (Oct. 2, 2014).

internal client, who was then free to buy services from the in-house department or on the open market, with in-house services billed in a time-based manner.[7] As an aside, this is another example of the use of a burning platform that presented itself to gather consensus for change (see chapter 13). Geoff comments:

> I was given a year, either to transform the service or to oversee its complete externalization; it was a sort of "shape up or ship out" situation. . . . I tried to do the first option, which was to transform it completely, but what I needed to do was to dramatically alter the basis on which the service was run and delivered. That meant convincing the people here to change all the things which had been established for generations about how legal services ran and operated. The first of those was the financial basis on which we operated. I wanted to model the in-house team very much more along the lines of a private law firm.[8]

At that time, that included time-based billing for the internal client, and for other local government entities that the department eventually served. Initially, and for quite a while, this pricing mechanism resulted in a much better alignment between legal department and clients, and a large increase in customer satisfaction. But the story does not end there, as Geoff describes:

> Going from the corporately-funded model to the charging model I just described required us to adopt a form of charging, and we used the form that was the most commonly used at the time and is still used, which is the hourly rate; the billable hour. That is still used for some of our clients who actually insist on it, believe it or not, because they recognize it, they are comfortable with it. They ask, still, to be billed on that basis.

> But increasingly, we are moving towards fixed cost pricing and value-based charging. Charging by results, we offer our clients all sorts of different methods now, to better suit their wishes and expectations. This requires a different way of thinking, and a different way of valuing and costing your work, because the temptation is simply to always go back to the hourly rate to calculate your fixed price. Whereas, in fact, what you should be looking at in the value-based charging method, is looking at what really is the benefit for the client of doing this work. Working out with them what value they place on doing this, according to very specific criteria.

> You sit down with the client, agree what the work is that is required by them, what the value is to the client. Is the value based on how quickly it could be done? How specifically it could be done in a certain way? You work out with the client what their parameters are for this piece of work, and price it according to that. Now that requires a different skill-set to the one we've been used to in billing by time. But it is far more attuned to what a number of our clients increasingly want.[9]

---

7. For a more detailed profile of Geoff's work with the department, see Diana Bentley, *Running Wild* (Feb. 2014), http://www.kent.gov.uk/__data/assets/pdf_file/0015/13335/Running-Wild-February-2014.pdf.
8. *Supra* note 6.
9. *Id.*

So the goal of high-quality client service was initially fostered through time-based pricing, until a better way came along. The new way of pricing is based on a careful ascertainment of what constitutes value to a specific client. The transformation of pricing structure from fixed-budget to hourly billing to value-based negotiated fixed-price billing at Kent County Legal over a number of years provides an example of what magnitude of change is possible even in the notoriously change-averse setting of local government legal services.

ALTERNATIVE FEE ARRANGEMENTS

A lack of creativity is the only limit to the types and variations of fee arrangements beyond those that are solely time based or, as they are sometimes called, cost-plus fee arrangements. The umbrella term "alternative fee arrangement," or AFA, is commonly used to designate anything other than a straight hourly rate per fee-earner as the basis of billing. We feel that blended, discounted, or capped rates that are still time-based do not qualify for the designation AFA, because they do not serve to align the interests of clients and law firms any better than simple hourly rates do (possibly with the exception of capped rates that effectively constitute a fixed maximum price).[10]

TRENDS IN PRICING STRATEGY AND AFA USE

There is a clear expectation in U.S. law firms that competition based on price is here to stay, with 94 percent of respondents seeing it as "permanent" in a 2015 Altman Weil survey.[11] Yet even among firms with over 250 partners, only 53 percent have changed their approach to pricing, and an additional 17 percent were considering such a change. Among firms with fewer than 250 partners, the numbers are even lower (only 24 percent have changed their approach, with 58 percent considering it).[12] This is against the backdrop of clients routinely asking for, and receiving, discounts for legal services. In another Altman Weil survey of the client side, CLOs quantified the average discount received, with about half of them naming 6 to 10 percent, but with an increasing trend toward more clients receiving discounts of more than 10 percent.[13] Add realization rates of around 83 percent into

---

10. *See, e.g.*, Law Technology Today, *What Is, and Is Not, An Alternative Fee Arrangement* (Dec. 10, 2014) (based on Patrick Lamb, Alternative Fees for Litigators and their Clients (ABA Publishing 2014)), http://www.lawtechnologytoday.org/2014/12/what-is-and-is-not-an-alternative-fee-arrangement/.

11. Altman Weil, *2015 Law Firms in Transition* (2015), http://www.altmanweil.com/dir_docs/resource/1c789e f2-5cff-463a-863a-2248d23882a7_document.pdf (last visited Nov. 14, 2015).

12. *Id*, at 57.

13. Altman Weil, *2014 Chief Legal Officer Survey* (2014), http://www.altmanweil.com/CLO2014/.

the mix[14] and it becomes clear that the billable hour has become a double-edged sword at the bottom of a slippery slope (excuse the catachresis).

Susan Hackett, formerly of the ACC, points to the trouble that lies ahead for law firms that simply engage in the discounting game:

> The firm that is responding to clients' requests for cost reductions by giving discounts usually does so—not because they want or believe that they should do the work at a lower cost, but because they are worried that they cannot afford to lose the client. Within a few years (or maybe sooner) that work will be unprofitable for them, and then they are in a real quandary, since raising rates or prices is not the norm in today's markets.
>
> The goal from my perspective is to get firms who hear those kinds of requests to figure out early on how they can start lowering their costs by improving their service efficiency, rather than simply saying, "OK, we have a 20 percent margin so we can afford to take 10 percent off." If a firm is discounting its rates year after year, it is either going out of business soon, or it is artificially raising its prices so that they can be discounted. Some firms have this wacky belief that having given a big discount in Year One, they think that in Year Two, the client will come back and say, "Wow, that was great, our economic pinch is over, take back the 10 percent that you took off last year, and add an additional 7 percent as you have always done in the past going forward." The increase is never coming back—firms that want to charge more and make more money from their work are going to have to change their focus from increasing revenue to increasing profitability: They will need to find new ways to deliver higher value work more efficiently (which increases margins), rather than playing shell games with rates or trying to trick clients into paying lower rates for lawyers who take longer to do the work: These strategies rarely lead to higher profitability, and they drive away clients.
>
> It may sound contradictory, but it's not: You have to learn how to deliver services more efficiently to drive the same profitability in the future—because it's no longer about falling rates times increased hours, but about fixed price for results delivered. It's not about cheap; it's about value.[15]

Figure 3.1 in chapter 3 confirms precisely the point made by Susan, that discounted prices are a one-way street, especially when clients perceive that the prices charged by their suppliers are falling.

The additional survey data on use and profitability of AFAs (defined as "nonhourly billing") in the Altman Weil 2015 survey points to the huge wasted opportunities by firms that do not invest in their ability to offer and profitably price with AFAs. In 2015, the percentage of firms that offered AFAs primarily proactively was 32 percent, compared to 68 percent reactive.[16] London-based pricing expert

---

14. Georgetown Law Center for the Legal Profession, *2015 Report on the State of the Legal Market* 5 (2015), http://www.law.georgetown.edu/academics/centers-institutes/legal-profession/upload/FINAL-Report-1-7-15.pdf.

15. Telephone interview by Eric Chin and Imme Kaschner with Susan Hackett, former Senior Vice-President and General Counsel of the Association of Corporate Counsel (Sept. 4, 2004).

16. Altman Weil, *supra* note 11, at 66.

Richard Burcher comments, "You've got this appetite for more creative pricing, smarter pricing, more of a Saville Row customized pricing for each client and matter. The appetite is undoubtedly there, and we have been seeing it for some years now."[17]

In addition, the survey asked respondents for the profitability of projects billed through AFAs versus those based on hourly billing, with 16 percent of respondents finding them more profitable, 38 percent of respondents as profitable, and 32 percent finding them less profitable overall. Of concern, 15 percent of respondents were not able to comment on the effect of AFAs on their profitability, pointing to a serious shortfall in the analytics capability or possibly application in these firms. Overall, this data indicates that AFAs offer clear opportunities to firms and their clients. It is also informative to look at profitability broken down by firms that offer AFAs proactively versus reactively. Of the proactive firms, 29 percent report that AFA-based projects are more profitable than others, with only 10 percent of firms offering them in a reactive manner reaping a similar benefit from them.[18]

As more law firms become comfortable that AFAs can be used profitably, this by itself will create positive feedback loops and the practice will grow increasingly rapidly. Andrew Perlman believes this is a significant factor in driving uptake of AFAs:

> As firms have more experience with AFAs and can show that they are profitable— as profitable as billing by the hour—and that lawyers are actually happier when they do not have to bill every tenth of an hour, that itself can drive change. Showing that they are profitable is a big part of this.[19]

We observe that firms that have invested in building pricing capabilities, that is, people, process, and technology, seem to be more competent in delivering pricing that is both profitable and competitive—and more confident in consistently leveraging this to their competitive advantage. They might also be the firms that have brought their costs down earlier and more than others, and are therefore better able to leverage their efficient operating model compared to firms using time-based billing.

BENEFITS OF VALUE-BASED PRICING FOR FIRMS

The most intuitive benefit that arises from AFAs is the immediate effect on realization rates that these fee agreements have. If firms can figure out how to achieve adequate results by doing less work on a matter, and quote and deliver a fixed price accordingly, realization rates will go up, as Mike Roster points out:

---

17. Interview by Imme Kaschner with Richard Burcher, Lawyer and Managing Director, Validatum, in London, U.K., (Sept. 30, 2014).

18. Altman Weil, *supra* note 11, at 67–68.

19. Perlman, *supra* note 4.

As a managing partner I was used to a 91 to 93 percent realization rate—that is, what we were paid after taking into account write-downs, discounts, and the like. Virtually all the firms, not just in the United States, but worldwide, are now in the 80s and plunging toward the 70s. This is how I have explained it to some chairmen: 'Do you understand, when you go to a fixed-price arrangement and you actually deliver, say, a 25 percent reduction of your client's cost—you are no longer trying to crank out hours, you are focusing instead on expertise and good results, and your realization rate, if you manage your work correctly, is going to exceed 100 percent?" And it does.[20]

So these are the benefit of AFAs to clients and firms alike in comparison with the billable hours approach. We have also heard anecdotal evidence that clients pay fixed-price bills more quickly than bills based on hourly rates.

But let us suppose that firms choose to remain competitive mainly by discounting their hourly rates. Such discounting may be enough to hold your clients when the opposition is also competing purely on discounts, as long as you can match those. But enter the procurement professionals, whose job it is to bring down unit cost without compromising quality—and the situation becomes very tricky. The increasing influence of procurement professionals in buying legal services was discussed in chapter 4. Here is how law professor Bill Henderson considers the current role of procurement professionals:

Procurement is putting downward pressure on law firm prices, but they are not really necessarily kicking the tires, to say, "How are you doing the work? I know that you are doing it for less money, but do you have systems and processes in place to make me believe that I am going to get the same quality work, even though we are paying less?" I don't think that procurement is quite that sophisticated yet.[21]

Not yet, but it can be confidently expected that quality control concerns are going to become more, not less, of an issue when prices are increasingly being driven down, and procurement will address those issues if and when they arise. Defining and tracking high-quality outcomes is therefore certain to become an important part of doing business for a firm, regardless of what pricing strategy is employed. So why not be proactive in developing the capability of demonstrating quality outcomes delivered through standardized and predictable processes, and use the insights gained to develop non–time-based pricing strategies?

To make this clear, we do not advocate the complete elimination of time recording. Time recorded on a matter is a relevant component of the cost of production. And of course revenue minus cost equals profit. Every firm must know the extent to which its units of production, that is, matters, are profitable—and that is the reason why time must be recorded to track efficiency and improvements.

---

20. Roster, *supra* note 2.

21. Telephone interview by George Beaton with William D. Henderson, Professor of Law and Val Nolan Faculty Fellow, Maurer School of Law (July 31, 2014).

The main benefit of AFAs to us is the opportunity to develop ways of risk sharing and cooperation with clients that fosters long-term business relationships that go beyond individual matters. The potential of reward strategies to drive behavior are not lost on the frequent buyers of legal services, as the following anecdote from Toby Brown, legal pricing specialist and Chief Practice Officer at Akin Gump Strauss Hauer & Feld LLP illustrates:

> A couple of months ago, I was doing a presentation to a group of general counsel, and I posed this question, using a list of different types of fees: "Okay, what behavior changes does each of these motivate in the outside counsel?" Silence, so I said, "A fixed fee is going to motivate some efficiency combined with results." And then I said, "Hold-back success fees, where you get your success fees based on results, are going to have more of a focus on results." And so I went down the list, and on the bottom I had put discounts, and I said, "What behavior motivation does a discount trigger in your outside counsel?" And everyone just looked at me for a minute. Finally someone said, "None." And I said, "Yes, I agree."[22]

AFAs play a large role in demonstrating a willingness to work collaboratively with clients in assessing how to best address their legal needs in a "better, faster, cheaper" manner. Particularly long-term retainer arrangements provide both sides with cost and income certainty—just as long as the law firm has done its homework on analyzing its cost structure and resource allocation. So overall, AFAs provide benefits that should cause firms to rethink their pricing structures and solutions, even before clients exert maximum pressure in asking for them.

PRICING IN THE BUSINESS MODEL AND STRATEGIC CONTEXT

If it is acknowledged that pricing strategies need to be changed in response to or to pre-empt changes in client demand, nothing less than a mandate from the top will suffice to enact a move toward outcome- or value-based pricing. This is because of the pervasive manner in which the billable hour has shaped the culture of the traditional law firm. Sustainable pricing has to be at the core of the business model, and it must relate to strategy through effective governance. The (deceptively simple) questions to be decided when building pricing competency in a firm were summed up by pricing expert Richard Burcher as follows:[23]

- How pricing is linked to strategic objectives (this includes the interplay between pricing and internal metrics and reward systems)
- Where the pricing function is located within the firm's departments

---

22. Telephone interview by George Beaton with Toby Brown, Chief Practice Officer at Akin Gump Strauss Hauer & Feld LLP (Aug. 8, 2014).

23. Richard Burcher, *Pricing Dissonance: Big Law Firms' International Pricing Strategy Dilemma*, MANAGING PARTNER MAGAZINE (Mar. 21, 2014), http://www.managingpartner.com/feature/business-development/pricing-dissonance-big-law-firms'-international-pricing-strategy-dilemm.

- How pricing authority and accountability are allocated
- What message is conveyed through pricing
- Thresholds and accountability for write-offs, and
- Policy decisions around the interactions between the interrelated functions of pricing, marketing, and business development.

Additional useful and more detailed resources on pricing can be found in *The Price Advantage*[24] and in Edward J. Wesemann's *Creating Dominance: Winning Strategies for Law Firms*.[25]

To make these decisions, there is a need for data about cost and time frames for work that has been done, and the availability of human and other resources. There is also a need for data on client demand, current and forecast future client needs, and competitors. Capturing and analyzing this data necessitates the analytics competencies discussed in chapter 12. A number of vendors, such as Thomson Reuters with Peer Monitor, Wolters Kluwer with TyMetrix® 360°, and Aderant with their various offerings, provide a starting point in analyzing costs and profitability using different pricing models. Not surprisingly, however, their approach and historical data is skewed toward time-based billing models. The process awareness and predictability that arise with the use of project management, discussed in chapter 11, are necessary to provide an accurate basis upon which to price matters profitably. Marketing and business development competencies, discussed in chapter 8, similarly increase a firm's ability to craft pricing strategies based on client demand and competitors' offerings. All these components of pricing strategy and planning need a whole-of-firm perspective and must be located at a level that has the necessary overview and authority to pull together practitioners, practice groups, and offices.

GUIDING PRINCIPLE: COST CONSCIOUSNESS

One underappreciated fact that has been demonstrated in our own research and by others is that price is far from being the most important driver in clients' legal services purchasing decisions. Altman Weil, for example, recently asked in-house lawyers what pricing scenarios they would want from their outside counsel if given a choice (excluding "bet the company" type matters). Notably, 37 percent of respondents chose "transparent pricing" (defined as understanding why and how a price was set, and having the opportunity to discuss changes); 27 percent chose "guaranteed pricing"; 26 percent chose "value-based pricing" (defined as variable

24. Michael V. Marn, Eric V. Roegner & Craig C. Zawada, The Price Advantage 43–73 (John Wiley & Sons 2004).

25. Edward J. Wesemann, Creating Dominance: Winning Strategies for Law Firms 53–75 (AuthorHouse 2005).

price based on clients' assessment of the value that they receive). Only 10 percent wanted the lowest price possible.[26]

What is far more important than price is clients' perception of their lawyers' "cost consciousness." Dr. Margaret Beaton coined this term when researching how members of the Australian Corporate Lawyers Association and Chartered Secretaries Australia perceived the value of solicitors' services for her doctoral thesis at the University of Melbourne in the 1990s.[27] She coined the term "cost consciousness" to designate a previously undescribed factor in explaining what drives perceived value in clients' minds, and the term stuck. Looking at a dictionary definition to unpack this concept, there is usually reference to an awareness of costs and caution about spending,[28] but it seems to be something of an "I-know-it-when-I-see-it" term. Based on an analysis of qualitative comments of clients drawn from a number of Beaton Research + Consulting surveys,[29] we discern that in the context of a law firm acting for a client, there are two elements to being cost conscious:

1. Acting as if the client's money were their own, by being thrifty in regard to additional expenses, and doing the right job, no more, no less, and as efficiently as possible; and

2. Communicating and demonstrating this behavior to the client from beginning to end, at the very least:
   - communicating estimates at the start of the matter;
   - seeking approval at any time when any material changes occur or with a threatened mismatch between budget and spend, and prior to incurring additional expenses unless practically impossible; and
   - billing in a transparent manner so that clients know exactly what the basis for any charges is, presented in an easily accessible way with appropriate data visualization where appropriate, rather than through reams of paper or endless electronic documents.

The importance of communication in the perception of service value goes beyond communicating costs to meaningful communication with the client in general, making them feel intimately involved in the service that they receive for the life of the matter.

Mel Anderson, former director of benchmarks at Beaton Research + Consulting and now head of information & insights at Grant Thornton Australia, summed up some internal data:

---

26. Altman Weil, *supra* note 13, at 13.

27. Margaret R. Beaton, The Role of Quality, Value and Structural Factors on Exit, Voice, Loyalty and Neglect in the Relationship Between Law Firms and Corporate Clients (1995) (unpublished Ph.D. dissertation, University of Melbourne) (on file with the authors).

28. *See, e.g.*, COLLINS DICTIONARIES "cost-conscious," available at http://www.collinsdictionary.com/dictionary/english/cost-conscious.

29. For some examples of qualitative client comments, see GEORGE BEATON, ERIC CHIN & TRISTAN FORRESTER, *Research on the Procurement of Legal Services, in* BUYING LEGAL- PROCUREMENT INSIGHTS AND PRACTICE 4–5 (Silvia Hodges ed., Ark Group 2012).

Beaton Benchmark's 2014 analysis of what is most important to clients in their selection of "top-end of town" firms when they assess a law firm's client service performance shows 12 statistically significant drivers. In no particular order these include attributes like "technical expertise," "reliability," "understanding the client's business and industry," and "ease of doing business" with the firm. Crucially, and ranking in third position of importance, is "cost consciousness." Also, for the first time in many years "innovation" appears in this list, putatively emphasizing the importance large clients are starting to place on LPO, LPM, alternative business models, and the like.

When we analyze what drives the way clients of these same firms perceive the value of the services they receive, we find cost consciousness plays a much more important role than price. In Figure 9.1, cost consciousness is in fourth position, contributing about 10 percent to the perceived value, compared with price at only 4 percent.

That is right! Price is positively correlated with value, not negatively. In other words, while the effect is small, only 4 percent, price adds to value, it does not subtract, which is not the way most people think about price. In business school texts this is known as the heuristic role of price; it is a signal of quality. Of course,

FIGURE 9.1

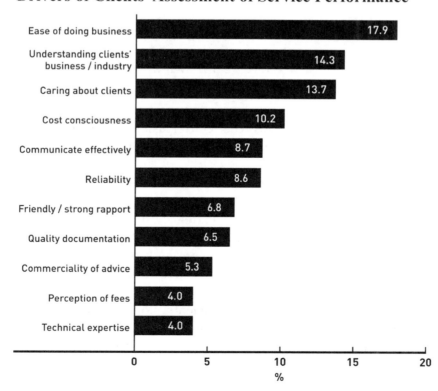

Drivers of Clients' Assessment of Service Performance

FIGURE 9.2

Performance on Cost Consciousness

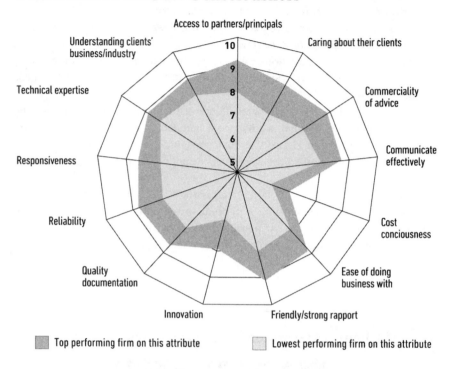

if a price is overly high, then it will reduce perceived value. Equally, it can be too low and damage perceived value. Like Goldilocks' porridge, the price level must be "just right" for clients.[30]

Examining how clients rate law firms' cost consciousness in our large-scale surveys shows performance of this important driver of client satisfaction is noticeably poorer than on other attributes.

Figure 9.2 shows how ten high-end law firms, selected because of their size and reputation overall, were ranked by clients in regard to the drivers shown, with zero being "extremely poor" and ten being "extremely strong." The band indicates the spread between the highest and lowest performers. The noticeable dents in the "circle" represent innovation and, more importantly for present purposes, the larger one for "cost consciousness." So the firms in the sample are falling behind in clients' perception of their cost consciousness.

Cost consciousness, that is, spending the clients' money as thriftily as if it were one's own, and communicating this to the client before, during, and after a matter, is more important than price itself in driving clients' perception of value, yet top

---

30. George Beaton, *More Evidence Why Cost Consciousness Is Valued by Clients*, RESEARCH. REVEAL. BLOG (Mar. 31, 2014), http://www.beatonglobal.com/law-firms-will-benefit-cost-conscious/.

law firms perform poorly in this regard. Any pricing strategies must be scrutinized as to how they will demonstrate the cost consciousness of a firm.

COMMUNICATION TO PRICE THE CLIENT AND THE MATTER

To develop pricing strategies in general, or to negotiate about a specific AFA with a client for a matter, necessitates a more collaborative approach to communicating with the client than that to which many lawyers are accustomed. Instead of a situation of information asymmetry, where the lawyer defines the problem and advises the solution to be implemented, the communication is between equals, that is, the client as expert in his subject area and business needs, and the lawyer as options expert. This change in dynamic may be compared with the shift toward patient empowerment embraced by the medical profession since the 1980s, resulting in developments like advance directives; comprehensive, scientifically sound and freely available patient information materials; and approaches that are more collaborative than directive in helping the patient to choose between care alternatives.

Geoff Wild has been in the position of both provider and buyer of legal services to support an internal client (Kent County Council) that in turn provides a wide range of services to end clients. He talks about pricing, and the changing dynamic in the lawyer–client relationship with fixed prices:

> What the clients get is a very transparent assessment of the work that will be done and a fixed price—which is what many of them really look for now in their legal service provider, and which they have not enjoyed before. We apply this to every matter type. The typical arguments I get from some of my lawyers are, "Well you cannot apply this to complex litigation," for example, where the outcome is simply unknown at the moment. "The scale, the complexity are too much to estimate at the outset; you cannot possibly know what it is going to be like and how long it is going to take." But what you can do is break that down into bite-sized pieces, into segments, into chunks, where you can cost each one of those segments.
>
> You can create a fanning tree where you say, "Well, if we go from here to this stage, the potential outcomes are one of these three. If we go down this route, this would be the next stage and we can price that. If we go down this route that is the consequence. This is the next piece of work that would be required and we can price that for you." It can be done. Lawyers do not like the extra work that this sometimes brings, but it does actually stimulate far greater and more intelligent analysis of the required work, and to work with the clients and analyzing that, as opposed to doing it remotely from the lawyer's desk. . . . This approach requires lawyers to roll up their sleeves, get down and dirty with their clients, and really sit alongside them and say, "Right, let us look at this problem. Let us work it out together. And let us solve this as a team." The value and pricing of legal services as a commodity are changing.[31]

---

31. Wild, *supra* note 6.

Pricing expert Richard Burcher shares his approach to assessing the client's motivations and constraints, and ultimately their willingness to pay, in the context of pricing negotiations:

> A typical phrase that I would use to open that aspect of the conversation with a client, and I think this holds true whether it is contentious or noncontentious work, is something as simple as, "What does a great result on this look like to you?" It is an open-ended question. Then away they go and say, "Well if you can get this done by the first of November then we can do this or that. Or, if we can get at least half of a certain sum," whatever. They know exactly in their own mind what a good result looks like. Getting them to articulate that and then understanding that, it becomes a lot easier to build a value proposition around it, and then price that value proposition. At the end of the day the client will pay what they think it's worth. Forget about hourly rates and everything else. . . .
>
> It is a concept that comes out of this pricing principle known as willingness to pay. It is sort of the holy grail of pricing. It's that number where the client goes, "Yeah, it was not cheap, but that was worth it." You know the L'Oréal hair care product, "Because you're worth it.". . . We have got used to applying a homogeneous, one-size-fits-all approach to pricing through the mechanism of the hourly rate. In other words, irrespective of who you are or what you are or what your particular issues or prejudices are, or objectives or underlying dynamics, I'm $400 an hour. Well, tell someone who cares. Clients do not. They might pay $600 an hour; they might only pay $250. They might pay $600 for some and $200 for other bits of the job. We do ourselves and our clients a huge disservice by not spending the time to price the client before pricing the job.[32]

So pricing strategies, and specific pricing negotiations, need to be based on an informed assessment of the client's expectations and constraints. Once these have been assessed, the project itself offers room to negotiate scope and outcome metrics, such as, for example, but certainly not limited to, delivery times, litigation outcomes, client satisfaction, or a decrease in complaints. Rick Kathuria, national director of project management and legal logistics at Canadian firm Gowlings, talks about scoping a project based on budgetary constraints:

> There is an example I use where the partner estimated it was going to be $400,000. When they did the plan, it went to $500,000. They realized, I cannot do it for $500,000, so let us adjust the plan and figure out who does what and let us move some stuff around. We were able to cut $100,000 out of the fees without taking a discount, just by putting together a good plan.
>
>   . . .
>
> Lawyers are very good at client service. When a client asks for something, the lawyer does it. What is missing in that step is the lawyer can do it but tells the client, "Here is the impact of me doing this. Do you still want to go ahead with this?".
>
> Back in my consulting days, because I used to bill my time by the hour as well, I found clients would ask me something and I would say, "Yeah, I can do this but it

---

32. Burcher, *supra* note 17.

is going to cost you an extra $10,000." The client would say either "Sure, go ahead and do it, it's important." Or, "$10,000, really? Forget about it. It is not that important." Or, "I still need it but I do not have any more money to spend." That is when you have a different conversation with a client about what do we do differently, how do we change the scope. At least you are having that conversation.[33]

Again, the overriding consideration is not what can be done, or what "should" be done unilaterally determined by lawyers: It is what solution can be offered that best meets the needs of the specific client and matter at a price acceptable to both the client and the firm. These communication tactics, paired with an understanding of pricing analytics, discussed later in the chapter, have to be taught to, and learned by, those who have pricing discussions with the clients, mostly still the partners, but also increasingly members of the sales teams. Changing the way that things have always been done, and have been successful in the past, is no small undertaking. Change management strategies are discussed in chapter 13.

PRICING MASS CUSTOMIZATION

The pricing discussion starts with assessing the client and the matter, and proceeds to offering solution options, and ways of pricing these. In order to price sustainably, that is, not to price so high that the service ceases to be competitive, and not so low that the firm cannot be profitable (though such pricing might of course be offered short-term as a loss leader, resulting in problems long-term, as Susan Hackett points out earlier), pricing options need to be based on in-depth analysis of internal costs and market competition. This involves cooperation among professionals with diverse skills across the firm, including analytics, knowledge management, legal project management, marketing, and, of course, legal practice. There is a growing trend to employ pricing experts in larger firms to advise on and train lawyers in pricing, and manage the coordination, to build overall pricing capabilities.

Sustainable pricing also needs a digitized platform that accesses and uses data from often multiple information systems. This analysis needs to be centrally located in the firm, and the firm needs to invest in its analytic capabilities. Ultimately, there must be inputs of client, matter cost, and market data informing all pricing decisions. The system should allow for modeling of price outcomes with changing parameters, such as the changing scope of a project that Rick Kathuria describes previously, or the litigation "fanning tree" that Geoff Wild suggests. Susan Hackett points to the client expectations of pricing options that go beyond an ad hoc approach:

---

33. Interview by George Beaton with Mark Tamminga, Leader, Innovation Initiatives, and Rick Kathuria, National Director, Project Management and Legal Logistics, Gowlings Lafleur LLP, in Toronto, Can. (Sept. 14, 2014).

Too many firms look at AFAs as activities they will engage in for a particular client who has made a specific demand, rather than a mandate that the firm should truly look at its business model, and think about how, even without being asked, they are going to become better, and more effective, and more innovative, and more value-based in their service approach. Right now, too many law firms will say, "Well if you tell us that you want an AFA, we will figure out how to crack one for you." And clients kind of look at them and say, "Why do I have to ask for an AFA? Why can't you come to me and say that there are four different ways that we can structure a fee here or there are three different ways that we can set a price for this service: Which one would you like, and which is best matched to the value that you're looking to drive for this matter?"[34]

IT IS A TEAM SPORT

Richard Burcher's questions of where in the firm the pricing function is located—and how it interacts with marketing, business development, and lawyers—point toward the need for pricing to be the result of cooperation between many stakeholders within the firm. Burcher Jennings' excellent overview *Contemporary Law Firm Pricing Challenges and Solutions* addresses common challenges and solutions in more depth, and similarly indicates the multidisciplinary nature of sustainable law firm pricing.[35]

Pricing skills and related competencies are becoming increasingly relevant to how a firm attracts work. This indicates a need to rethink performance assessment and rewards in the future, as the market for pricing talent and professionals from various disciplines who support legal services providers becomes more competitive. This is, of course, not limited to affiliated professionals who assist with pricing; the same goes for experts in technology, data analytics, project management, and marketing. The time of grouping law firm personnel into lawyers and non-lawyers, with pejorative connotations, are numbered. William (Bill) Henderson, whose empirical research on the U.S. legal market puts him at a unique vantage point, describes a snippet of conversation that illustrates the increasing importance of law-affiliated professionals:

> Support attorneys, project managers, process improvement persons, artificial intelligence persons, technologists, et cetera, et cetera, those folks said they were getting 80 to 90 percent of the airtime in the client pitches. Their presence was landing work for the firm, so I asked one of them, "How long is it going to be until all of you, none of you being equity partners, are perceived to be as valuable or more valuable than an equity partner who brings in a lot of business?" He said, "Five years, max." I think that this is true.[36]

---

34. Hackett, *supra* note 15.
35. (2014), http://www.burcherjennings.com/img/resources/Contemporary_Pricing_Challenges_and _Solutions_2014.pdf.
36. Henderson, *supra* note 21.

COMPONENTS OF AFAS

This section describes some examples of commonly used components and types of AFAs that are at one end of the risk allocation spectrum.

There are many brief[37] and detailed[38] overviews of pricing models, especially AFAs, for the interested reader. For our purposes, the importance of AFAs lies in the opportunity to demonstrate how they align law firm and client interests, and how quality, defined as managing and meeting (or even better, exceeding) the clients' expectations, is maintained—particularly with lower prices. All of this is in addition to making the client's legal spend transparent and predictable. In this sense, a capped budget based on an hourly rate, for example, can achieve a risk allocation that is similar to a fixed price at the level of the cap. Similarly, an agreed progressive decrease in rates based on a threshold number of hours spent on a project can align law firm and client interests.

Fixed fees based on matter type, or specific smaller or larger tasks or projects, like, for example, predictable stages of litigation, have the advantage of transparency and compatibility. From the perspective of the client, this includes compatibility across firms. One problem in this respect is still a lack of industry standards, meaning that when a client puts out a request for proposal, the specifications might not be clear enough to result in truly comparable bids by different law firms. There can, therefore, be a need for additional communication with the client to clarify the exact scope. The precise risk allocation with fixed price arrangements depends on the specifics. For example, a set price without fixing the number of service units, be they units of time or specific results to be bought, might turn out to favor the seller, if a high number of units is sold that would possibly lead to a discount if set in advance. As in any business negotiation, risk limitation in the form of guarantees either way will come at a price.

Fixed prices can be combined with arrangements that provide additional incentives to achieve desired outcomes. Jeremy Szwider of Bespoke comments on their pricing approaches:

> We provide value-based pricing. We have a product called "D.cubed."[39] We feel that our product is so unique and proprietary that we have given it a brand name. . . . As part of value-based pricing for this D.cubed product, one important aspect is fixed pricing, and we have a heavy focus on fixed pricing. There are other formulas we will look at, such as retainer fees, percentages, uplift fees, or abort fees. We

---

37. *E.g.*, Darren Van Puymbrouck and Joshua Kurtzman, *The Rise of Alternative Fee Arrangements,* 28 Corporate Counsel 10 (2013); Silvia Hodges-Silverstein, *Professionalizing Pricing and Procurement Process,* in Law Firm Strategies for the 21st Century 164–71 (Christoph H Vaagt ed., Globe Business Publishing 2013).

38. For more comprehensive material on specific types of AFAs, see, e.g., Legal Procurement Handbook (Silvia Hodges-Silverstein ed., Buying Legal Council 2015); Patrick Lamb, Alternative Fees for Litigators and Their Clients (ABA Publishing 2014); Mark A. Robertson, Alternative Fees for Business Lawyers and Their Clients (ABA Publishing 2014).

39. An explanation of the name is given on the Bespoke webpage http://bespokelaw.com/more-about -d-cubed/ (last viewed Feb. 11, 2015).

do not offer hourly rates; that is not within our offering. It is all based on value propositions.

We will assess what the task at hand is. A team will go away and assess it and price it accordingly. More often than not, it will be a fixed pricing or a retainer fee model. Sometimes, for a particular transaction we may "have a bit more fun," where we will directly align the price with the upside, such as an uplift or a percentage-type concept based on success. With our pricing models across the board, we look to invest in a future partnership relationship with our clients. We do not act for endless numbers of clients. We selectively chose who is the right client. We hope that most times we get it right, and we may say "No" to prospective clients.[40]

Nick West, managing director U.K. at NewLaw provider Axiom, describes a commoditized, fixed legal service unit price as follows:

We try as far as possible to provide fixed price options to our client when working on large projects, though it is not always possible to do that. We start by working out with the client what needs to get done. The more transparent the task is, the easier it is. For example, let's say we need to review 10,000 documents within the next six weeks, determine whether there's an assignment clause, and, if so, send a letter to the counterparty. Once we've reviewed a sample of the documents, we can almost write down the playbook in advance, and that enables us to determine what resources it will require. We can say, "For that volume, we estimate it will take two subject matter experts and fourteen paralegals," or whatever. Therefore we can boil it down to a whole document price, that is, a whole unit price. If the number of documents goes up by 25 percent but the timeline is the same, we'll need 25 percent more resources, so the price will go up by 25 percent, give or take.[41]

Other examples include bonuses for completion within certain time frames or any other client-defined metric, or hold-backs if the client is not satisfied with aspects of services (or again, if metrics are not met). Particularly in litigation, additional elements that take into account the somewhat unpredictable nature of the process, by, for example, providing for a discount from a fixed fee if an early settlement occurs (thereby incentivising the law firm to settle, since the payment in relation to their costs would be higher than if the matter ran all the way to trial, even though the payment is less in absolute terms) may be suitable to align client and firm interests.

Portfolio or retainer arrangements are suited to long-term relationships in a situation where the parties have a sound grasp of the overall volume of work that is necessary to serve the needs of a client. Usually such arrangements arise in situations where the volume of work is large enough that commonly observed variations in legal needs even out over the duration of the retainer arrangement, or where firms are in a position to offer services to a number of smaller businesses

---

40. Interview by Imme Kaschner with Jeremy Szwider, Managing Director, Bespoke, in Melbourne, Australia (Jan. 30, 2015).

41. Interview by David Goener, Eric Chin, and Imme Kaschner with Nick West, Managing Director, Axiom U.K., in London, U.K. (Sept. 29, 2014).

with similar legal needs so that the law firm can build a portfolio. Such retainer arrangements leading to in-depth understanding of the client business can provide a suitable background for shared investments in innovation. If, for example, a law firm identifies the potential for a large in-house legal department that serves not just internal, but also external clients to serve those clients through a self-service portal, and sets up and runs such a portal leveraging their legal and knowledge management expertise, the in-house department can commit to buying a certain volume of services from the firm in return. They may also contribute to financing and contributing to the development of the system as a joint venture, with both parties benefitting if the system is also offered to other entities.

True contingency fees will probably remain mostly limited to the no-win-no-fee consumer law arena, but firms providing litigation services for commercial entities should not exclude the possibility of working with litigation funders if this is allowed in their jurisdiction. A major 2014 survey (unfortunately, with no 2015 follow-up available yet) by litigation funder Burford Capital LLC yielded a number of insights into the increasing use of this option in the U.S. legal market. The survey respondents were grouped into outside private practice lawyers (PP), in-house lawyers (IH), and finance executives (FE) for analysis.[42] There was a clear acceptance of litigation funding, with a majority of respondents considering it a "useful tool" (72 percent of PP, 69 percent of IH, 78 percent of FE).[43] There was a strong year-on-year growth compared to 2013 in the number of respondents who had "done it," that is, used litigation finance for a matter (PP 7 percent to 11 percent, IH 2 percent to 5 percent, FE 3 percent to 8 percent).[44] Many respondents had active cases they thought would benefit from litigation funding (23 percent PP, 5 percent IH, 7 percent FE),[45] indicating further growth potential. Many respondents also considered that the option of litigation funding should be communicated to clients at the outset of each case (PP 41 percent, IH 32 percent, FE 40 percent).[46] Not just for smaller firms, the cost and risk of litigation even with a meritorious claim can be prohibitive. The Burford survey demonstrated that many respondents considered litigation funding to lead to meritorious cases being brought that otherwise would not be (PP 59 percent, IH 36 percent, FE 58 percent).[47] And among the holders of the purse strings, the finance executives, a clear majority expected demand for litigation funding to rise over the following 18 months (62 percent FE).[48] Fee arrangements that incorporate an element of litigation insurance enabled by cooperation with litigation funders, subject of course to applicable professional regulation, can

---

42. Burford Capital LLC and Briefcase Analytics, *Summary of Findings: Third Annual Litigation Finance Survey* (2014), *available at* http://www.burfordcapital.com/wp-content/uploads/2014/12/BURFORD_3RDSURVEY2014.pdf.

43. *Id.* at 3.

44. *Id.* at 8, 9.

45. *Id.* at 13.

46. *Id.* at 14.

47. *Id.* at 11, 12.

48. *Id.* at 15.

let a firm access this market segment. Increasing access to justice for smaller enti-ties that would not seek to enforce their legal claims otherwise may be a positive consequence.

So really, there is no limit to the variations of fee arrangements that can be agreed on between clients and law firms, but law firms need to do their home-work on clients, matters, and competition to identify what they want to offer, and become adept in quickly and efficiently providing sustainable pricing options.

CONCLUSION

The billable hour might still have a place as one of many available pricing options that can be agreed between law firms and their clients. But because it largely coun-termands the incentive for law firms to become more efficient, it is not desirable to retain it as the main pricing mechanism and chief metric that governs client relationships as well as internal law firm operations.

When instituting change initiatives in any entity, one relevant question is always what will stand in the way of change occurring, and the billable hour clearly incentivizes against the implementation of any alternative sourcing and LPM initia-tives leading to greater efficiency in the provision of legal services (see chapters 10 and 11). Clients are increasingly demanding other pricing options that better align the law firms' interests with their own. If researched and crafted appropriately, tak-ing into account internal data and market data as well as client- and matter-specific factors, AFAs are sustainably as or more profitable as time-based charging. Chang-ing pricing strategy and building capacity and competencies around new ways of pricing takes significant effort, and goes to the core of law firm structure as we know it. To quote the wise words of Ecclesiastes chapter 3, "To everything there is a season, and a time for every purpose under the heaven . . . a time to get, and a time to lose, a time to keep and a time to cast away."[49]

---

49. *Ecclesiastes* 3:1, 3:7 (King James).

Chapter 10

Sourcing and Outsourcing

Key Points

- A supply chain is a system of inputs or building blocks—including organizations, people, activities, and information—that enables the provision of defined deliverables to a client.
- In the legal services industry, the concept of outsourcing is becoming more established. Options for sourcing include on-demand workers, captive entities, and third-party outsourcing as parts of the legal services ecosystem. Near-shoring is increasingly common in both the United States and the United Kingdom.
- Clients are frequently the driving force that leads law firms to explore alternative sourcing options.
- A clear understanding of how legal work is produced, at what cost, and how it relates to risk is necessary to identify appropriate outsourcing targets.
- Large law firms in the United States and the United Kingdom have recently built or expanded captive centers to provide support services and low-complexity, high-volume legal services. In some cases, complex captives provide services to organizations beyond the parent.
- Law firms working with Legal Services Outsourcers are understandably concerned about quality and client confidentiality. These potential issues have to be managed by appropriate communication, procedures, and agreements.

INTRODUCTION

Outsourcing in the legal services industry today can take a variety of forms. A broad definition by Mary Lacity and others in the book *The Rise of Legal Services Outsourcing: Risk and Opportunity* proposes that

> Legal Services Outsourcing (LSO) is when a company, organi[z]ation, or law firm procures services from an external provider. . . . [T]he external provider may be located domestically, offshore, or internationally and the "service" may include

any service that supports a legal organi[z]ation, from legal support services performed by office workers, IT professionals, and paralegals to complex end-to-end legal services.[1]

LSO and LPO (legal services outsourcing/outsourcer and legal process outsourcing/outsourcer) are often used synonymously. We will use the acronym LSO in accordance with the definition above. The broad scope of this definition illustrates that outsourcing options today have expanded from the "discovery to India" option where a law firm outsources distinct high-volume, low-complexity projects, frequently in the context of litigation. Firms like Axiom or Elevate have moved up the value chain and offer end-to-end legal services for complex projects. Interactions between law firms, their captives, LSOs, and clients in the traditional sense can be complex, as this chapter will demonstrate. The term "ecosystem," alluding to multiple interdependent parties that concurrently interact, cooperate, and compete, is an apt metaphor to describe sourcing options and supplier/client interactions in the legal services industry today.

This chapter draws on examples from both the United States and the United Kingdom to illustrate the possibility of complex sourcing strategies that go beyond the traditional law firm model generating all aspects of legal services under one roof (literally and figuratively). Possibly spurred by more permissive regulatory structures, the United Kingdom offers a testing ground for providers offering building blocks or innovative delivery of legal services. This has already attracted the attention of U.S. firms in the traditional and nontraditional legal services space. LegalZoom, provider of automated, individualized legal documents, and subscription-based legal services through a referral network, has entered into a partnership with U.K. franchised law firm network QualitySolicitors to trial offerings of blended automated and lawyer-generated legal services that can be combined in a more seamless manner under U.K. law than in the United States.[2] Consumer law giant Jacoby & Myers is similarly using a U.K. joint venture company to explore legal services offerings for consumers and small businesses provided as a mixture of traditional and "virtual" services by an Alternative Business Structure (ABS).[3]

Veteran buyer and provider of outsourced legal services Richard Tapp, Company Secretary and Director of Legal Services at the U.K.'s Carillion plc, an international support services and construction company, puts legal outsourcing into the context of commercial developments in equivalent service functions:

> If you look at comparable professional services, and finance or HR functions, we are in step with most large corporations that outsource those, and have done so for decades. The question becomes how different really is law compared to other functions. The

---

1. MARY LACITY, LESLIE WILLCOCKS & ANDREW BURGESS, THE RISE OF LEGAL SERVICES OUTSOURCING xiv (Bloomsbury 2014).

2. Laura Snyder, *Does the UK Know Something We Don't About Alternative Business Structures?* A.B.A. J. (Jan. 1, 2015), http://www.abajournal.com/magazine/article/does_the_uk_know_something_we _dont_about_alternative_business_structures.

3. *Id.*

trick with any outsourcing is know what you need to retain, and you need to understand what you're outsourcing and why. You need to retain the controlling mind and management, and make sure you have the right management information.

Once you have those in place, the question you have to ask is, how different is law to other professional functions? You can argue that most law departments will outsource anyway, because they can't do everything themselves. A majority will use law firms to some degree. And once you do that, it almost becomes a question of "Okay, so what do you outsource, and to where?" as opposed to "Why should you outsource anything?"[4]

Richard is referring to the setting of a corporate law department, but the considerations are equally applicable to law firms. As Richard puts it, "if you look at the reasons why people outsource in a range of professions and functions, it's basically to ensure the service is delivered as efficiently as possible, and to achieve cost certainty."[5]

THE LEGAL SERVICES SUPPLY CHAIN

Asking commercial lawyers about supply chains is likely to yield sophisticated advice about how companies need to structure contracts to protect themselves against risks arising from suppliers, how tax obligations throughout the supply chain can be optimized, how those contracts can be negotiated, and a range of other legal issues. "Supply chain," a term coined by Keith Oliver in 1982,[6] denotes a complex system that ultimately results in getting products or services to a buyer. There are about as many definitions as there are consultants interested in the topic. Oliver's own understanding of supply chain management is as follows:

> Supply chain management (SCM) is the process of planning, implementing, and controlling the operations of the supply chain with the purpose to satisfy customer requirements as efficiently as possible.[7]

Lawyers readily accept that a supply chain that supports delivering efficient, timely, and high-quality inputs is crucial to the success of any business, regardless of whether it sells goods or services. An optimized supply chain allows a company to concentrate on those steps in the chain where it is best able to add value, and therefore compete effectively. Insisting on keeping all or at least most of the steps

---

4. Telephone interview by Eric Chin with Richard Tapp, Company Secretary and Director of Legal Services at the U.K.'s Carillion plc (Sept. 11, 2014). Richard is coauthor of two insightful and concise books on the sourcing of legal services from the in-house perspective: Ann Page & Richard Tapp, Managing External Legal Resources (ICSA Publishing 2007) and Ann Page & Richard Tapp, In-house Lawyers' Toolkit (Law Society Publishing 2014).

5. Tapp, *supra* note 4.

6. Keith Oliver's initial definition of supply chain management only applied to goods, not services. *See generally* R. Keith Oliver & Michael D. Webber, *Supply-Chain Management: Logistics Catches Up with Strategy*, 1 Outlook 5, 42–47 (1982).

7. Quoted in Aspects of Computational Intelligence: Theory and Applications 300 (Ladislav Madarsz & Jozef Zivcac eds., Springer 2011), original source unclear.

within the company if other parties are willing and able to supply intermediate products and services at lower cost and comparable quality does not make economic sense. In choosing which parts of the supply chain a firm makes and which ones it buys, it is crucial to be clear about the answer to the strategic question, "What are the core competencies of the firm?" or the colloquial version, "What business are we in?"[8]

Supply chain management that identifies and procures appropriate inputs is a well-established function in large companies. For the legal services industry, the idea that their services would partly be composed of commoditized building blocks provided by outside parties is not necessarily appealing. Stephen Allen, Head of Marketing Strategies at DLA Piper, describes this as follows:

> The very nature of our training as lawyers is not just to perfect what we do, but also at every single level. There is a need to be perfectionist and because most of the work is built from scratch by lawyers on a reactive basis, the perfectionism is about re-building the building blocks.[9]

One everyday example illustrates that such an approach might not be the most productive. Let's talk about dinner here. If any readers have the time and headspace to cook a delicious dinner from fresh, seasonal ingredients every evening from scratch, more power to you. Likewise if you can afford to patronize your favorite upscale restaurant every night. But in reality, you will probably cook sometimes, using some prepared ingredients to save time. If children come into the equation, the golden arches might be the path of least resistance. A bag of chips (crisps in U.K. and Aussie parlance) is perfectly suitable when consumed while getting through things to get home before midnight. On the other hand, anything with less than a few stars will simply not do for that special occasion dinner. And for an impressive first date, nothing says "I care" like a relaxed home-cooked dinner that took at least a day to prepare. Depending on the circumstances and objectives, the best option to source a dinner varies dramatically. The same applies to legal services.

For the legal services industry, the importance of supply chain management is only starting to be recognized, probably because the availability of large-scale input services for law firms is a relatively new development, at least when thinking in time frames of legal industry changes. Pangea3, for example, a provider of a range of legal outsourcing services with offices in the United States and India, was founded in 2004.[10] It provides a range of project-based offerings for litigation and transactions, but also ongoing support, for example related to regulatory compliance. Major U.K. law firm Clifford Chance opened its support services and

---

8. *See* C.K. Prahalad & Gary Hamel, *The Core Competence of the Corporation*, Harvard Business Review, May 1990.

9. Telephone interview by George Beaton with Stephen Allen, Head of Marketing Strategies at DLA Piper (July 29, 2014).

10. Pangea3, www.pangea3.com.

knowledge management center in Delhi, India, in 2007.[11] Major deals highlighting the increasing acceptance of LSOs by major corporations include the contract between Rio Tinto and LSO CPA Global in 2009, which subsequently put pressure on Australian law firms Allens Arthur Robinson (now Allens Linklaters) and Blake Dawson (now Ashurst), who provided services to Rio Tinto, to similarly embrace outsourcing.[12] In 2014, Rio Tinto switched over its outsourced legal work to Elevate, proving once again the competitive nature of the legal outsourcing business.[13] BT's contract with outsourcer UnitedLex in 2010 for contracting and antitrust regulation services similarly demonstrated corporate acceptance of LSOs.[14] Since 2014, BT is working with alternative legal services provider Axiom.[15]

Setting up captive entities that provide ongoing legal and other support services for large law firms or law departments, leveraging lower overhead costs for labor and facilities, and using skilled-for-purpose professionals who might not be lawyers or paralegals, is one strategy to optimize the supply chain. Compared to third-party outsourcing, it has the potential to better integrate the building blocks through the close connections and ongoing relationships between captive and parent. Not surprisingly, early creators of captive centers were legal departments in corporations that had a history of outsourcing other business processes, such as General Electric[16] and Cisco Systems.[17]

Using independent lawyers and other professionals to provide additional human resources on an as-needed basis, rather than employing them on a fixed cost basis, is another strategy for effective supply chain management. Individuals who are not partners or employees of the firm may generate legal advice or intermediate steps. These professionals can be independent, or may be employed by an entity that makes their services available to law firms or in-house departments. One example in this regard is the U.K. company Lawyers On Demand (LOD), affiliated with commercial law firm Berwin Leighton Paisner.[18] LOD was founded in 2007 to connect lawyers interested in more flexible work practices with law firms and companies looking for nonpermanent staff. The co-branding effect provides both an endorsement of lawyer quality for clients, as well as proximity to the brand of a well-established firm for lawyers. Additional U.K. examples are Peerpoint (an

---

11. Clifford Chance, *Applying Continuous Improvement to High-end Legal Services* 10 (2014), http://www .cliffordchance.com/content/dam/cliffordchance/About_us/Continuous_Improvement_White_Paper.pdf.

12. *See* Leah Cooper, *Corporate Clients Embrace Outsourcing*, The Australian, Nov. 12, 2010, at 39; *Governments Waking Up to LSO*, Lawyers Weekly Blog (Dec. 9, 2011), http://www.lawyersweekly.com.au /news/9612-governments-waking-up-to-LSO.

13. See Liam Brown, *2015: Looking Back, Looking Ahead* (Jan. 20, 2015), http://elevateservices .com/2015-new-year/.

14. For more details, see Lacity et al., *supra* note 1, at 3.

15. Global Legal Post, *BT Opts for Axiom* (Feb. 7, 2014, 11:18 AM), http://www.globallegalpost.com /management-speak/bt-opts-for-axiom-28507494/ (last visited 14 Nov 2015).

16. Lacity et al., *supra* note 1, at 4.

17. *See generally Law Department Operations Profile: Steve Harmon, Cisco Systems, Inc.*, LDO Buzz, http://ldobuzz.com/ldo-profiles-2/law-department-operations-profile-steve-harmon-cisco-systems-inc/ (last visited July 2, 2014).

18. Lawyers On Demand, www.LOD.co.uk.

initiative of Allen & Overy),[19] Agile (which is connected with Eversheds),[20] and Vario (arising from Pinsent Masons),[21] all providing freelance lawyers—as well as Axiom, originating in the United States and now present in the United Kingdom, providing lawyers who are Axiom employees. U.K. legal services provider Riverview Law is an example of an outsourcer that provides legal services that are fully integrated with the legal departments of their corporate clients.[22]

Overall, it is clear that commercial legal services can be provided using supply chains that extend beyond law firms and corporate law departments, and this does not depend on alternative business structures or deregulation. But what are the advantages of remaking a firm's supply chain?

FOR CLIENTS, FULL SERVICE INCLUDES ALTERNATIVE PROVIDER USE

Corporate clients are familiar with the increased efficiency that results from sourcing goods and services from outside providers, rather than generating every step of a desired service themselves. There is an increasing client expectation that large law firms will rely on alternative providers in generating legal services, or will cooperate to some extent with entities outside the firm for low-stakes, high-volume work. Requests for proposals increasingly require law firms to give details of proven LSO co-operations, not just aspirational agreements. A recent survey commissioned by an international law firm showed that there was an anticipation of clear reductions in spending on services from traditional law firms by corporate buyers. This was coupled with an expectation to spend more on alternative service providers, but also showed that the buyers were aware of the project management challenges that resulted from unbundling to multiple providers, and were looking for "one-stop shops" if the cost and efficiency improvements could be preserved.[23] A survey by the Australian Corporate Lawyer's Association similarly demonstrated an increasing trend by corporate counsel to outsource different aspects of legal work to separate providers, based on work type and cost.[24]

These client expectations open up opportunities for established law firms through the cooperation with alternative legal services providers. Law firms that are experienced LSO clients can add value by providing guidance and project management expertise in dealing with LSOs. They can also offer mission-critical work as necessary, while identifying legal needs that can be met more efficiently through

---

19. *See* http://www.allenovery.com/peerpoint/Pages/default.aspx.

20. *See* http://www.evershedsconsulting.com/eversheds-agile/.

21. *See* http://www.pinsentmasonsvario.com.

22. *See* http://www.riverviewlaw.com/our-approach/.

23. Allen & Overy, *Unbundling a Market: The Appetite for New Legal Services Models* 5, 7 (2014), *available at* http://www.allenovery.com/SiteCollectionDocuments/Unbundling_a_market.PDF.

24. Australian Corporate Lawyers' Association, *2012 ACLA/CLANZ In-house Counsel Report: Benchmarks and Leading Practices* 47.

alternative sources. One example of a firm that has leveraged their own expertise in the area of alternative sourcing is Seyfarth Shaw LLP with their SeyfarthLean consulting business.[25]

William (Bill) Henderson points to experiences with comprehensive long-term supply chain agreements in other industries, where suppliers and customers cooperate closely and share information in order to decrease costs, demand is linked to prices that decrease year-on-year, and realized surpluses are shared between the participating entities:

> State of the art procurement [of legal services] is still in its infancy. Really, what you need is a general counsel who is willing to enter fully into it. Instead of procurement that puts a lot of price pressure on law firms, what we really need is a Japanese supply chain model where we are going to be in a five-year partnership, and we are going to share information, and I am going to guarantee you this work, but we are going to have to drive down costs over time.[26]

So looking at the supply chain that extends all the way from a law firm's sources to its final clients opens the way for agreements that integrate law firms more closely with their clients, and deliver ongoing price decreases to them in return for guaranteed volumes of work.

CASE STUDY: COOPERATION AXIOM-STYLE

Nick West, managing director at nontraditional legal services provider Axiom in the United Kingdom, describes how relationships between law firms and nontraditional providers can work:

> We work with traditional law firms quite regularly, but we take a bullish view of how we do it. It is not our role to serve you, Mr. Law Firm, while you serve your client. That is not how we work. We work exclusively for General Counsel and their teams. So, we are both going to have to get comfortable that we can partner together for the benefit of a mutual client. That means that you are going to have to get comfortable that we'll have a direct relationship with your client, but you'll get the credit from them for having helped them solve their problem better than if you'd have just tried to do it yourself.
>
> This allows the traditional law firm to position itself as the front-end advisor, doing the strategic advice, which is where it wants to be. We are certainly comfortable with the positioning that we are doing the execution work, because that's what we're cut out to do. Let me give an example—right now, in the context of a multi-jurisdictional cross border M&A transaction, we would never hold ourselves out as being capable of being the lead advisor. But we know that we

---

25. *See* Seyfarth Shaw LLP, *Sourcing Business Strategies* (2009) http://www.seyfarth.com/dir_docs/brochure/2aabc10b-8f8c-40f9-91ac-2cf026930de0_brochure.pdf.

26. Telephone interview by George Beaton with William D. Henderson, Professor of Law and Val Nolan Faculty Fellow, Maurer School of Law (July 31, 2014).

can do the post-merger integration work far faster and with a far better guaran-
tee around quality than a traditional law firm can.

Taking such a bullish approach does require us to build relationships with
the firm so they do not worry we are in there to steal the work that they want.
Here is a real example from the last month: a Magic Circle firm rings us up. We
are both on a bank's law firm panel. That bank is demanding for its law firms to
collaborate, to make sure work is being done by the appropriate cost provider.
So that firm rang us up and said, "We have been asked by that bank to pitch for
some work, and there is no way we can win this all by ourselves, because we are
just too expensive. Would you work with us on this?" I said, "We would love to,
thanks for asking." We spoke with them about our capabilities and they tweaked
their proposal, taking on board some of our experience, saying, "Here is how we
are going to do it. We are going to do this and this, Axiom is going to do that,
that, and that, and the price for the whole project is X."

We have built a good enough relationship with that particular firm that we
felt comfortable with them putting a bid forward on our behalf. We won the
work together and we are doing it right now.[27]

Given the pressures to reduce overall and outside spending, clients are simply unwilling to forego benefits offered by alternative providers by remaining blindly loyal to
incumbent traditional firms. Clients are also no longer accepting law firms' pro forma
relationships with alternative providers that do not result in any substantial work being
done by the outsourcer, and at a lower price point (what Mark Ross aptly terms the
"checking the box" approach to legal outsourcing),[28] as sufficient to fulfill, for example,
panel appointment or RFP criteria.

IDENTIFICATION OF ALTERNATIVE SOURCING TARGETS

When considering sourcing options beyond the firm, the first step is to identify
promising targets within the services the firm offers to its clients. Mary Lacity has
extensively researched outsourcing across different industries, more recently in
the legal context. She identifies two possible starting points for outsourcing of
legal activity, based on a pyramid model of legal tasks of increasing complexity.[29]
For a "horizontal slice," one type of activity of low or intermediate complexity that
occurs across different practice groups is identified for outsourcing. For a "vertical
slice," a project type in one area comprises different tasks of different levels of low
to intermediate complexity is chosen. LSOs will often specialize in offering either

---

27. Interview by Eric Chin, Imme Kaschner, and David Goener with Nick West, in London, U.K. (Sept.
29, 2014).

28. Mark Ross, *Redefining the Law Firm Delivery Model* 31 Outsource Magazine (2013), *available at*
http://outsourcemag.com/redefining-the-law-firm-delivery-model/.

29. Lacity et al., *supra* note 1, at 88–90.

"horizontal-type" or "vertical-type" work, since the qualifications and experience of the human resources that are needed to provide either one are different.

For either approach, detailed analysis of all the steps involved in generating legal services, and the necessary resources (and based on that, costs) for each step are necessary. This process mapping to identify where and how outsourcing can make processes more efficient does take considerable resources. U.S. firm Seyfarth Shaw LLP has mapped over 100 processes for its SeyfarthLean initiative. On its webpage, Seyfarth Shaw describes its approach and the chances for client relationship management and improved services that it offers in this manner:

> When we map legal service delivery from beginning to end, we identify steps that deliver the right results and identify where we need to modify or re-engineer the process—often using best practices, knowledge management, or a technology solution. Joint process mapping sessions with clients have proven to build stronger client relationships. We use these sessions to help define business outcomes that support our client's strategic goals. Frequently, the client's own internal steps in key process areas are defined and incorporated into an overall plan that more clearly defines roles/responsibilities between client and outside counsel.[30]

U.K. law firm Addelshaw Goddard for example mapped 46 common processes in the areas of banking, corporate, litigation, and real estate in preparation for the launch of their captive Transaction Services Team.[31]

Such business process mapping is equally necessary for sophisticated pricing strategies, as discussed in chapter 9, and internal process improvement through legal project management (LPM) that will be discussed in chapter 11. This analysis usually needs external consultant input.

Liam Brown, founder and chairman of major nontraditional legal services provider Elevate Services, gives an example of how different aspects of one transaction project are sourced efficiently:

> We offer a full range of legal services, ranging from automation, through process-driven, by non-lawyers and junior lawyers, through to highly sophisticated legal services, by senior lawyers. A perfect example is handling a demerger for a corporation. We use technology to identify and locate contracts around the enterprise. Then we use technology to automate/assist junior lawyer review of the contract provisions to identify provisions that require we take business or legal action. We then use non-lawyers and software to manage sending notices, tracking status. Then we use more senior lawyers to negotiate revised contracts with the counter-parties, escalating to the company's in-house legal team as appropriate, e.g., for sensitive customer contracts.[32]

---

30. Seyfarth Shaw LLP, http://www.seyfarth.com/seyfarthlean-background.
31. Lucy Burton, *Alternative Workstyles*, THE LAWYER BLOG (June 16, 2014), http://www.thelawyer.com/analysis/alternative-workstyles/3021683.article.
32. E-mail from Liam Brown to authors (Aug. 17, 2014) (on file with authors).

SELECTING PRICE-SENSITIVE WORK FOR ALTERNATIVE SOURCING

Beyond an identification of process elements that are fit for outsourcing, the identification should also include an assessment of clients' perception of the value of
the work, which translates into price sensitivity, or lack thereof. Value, in turn, is
based on perceived or measured risk inherent in a transaction or other matter.
This risk is managed at least in part through the involvement of the law firm. Price
sensitivity and risk are negatively correlated, meaning price sensitivity decreases
with increasing risks and complexity (those are of course not the same, but are
often positively correlated) of legal services. Clients are therefore less likely to
seek critical legal services elsewhere solely because they are offered for a lower
price.

Firms need to identify price-insensitive demands and continue to service those
demands themselves, allowing them to directly control quality and maintain margins. In this manner, they can fully leverage their technical expertise. Mark Jones
of Addleshaw Goddard LLP uses the image of a modified and multisourced value
pyramid in his succinct analysis of changing law firm–client interactions.[33] Law
firms might also be able to provide the lower-risk, commodity-type services, if they
are willing to invest in captives or find some other way to use technology, project
management, and legal professionals (though not necessarily lawyers) to be able
to match LSO prices. Stuart Fuller of King & Wood Mallesons identifies this as "the
business model challenge for law firms—how you keep different types of work at
different price points under one firm's brand. The drive for efficiency and productivity demands greater flexibility from our business model."[34] Paul Carr, president
of Axiom Law in the United States (and a former student of George Beaton's, going
back to Melbourne Business School days for both), sees the strategic choice of
where in the high-risk segment of the legal market a firm wants to compete as intri-
cately linked to choices about how connected, but lower-risk, work is dealt with:

> There will always be work that is of a risk profile, whether that be legal, reputa-
> tional, or business risk where clients are relatively price insensitive. Maybe the
> work involves novel questions of law or the client wants to off-load liability. BigLaw
> firms absolutely fit this purpose; that just has to be a bulls-eye.
>
> This creates choices for law firms around questions like "Is my competitive
> advantage in litigation, or in transactions, or in regulatory work?" This kind of
> work, or at least a segment of it, is probably the center of gravity for which BigLaw
> is ideally designed.
>
> This leaves BigLaw with another choice: How do we service sub-adjacent mat-
> ters and related lower risk work? Do I compete for it? Do I partner with other
> types of providers to provide more of a commoditized solution? Do I build a set of

---

33. MARK JONES, *The Changing Relationship Between Clients and Law Firms, in* LAW FIRM STRATEGIES FOR
THE 21ST CENTURY 175–89 (Christoph H. Vaagt ed., Globe Business Publishing 2013).
34. Telephone interview by George Beaton and Eric Chin with Stuart Fuller (Sept. 8, 2014).

capabilities at a different cost point or in a different operating structure? How do I deal with the adjacent work that is in and around the big ticket items in order to provide clients with more of an "in-to-win, one-stop-shop" solution?[35]

There can be no question that the strength of large law firms lies in their expertise in dealing with complex legal matters, and managing the legal and business risks involved in those. In order to continue to attract such matters, firms need to identify routine aspects of such work that carry a lower risk and need to find ways of sourcing those at a lower price point, be it through cooperation with alternative service providers as providers to the firm or directly to the client, or through lower-cost captive centers, as we discuss further on.

THE MAKE-VERSUS-BUY DECISION

In weighing up the different sourcing options, work done within a law firm (by employees or temporary staff) can be compared to work done at a captive center and work that is outsourced to an LSO. A summary of such considerations is given in Figure 10.1. The make-versus-buy decision is obviously one that has to be made on a factual matrix for groups of projects or specific common processes. Stuart Fuller, global managing partner at King & Wood Mallesons, acknowledges "We need to be very flexible about the make-or-buy decision. Law firms tend to convince themselves that they can do things better than others, and I do not believe that is the case."[36]

For a more academic discussion of the subject of make-versus-buy considerations, see Mari Sako's White Paper *Make-or-Buy Decisions in Legal Services: A Strategic Perspective*.[37]

Ultimately, sourcing decisions are not of a one-size-fits-all nature; rather, the challenge is to generate an integrated sourcing mix that delivers the desired end-result at the best possible profit margin. Each possible solution has advantages and disadvantages. Such a mix can put lawyers in a firm in the position of both buyers and sellers of legal services, with their clients sometimes becoming suppliers of building blocks of the services that they ultimately buy (see the example of Carillion plc that follows). An integrated sourcing strategy can therefore become a means not only to save costs, but also to generate revenue.

FLEXIBLE STAFF

Instead of employing legal personnel on a fixed cost basis, options are increasingly available to add members to legal teams for defined periods of time as and

---

35. Telephone interview by George Beaton with Paul Carr, President, Axiom (Aug. 8, 2014).
36. Fuller, *supra* note 34.
37. Mari Sako, *Make-Or-Buy Decisions in Legal Services: A Strategic Perspective* (2010), *available at* http://www.sbs.ox.ac.uk/ideas-impact/novakdrucecentre/research/working-papers/make-or-buy-decisions-legal-services-strategic-perspective.

FIGURE 10.1
Make-versus-Buy Considerations: Ways to address potential issues with aspects of work done within the firm, by a captive entity, or by a third party

Make Versus Buy Considerations

Issue	Work Done by Law Firm	Work Done by Captive	Work Done by Legal Services Outsourcer
Quality control	Through direct supervision	Through close supervision and control over general process	Indirect through contractual agreement
Process control	Through direct supervision	Process controlled at set-up	Only control over process through contractual agreement and control of intermediate steps as agreed
Level of fixed costs	High fixed costs for facilities and labor in prime business locations	Lower fixed costs through lower cost of facilities and labor, but need to consider sunk costs for set-up	Costs per project or other basis
Cost certainty	Achieved through measurement/ project management	Achieved through measurement/ project management	Based on contract
Flexible capacity	Flexibility limited by need to hire/dismiss staff, but can be increased through temporary staff	Flexibility limited by need to hire/ dismiss staff but can be increased through temporary staff	Can be scaled as desired, with expertise as desired
Profit	Profit remains with firm, but possibly low margin	Profit flows back to firm, likely higher margin	Possibly lower cost, but no income generated
Potential to leverage firm's intellectual capital	Intellectual capital leveraged at low volume	Intellectual capital leveraged at high volume	Low (only through advice to LSO)
Access to innovative technology and non-law competencies (data analysis etc.)	Possibly some	Possibly some	Easy through selecting appropriate LSO
Economies of scale	Possibly some	Likely some if combining for multiple offices	Large through selecting appropriate LSO

when needed for specific projects, at times of peak demand, or for rapidly growing companies. In a way, this is an extension of the well-established secondment model. Flex by Fenwick offers such on-demand in-house resources in the United States. As noted previously, in the United Kingdom, a number of law firms have responded to client demand by building their "own" hubs of flexible talent, often from their alumni bases, to be available to clients on an as-needed basis. These entities also provide a reservoir of experienced talent for the firm without adding fixed costs. In addition, depending on the structural set-up of these entities, they can be additional sources of profit for a law firm. Since these flexible lawyers are fully immersed in the team, whether working on-site or remotely, it is comparatively easy to integrate them into work flow and processes, and to control the quality of their work.

CAPTIVES IN THE UNITED STATES

One option for alternative sourcing is setting up captive centers, also called shared services. Consulting, technology, and outsourcing provider Accenture defines shared services as

> [t]he consolidation of support functions (such as human resources, finance, information technology and procurement) from several departments into a standalone organizational entity whose only mission is to provide services as efficiently and effectively as possible.[38]

This broad definition does not limit to whom the services are provided, and therefore can cover services to the parent entity as well as outside clients. Because of the different long-term options for captives that only serve the parent entity, and captives that serve clients outside the parent entity, we refer to the latter as "complex captives." In the legal sector, captive centers have been set up by law firms to service their own needs, but also by legal departments of corporations to provide specialized services to outside clients in addition to the internal client, in the process turning a cost center into a profit center. Theoretically, there is no need to design law firm captive centers as brick-and-mortar, fixed-cost entities with permanent staff. In reality, the set-up cost and desire for close and dependable integration with the parent, as well as quality control considerations, usually lead to such organizational structures, and therefore still result in fixed, though lower, costs. Such captives are often formed as a part of multifaceted sourcing strategies that also incorporate third-party outsourcing and on-demand legal talent.

Captive centers are usually set up to take advantage of any or all of lower labor cost (in general or through giving tasks to staff with lower levels of formal legal or other education), lower facilities cost, process and project management

---

38. Accenture Report, *Driving High Performance in Government: Maximising the Value of Public-Sector Shared Services* 3 (2005).

optimization, and in some cases government subsidies. Setting up a captive often necessitates significant staff redundancies, since many members of staff are frequently unwilling to relocate and accept the lower remuneration, but the upside of this is the possibility to start out with staff willing to accept different ways of working. An example of such a change management challenge is discussed in chapter 13. For a captive to provide an advantage, the cost savings through these combined factors have to outweigh the losses of talent and face-to-face communication, and other interface problems that arise in the cooperation between parent and captive due to cultural and geographical distances. Any consideration of, or proposals for, designing a captive in a certain location must address these factors. Increasingly, law firms in the United States use near-shoring, through captive centers or by LSOs, to take advantage of lower cost facilities and labor.[39] This allows them access to a culturally and educationally identical or very similar talent pool, which decreases losses through incompatible work and management cultures. One example is Pillsbury Winthrop Shaw Pittman's operational center in Nashville, Tennessee, which has been combining back office functions for the firm's other offices since 2012.[40] Kaye Scholer LLP's shared services center in Tallahassee, Florida,[41] and Sedgwick LLP's center in Kansas City[42] are additional examples of U.S. captives.

CAPTIVES IN THE UNITED KINGDOM

For U.K. law firms, moving from London to regional centers like Birmingham, Manchester, or Bristol, or to other parts of the United Kingdom, like Scotland or Northern Ireland, provides sufficient decreases in fixed facilities and employment costs to justify setting up a captive. In 2011, Herbert Smith Freehills opened a captive center in Belfast, Northern Ireland, that focused on document review. Another example is the firm of Hogan Lovells, formed through a trans-Atlantic merger in 2010. The firm has over 2,500 lawyers including 800 partners worldwide, with particular strengths in the areas of financial services, energy, and pharmaceuticals.[43] The Birmingham Legal Services Centre with about 20 lawyers was launched in late 2014. While this seems rather small, there is no magical threshold size for a captive, rather the return on investment depends on the balance between set-up and running costs per output compared to what the cost–return ratio would be if the work were done within the structure and facilities of the parent. Hogan Lovell has

---

39. See, e.g., Rebekah Mintzer, *Legal Process Outsourcing Comes Back Onshore*, Corporate Counsel Online (July 29, 2015), http://www.corpcounsel.com/id=1202733303001/Legal-Process-Outsourcing-Comes-Back-Onshore?slreturn=20151017074107.

40. *See also* http://www.pillsburylaw.com/news/sean-whelan-comments-on-law-firms-relocating-back-office-tasks.

41. *See* http://www.kayescholer.com/offices/tallahassee.

42. Sedgwick, http://www.sdma.com/sedgwicks-global-administrative-operations-to-be-relocated-to-kansas-city-02-06-2014/.

43. *See* www.Hoganlovells.com.

a complex sourcing strategy encompassing the Birmingham Centre to support the London office through completing lower-complexity legal work and outsourced back-office functions through the office in Johannesburg, South Africa, following a merger with South African firm Routledge Modise.[44]

Berwin Leighton Paisner, a U.K.-based international law firm with over 200 partners, similarly has a Manchester captive as part of a complex sourcing strategy. Following a major process mapping initiative, the Manchester hub is posed to support other offices.[45] Complementing the fixed in-sourcing, Berwin Leighton Paisner was also the driving force behind the creation of Lawyers On Demand (LOD) in 2007, a company that offers flexible legal talent as needed for law firms and in-house legal departments.[46] On June 1, 2012, LOD was spun out into a separate company, with Berwin Leighton Paisner holding an 80 percent stake initially. As Neville Eisenberg of Berwin Leighton Paisner explained, this change was intended to

> [g]ive the LOD business a more independent and accountable platform to pursue its future development. LOD is now a known and respected entity in the marketplace with an impressive track record, and will have greater opportunity to pursue future growth plans in the new structure.[47]

The entities still maintain close ties that benefit the recruitment and professional development of LOD lawyers.

Addleshaw Goddard is another U.K.-based international firm with a Manchester captive. The transaction services team was formed following extensive process mapping, in part to carry out identified repetitive tasks that do not necessitate legal qualifications.[48] Further examples of on-shore captives include Clyde & Co LLP and Nabarro, both with offices in Manchester, and Simmons & Simmons' office in Bristol.

Beyond England, Scotland and Northern Ireland offer culturally similar locations with substantial government subsidies if the jobs created are maintained over a period of time. So-called Magic Circle firm Allen & Overy has a captive center in Belfast, Northern Ireland, that delivers both business support and lower-complexity legal work. David Morley, Senior Partner at Allen & Overy, commented on the structural changes in the market in an interview (more on setting up the captive center in chapter 13):

> It is clear that there is a big shift going on in the legal industry, although there are still quite a few lawyers, particularly partners in private practice, who either don't believe that or prefer not to believe that . . . . This is a structural change, I don't think it is purely a cyclical response to a tough economic environment over the

---

44. Burton, *supra* note 31.

45. *Id.*

46. *See* www.LOD.co.uk.

47. *See* Press Release, Neville Eisenberg, Lawyers on Demand Comes of Age (May 24, 2012), http://www .blplaw.com/media/press-releases/lawyers-on-demand-comes-of-age/.

48. *See* Burton, *supra* note 31.

last five years. The financial crisis started it of course, but businesses got used to accepting better value for legal services. Controlling that cost and seeking out value is strategic and will not go away.[49]

So captive centers are very much a part of the complex sourcing landscape for legal services, at least in the mid-term, given the length of agreements for public funding and facilities in general and the volume of investment by law firms in the captives. As can be seen from the previous examples, the main considerations in contemplating setting up a captive entity include an assessment of which aspects of the work generated by a law firm are suitable for being generated by such an entity and the cost and availability of appropriate facilities and human resources, as well as possibly public funding, in the target area. Captives can also form an intermediate step prior to back-office and low-complexity legal functions being outsourced to third-party providers. In this regard, a captive also offers the option to leverage the firm's intellectual property that went into setting up the structures and processes by eventually selling it of to a third party or having it diversify into providing services to other organizations, that is, turning it into a "complex captive."

COMPLEX CAPTIVES

Beyond captives that serve only the parent entity, there is the possibility of setting up captives that provide services to additional corporate, law firm, or private parties. We are coining the term "complex captives" for these types of captives. These complex captives overcome the one-client limitation in the captive business model, and they provide a way to monetize the significant intellectual capital that the parent entity invests in building and optimizing high-volume solutions through the captive, and the significant expertise that is built in the provision of high-volume services. One example of such a complex captive is BT Legal, an ABS (alternative business structure) under British law that is a subsidy of British telecommunications giant BT. The group originated as a team that was dedicated to handling small claims that arose from minor damages caused by about 30,000 telecommunications engineers in the course of their work. The group consisted mostly of non-lawyer claims handlers supervised by a few attorneys. Spun out as an ABS, the large-volume, small-claims handling capabilities of BT Legal are now provided to other firms. In addition, BT is considering making the expertise of its in-house team in the area of employment law and human resources available for outside clients.[50]

---

49. Telephone interview by George Beaton with David Morley, Worldwide Senior Partner, Allen & Overy (Oct. 21, 2014).

50. Neil Rose, *BT Legal Chief Warns Firms of New Entrant Threat as Its ABS Eyes Expansion,* LEGAL FUTURES BLOG (Mar. 25, 2014), http://www.legalfutures.co.uk/latest-news/bt-legal-chief-warns-firms-new-entrant -threat-abs-eyes-expansion.

Other interesting U.K. examples are the offerings of some members of the Carillion group of companies. Carillion plc is a large company providing construction and general support services, with a long history of public–private partnership projects.

The company's legal department is Carillion Legal. Another entity, Carillion Advice services, provides high-volume, low-complexity services to Carillion Legal, but also to other law firms that receive work from Carillion Legal.[51] In addition, the captive has built a track record of providing cost-effective advice for legal aid recipients, as well as considerable process expertise around employment law matters. Both of these competencies (provision of high-volume advice to private individuals along with employment law expertise) are now being leveraged in yet another co-operation with employment law specialist firm Clarkslegal LLP for integrated employment law services to individuals, adding a dimension of cost-efficient delivery of low-complexity advice and managed legal services for other corporates. Richard Tapp, company secretary and director of legal services at Carillion, comments on the general outsourcing trends:

> Increasingly, corporates are outsourcing all manner of their non-core work, often now second-generation. Taking Carillion as an example, we are an outsourcer for others, but outsource all our own back-office functions in three towers of finance, HR, and IT, with a mix of in-placed staff, onshore and offshore. First generation process outsourcing through consultancies such as Accenture saw the process as transformational; second generation sees it as a process improvement task with significant cost benefits. Corporates may ask, why can't they do the same for legal work? . . . Corporates' own customers are demanding more for less and are pushing for commoditization—corporates have no alternative, if they are to remain competitive and survive—to make the same demands of their suppliers, law firms included.[52]

These two examples illustrate possible long-term strategies for captives, that is, to develop a customer base beyond the parent entity. Another radical example of a local government legal department (Kent Legal Services, U.K.) that turned into a law firm providing services to other local government clients, and is now looking to restructuring itself as joint venture ABS benefiting from external capital and additional work streams to "future-proof" itself, was discussed in detail in chapter 9.

Law firms might also be able to sell or partly sell captives off to legal process outsourcers looking to expand their portfolio and acquire an asset that has a close working relationship with the parent firm, as suggested, for example, by Mark Ross.[53] However, it is hard to predict the future demand for part or full ownership of such entities. When setting up a captive, an expected return on investment

---

51. *See also* http://www.carillionplc.com/capabilities/support-services/advice-services.aspx#.U_vg LFaKjFl.

52. E-mail from Richard Tapp to authors (Aug. 12, 2014) (on file with authors).

53. Ross, *supra* note 28.

through selling the captive as a whole or in parts, or through turning it into a publicly traded company, should therefore be estimated in a very conservative manner.

In summary, many law firms in the United States as well as in the United Kingdom have chosen to set up captive centers as an alternative to generating services within their main operating structure. Such centers offer many advantages, but they also contribute to ongoing fixed costs. Outsourcing to LSOs, in contrast, does not result in fixed costs.

OUTSOURCING AND QUALITY CONTROL

The advantages and disadvantages of third-party outsourcing compared to working with a firm's own captive or not outsourcing at all are listed in Figure 10.1. The advantages mainly relate to added flexibility and a decrease in fixed costs, the disadvantages to a lack of control and a perception of potentially inferior work, and risks through interface problems between the outsourcer and the law firm, including through data security breaches. David Perla, founder of Pangea3, sums up why large law firms might give more weight to those disadvantages than is justified: "The hardest thing in the legal market is the perception, rightly or wrongly, that lawyers have to be right all the time. They see quality as binary (right or wrong), and to be wrong is fatal."[54]

Looking at the trend toward law firm captive centers in low-cost areas as previously described, it is interesting to note the move in the other direction in LSOs. Near-shoring or on-shoring, as opposed to off-shoring, is increasingly common, with LSO providers opening up offices closer to their clients. One example is Integreon, which opened a substantial (100-seat) document review center in London in 2012, in addition to their regional (Bristol) center.[55] This is in stark contrast to law firms moving their captives away from the city. It would of course be unjustified to take this trend as a portent of the decline of traditional law firms, but it does demonstrate the potential of LSOs. Mary Lacity quotes sources estimating a value of US\$ 2.4 billion in the global LSO market in 2012, with predicted annual growth rates between 26 and 60 percent;[56] Alex Hamilton and Kevin Colangelo estimated US\$ 1 billion in 2012 and annual growth rates between 25 and 35 percent.[57] Without attempting to resolve the disparity in the numbers, the volume is significant. And the future for many of these outsourcers is likely to lie in cooperation with traditional law firms, as Mark Ross of Integreon opines:

---

54. Telephone interview by George Beaton with David Perla, President, Bloomberg BNA Legal Division /Bloomberg Law (Aug. 14, 2014).

55. Integreon, *Integreon Opens Legal Document Review Centre in London,* http://www.integreon.com /BlogDetails?BGID=292 (last visited Nov. 14, 2015).

56. LACITY ET AL., *supra* note 1, at 1.

57. Alex Hamilton & Kevin Colangelo, *Making LPO Work*, 28 OUTSOURCE MAGAZINE (2012), *available at* http://outsourcemag.com/making-lpo-work/.

The end of this journey . . . is when LPO solutions are so closely integrated into the firm's overall value proposition that they are simply viewed as part of a suite of re-engineered solutions that the firm provides to its clients across all its practice groups.[58]

This sentiment is shared by Peter Kalis, chairman and global managing partner of K&L Gates:

BigLaw need not fear LPOs or other alternative providers because they are part of an efficiency-enhancing ecosystem that refreshes the legal services industry and brings value to clients—as a complement and not a threat to classical lawyering.[59]

Lawyers are possibly more concerned about the level of quality they will receive from, and the level of control over, an outsourcer than are professionals in other industries. In view of the confidential nature of any information provided to an LSO to do the work, this is understandable, since any data security breach can result in serious damage to a firm's reputation, in addition to formal liability. But beyond data security, concerns over a general lack of control appear to be unfounded, as long as there is an adequately documented and shared understanding and language between the law firm and the LSO. Kevin Colangelo, vice president of client relations and strategic communications at Elevate Services, points out that

[i]n this context, "control" can encompass both risk management and commercial elements, and it includes considerations such as: (1) the ability to hire and fire, (2) the ability to ensure a consistent quality of service, (3) control in terms of investments in, and ownership of, infrastructure (e.g., capital assets), (4) protection of confidential information and/or intellectual property, (5) control in terms of ownership of something of value, and (6) control in terms of a somewhat-unexplainable discomfort (e.g., "I just mean control, know what I mean?").[60]

All of these aspects need to be addressed contractually in a service level agreement, but provided they are, Kevin Colangelo states that the level of process scrutiny and measurement at any point is likely to be higher within an LSO that is based on a business model of high volume and low margins with clearly defined outputs than within a law firm where technical excellence, possibly at the expense of timeliness and efficiency, is the overriding consideration. But for a law firm to take advantage of LSO offerings, probably the greatest challenge is to articulate, and clearly communicate, exactly what deliverable the firm seeks (beyond a general standard of excellence). And quality is a two-way street—a service level agreement also needs to codify the obligations of the law firm in enabling efficient processes,

---

58. Ross, *supra* note 28.

59. Peter Kalis, *There's Room Enough for BigLaw and LPOs*, The Lawyer Blog (June 30, 2014), http://www.thelawyer.com/analysis/behind-the-law/industry-leaders/peter-kalis-theres-room-enough-for-big-law-and-LSOs/3022283.article.

60. Kevin Colangelo, *The Business of Law: Addressing Law Firms' Concerns Over "Control" in Managed Services Relationships*, LinkedIn (July 15, 2014), https://www.linkedin.com/pulse/article/20140715134921-327998-the-business-of-law-addressing-law-firms-concerns-over-control-in-managed-services-relationships.

such as submitting relevant information on time and with clear instructions for the exact scope of the work.

OUTSOURCING EXAMPLE

One illustration of strategic collaboration between a corporate law department and an outsourcer is an ongoing contract management project delivered for Microsoft by Integreon.[61] The scope of the project included review of large numbers of routine procurement contracts that had previously been handled by an in-house team of paralegals not exclusively dedicated to the role. The outsourcing goal was to improve efficiency, quality, and delivery times, as well as allowing for the up-skilling of the in-house team for review of nonroutine contracts. The project proceeded from an internal study commissioned by Microsoft highlighting the repetitive nature of the review process, making it well suited for outsourcing, as well as the expected ongoing increase in the number of contracts to be reviewed. The service level agreements included specific KPIs and set metrics as well as detailed playbooks that were then updated on an ongoing basis as the project progressed. Integreon maintained a dedicated team to work on the project, with physical and electronic firewalling of the work. From its beginnings, the number of team members has tripled, and the project has grown to include support in multiple languages other than English. The outcome so far is a significant increase in cost, quality, and user satisfaction, combined with a clear decrease in turnaround time and number of contracts triaged to more expensive outside review. When thinking about options for strategic co-operations between client company, outsourcer, and law firm, such a co-operation in a similar situation can include arrangements for less routine contracts to be triaged to a law firm, with integrated data management systems to avoid interface problems and inefficient hand over, with the in-house department reducing involvement to strategic process supervision. An example of how technological innovations from LSOs can support similar projects can be found in chapter 12, which describes Axiom's proprietary IRIS system.

QUO VADIS?

In attempting to predict trends for both LSOs and legal captives, developments in other industries provide insight. In his seminal book *The Innovator's Dilemma*, Harvard Business School's Clayton Christensen provides many examples of industries where new entrants start at the low-margin, commoditized end of the market to build scale, usually through disruptive technologies, and eventually challenge strong incumbents on their home ground of high-quality services.[62] LSOs have

---

61. *See also* Integreon, *Contract Management for a Fortune 100 Software Developer* (2013), *available at* http://www.integreon.com/WhatWeDo/LegalServices/CaseStudyDetails?CSID=372.

62. Clayton M. Christensen, The Innovator's Dilemma (Harvard Business School Press 1997).

already significantly increased the complexity and breadth of services that they provide compared to the early offerings ten years ago, and they provide services to in-house law departments that in the past relied on law firms for their entire external supply of legal services. LSOs might be in a better position than law firms to quickly acquire and leverage disruptive technological innovations because of their strong technological expertise, clear governance structures, and access to (and willingness to leverage) significant capital. But even in the absence of technological game changers that might, for example, come from advances in artificial intelligence, at least some LSOs can be expected to move their offerings up the value chain as both their expertise and competition in the LSO market increases. Depending on one's view, this can be seen as allowing traditional law firms to position themselves even more clearly in the high-complexity segment of the legal services market, or as a threat to those firms, or as a classic example of co-opetition.

While captive centers are a significant trend at this point, it remains to be seen if their number continues to grow, or if they will constitute intermediate steps in law firms increasingly outsourcing building blocks of their services as they develop and increase their supply chain management competencies. As more firms build captives, a market for ownership or part ownership for those captives might develop. This would generate some data to gauge the market value in relation to the set-up costs of these assets. Such ROI data might further influence firms' make-versus-buy decisions.

CONCLUSION

Law firms have an unprecedented array of options available to them in order to not produce every step and building block of the work that they deliver to clients, and they should assess and use these options to remain competitive. Remaking their supply chains in a flexible way is a necessary step in positioning themselves in a mature market. In order to arrive at an optimal sourcing strategy, a firm needs to map its work flow and processes to identify what segment of work is to be sourced differently, and with what goal. One option is in-sourcing through hiring flexible talent on a temporary basis as needed. Another option is the formation of captive centers, that is, dedicated centers to provide lower-complexity work or support services that leverage lower facilities and labor costs, and also economies of scale and project management competencies in the same or a different jurisdiction. Complex captives, which provide services beyond the parent company, overcome one-client limitations and offer a way to leverage the parent entities' intellectual capital and other investments in the center for profit. Third-party outsourcing poses challenges in terms of control over the flow of confidential information and the resulting product, but those can be addressed through service level agreements. The breadth and diversity of sourcing options is likely to increase, given the significant investment and growth in the LSO industry.

Chapter 11

Legal Project Management and Process Improvement

Key Points

- Legal project management (LPM) is about a structured approach to the management of legal matters to meet the clients' and the firm's expectations in respect of quality, time, and budget. Legal process improvement (LPI) on the other hand is about optimizing processes to achieve a balance of quality, cycle time, and efficiency. The two methods need to be combined in any initiative aimed at reducing costs and improving service levels.
- Law firms need to use LPM and LPI for complex matters with many unpredictable facets, as well as for routine matters.
- Technology enables effective and efficient project management and process improvement, but relying too heavily on technology in implementing LPM, and neglecting the significant challenge in helping lawyers to learn to work differently, will not be successful.
- Innovation initiatives in a firm need to select approaches to LPM and related tools that are suited to the firm's culture and its clients' needs.
- Bringing it all together requires significant time, investment, and dedicated project management expertise. Monitoring of key metrics during and after implementation is important to reap the greatest possible benefits, and make adjustments as needed.

INTRODUCTION

Legal project management and legal process improvement—abbreviated LPM and LPI in this book—enable the predictable delivery of high-quality legal services in an efficient and timely manner, and within set budgets. To move from running legal matters on a one-off basis, with one of the younger attorneys or experienced paralegals having a spreadsheet somewhere to keep track of "things," with the partner in charge somehow keeping "things" from completely blowing out beyond a budget (if there is one), to the disciplined, predictable, efficient running of defined matter types requires significant resources, expert assistance, and willingness to embrace substantial change within the firm.

Optimizing the building blocks of matters and standardized work flows allows for the delivery of services for fixed fees, effective resource allocation within the firm, and implementation of technology-driven solutions to bring down the cost of human resources. Project management professionals and tools can make coordination between different practice groups or external legal service providers smoother by planning for hand-offs and time lines. Project management as a discipline is well established in other industries that deal with complex projects, but remains something of a novelty for many law firms.

One development that illustrates the growing importance of strategies relating to the process, and not just the content, of delivering legal services, is the launch of a section of the Association for Corporate Counsel (ACC) for legal operations professionals in June 2015.[1] Interest groups within the section include project and process management, but also external and internal resource management, metrics and analysis, litigation support and e-discovery (no surprises there), strategic planning, and technology and tools. The section has received a good deal of interest from the in-house community. It also illustrates the multidisciplinary nature and the importance of professionals with primarily nonlegal expertise in the talent mix of legal services providers today.

This chapter details reasons why law firms should embrace LPM (as clients are clearly doing), and provides examples of how firms have implemented LPM, changing the manner in which they provide services from the ground up in response to client demand. It does not discuss or teach specific LPM strategies in detail, as other excellent books and resources do.[2] Rather, it sets out how LPM and LPI fit into the context of a comprehensive remade business model, in conjunction with pricing, technology, interdisciplinary cooperation, marketing, and alternative sourcing.

---

1. *See* the ACC webpage, https://www.acc.com/legalops/interest/.

2. *See, e.g.*, The Project Management Institute Legal Project Management Community of Practice http://legalpm.vc.pmi.org/Public/Home.aspx (last visited Dec. 5, 2014); Susan Raridon Lambreth & David A. Rueff Jr., The Power of Legal Project Management: A Practical Handbook (ABA Publishing 2014); Jim Hassett, Legal Project Management Quick Reference Guide (LegalBizDev 2013); Stephen B. Levy, Legal Project Management: Control Costs, Meet Schedules, Manage Risks, and Maintain Sanity (Day Pack Books 2009); Barbara Boake & Rick Kathuria, Project Management for Lawyers (Ark 2011); and, for the time-poor, Pam Woldow & Douglas H. Richardson, Legal Project Management in One Hour for Lawyers (ABA Law Practice Division, 2014).

CASE STUDY: STARTING THE SEYFARTHLEAN JOURNEY

Lisa Damon, a partner at Seyfarth Shaw LLP, recalls the beginning of implementing LPM at the firm:

> When we began our journey in 2005, a primary catalyst was our clients asking for alternative fees. At first, we were like all law firms—we relied on our experience and, in the end, just made an educated guess. Our Executive Committee, led by Steve Poor, our Managing Partner, knew there had to be a better way to understand our work, find ways to be more efficient and then price the work accurately. This realization led us to a series of tremendous client conversations and eventually to Lean Six Sigma. We spent time with the legal departments at Motorola and Caterpillar and a lot of time with Tom Sager and the DuPont team. In the end, Lean Six Sigma felt right to us—fundamentally, it relied on a true listening to the client and then a process-driven way to design a solution that fit the client need.
>
> Lean Six Sigma's razor-focused emphasis on the client and the client needs fit our culture and drove our lawyers toward change. Lean's focus on continuous improvement also fit our culture—process improvement is a journey, where you make mistakes and then you come back, you look at results, data, and process. Then you redesign and try to make it better for the client. It fit us beautifully and allowed our lawyers to truly deliver a partnership with clients as they sought to solve business and legal problems with a fresh eye. This was a whole new way to look at helping clients and inspired us to begin the journey that has transformed our firm.[3]

So far the start of the LPM journey at Seyfarth Shaw.

LPM DEFINITION

Picking an LPM definition is a bit like picking your favorite ice cream chain franchise—it is all about the flavor. The following definition, however, is a good starting point:

Legal project management is the defining, planning, executing, and evaluating of legal matters to meet the client's and firm's desired objectives and expectations (typically including budget). It is not about changing the entire way a matter is handled—as legal process improvement is. It is fundamentally about a more proactive, disciplined approach to managing your existing work to enhance the likelihood of meeting client and firm expectations. A major theme throughout all the phases of

---

3. Telephone interview by George Beaton with Lisa Damon, National Chair, Labor & Employment Department, Seyfarth Shaw LLP (Aug. 21, 2014).

legal project management is greater communication with the client's key contacts and with the project team within the law firm.[4]

We would add that the objectives also typically include set time frames. In the commercial world, delays kill deals and drive up costs. The time frames that apply to legal matters are often hard to comprehend for business professionals who are used to completing complex projects in much shorter times. We would also not limit the definition to the context of a law firm, but would include in-house departments and nontraditional legal services providers. Mark Tamminga of Canadian law firm Gowlings refers to the "structured delivery of sophisticated legal services," an excellent shorthand for the goals of LPM and LPI. The implication of a comprehensive project management initiative at Gowlings will be described in detail later on in the chapter. The firm has recently announced the launch of a new international law firm together with U.K. firm Wragge Lawrence Graham & Co to be called Gowling WLG in January 2016.[5]

There are numerous branded and nonbranded methods for a structured approach to legal work, to keep legal matters predictably on budget and on time. LPM tools include software systems that provide templates for certain matter types, with built-in functionalities to obtain relevant information from clients, and generate documents or correspondence that is necessary at certain points. The methods share a focus on a diligent assessment of exactly what is done, and when, and by whom, and at what cost, and comparing that to budget. In addition, process improvement assesses how discrete processes or entire systems are executed, by mapping each step, and considering how it fits into the overall goals for the process, as defined by the firm, or the client, or both. It is intuitive that neither the structured, repeated delivery of inefficient processes, nor an inconsistent, piece-meal application of optimized processes will result in the best possible system overall. Today, project management approaches incorporate technological elements to collect, analyze, and disseminate pertinent information. Project management and process improvement are accepted tools to ensure efficiency and quality, and thereby profitability, in the corporate world. For law firms, they offer similar advantages when faced with the more-for-less challenge.

WHY LAW FIRMS NEED LPM

Lisa Damon's insights suggest it will be hard for law firms to provide services of the same quality at a lower cost without a clear knowledge of how and at what cost services are presently provided. This allows for the identification of steps with low or no added value. It will also be hard to provide services predictably at the lowest possible cost without a clear understanding of the processes, and

---

4. Susan Raridon Lambreth, White Paper: *Legal Project Management: Transforming Legal Services*, 1 (2011).

5. *See* the Gowlings webpage, http://www.gowlings.com/news/news.asp?newsID=983 (July 8, 2015).

standardization that allows for greater efficiency through automation of repetitive elements, whether completed by lawyers or others, within or outside the firm (see chapter 10 for more detailed considerations of sourcing options). Susan Hackett, former senior vice-president and general counsel of the ACC, links the success of any alternative fee structures (or what she calls "customized" fee arrangements) to awareness, reengineering and consistent delivery of internal processes in a law firm:

> You really cannot provide value-based services without having reinvented the way the law firm does the work. In other words, if a firm tries to provide a flat fee for a client when they really do not understand what their costs are, and they simply look at matters they have handled in the past on a billable hour basis, look at the average rates and time billed, add a safety margin by pasting on another 20 percent and say, "Ahhhh, here is your flat fee," both the firm and the client are likely to suffer. If the firm does not understand their costs in producing the service to be provided (rather than just an average of previous billings for somewhat similar work), and they do not understand how to replicate that work consistently with a team that has been carefully trained to perform just those services as efficiently as possible, they will regularly fail to provide value—both by producing the work profitably for the firm and by asking the client to pay for work that has not been efficiently produced. They simply won't have their pricing right.
>
> It is kind of a big "duh"; firms assume they can "name a price" for a matter one day, while continuing to bill on matters by the hour with the full expectation that there will be variances in how long each project takes and by what process different lawyers in the firm will do the work. That's not how any great business either guarantees consistently high quality or high efficiency results. That's just making it up as you go.
>
> What I am getting at is you need a much larger, more systematic reengineering of how your firm does its work. You cannot say, "I will respond ad hoc on an irregular basis as a client demands it for each different kind of service." You must say, "I am going to reinvent the entire line of this kind of service that we offer. I am going to cost it. I am going to make it more efficient. I am going to train the team who does it to do it consistently. I am going to be able to deliver it on a project basis, over and over and over again, in a very predictably priced manner." You have to change the way you work; you cannot just bid a price and expect to hit that mark consistently, efficiently, or profitably.[6]

Instituting LPM in this manner requires people to change the way they have worked for a long time, and where their habits have been reinforced by consistent rewards. (Chapter 13 provides examples of change management strategies to achieve such far-reaching change initiatives.)

Nick West of nontraditional legal services provider Axiom points to the need to limit use of lawyers as a high-cost resource in legal projects, and the value

---

6. Telephone interview by Eric Chin and Imme Kaschner with Susan Hackett (Sept. 4, 2014).

that project management professionals add to secure cooperation and hand-offs between several legal services providers:

> What we try to do on a complex project, such as the novation of 50,000 contracts, is to get the right balance between our lawyers and paralegals on the one hand and our bench of operational experts on the other. Lawyers are usually the most expensive cog in the wheel, so we need to get the balance right—there needs to be sufficient legal expertise that we can deal with the technical legal questions, but not too many lawyers so the whole system is really expensive.
>
> So, we spend a lot of time structuring the work up front, breaking down exactly what needs to be done—for example, which clauses in the contracts need to be reviewed, what kind of counterparty outreach needs to happen, and so on—and building playbooks and workflows. That allows us to work out how much lawyer time versus paralegal time versus contract negotiator time we need. We aim to build a team where the lawyers act as subject matter experts, framing exactly what needs to be done and acting as a point of escalation for tricky issues, but the junior team members do as much of the doing as possible. And we think hard about how we can use technology to support the legal work as well.
>
> Teams like this require skilled management. Particularly when we're dealing with huge volumes of documents and huge numbers of counterparties. And, of course, the client wants to know exactly where things stand on a regular basis. Why would you not ask people who are professional project managers to do all this? In any other industry, that is who you give the job to. So, at Axiom we hire project managers to do it; it doesn't get any more complicated than that.
>
> I guess we assume the idea that you can expect a lawyer to be a great communicator, great at advising, great at administrating, a great project manager, and a great whatever else is unreal. And so for us, the project manager is an integral part of the system. We deploy them as you would expect to see on an IT project or any other project.[7]

Nick points to the need for the coordination and oversight that project managers provide and that this need increases with the complexity of a matter. Complex matters or transactions often necessitate cooperation between offices of the same firm within or across jurisdictions—this is just the type of situation where experienced project managers add great value. Even if partners who buy into the need for LPM have obtained additional qualifications as project managers, this role can probably be filled just as well if not better by other specifically trained professionals (at a lower cost). As one observer put it, "Would you trust a person with only two days' training to undertake a major service of your fancy sports car?"

IS LAW DIFFERENT?

Probably the most commonly proffered argument against instituting project management in law firms is that while its techniques are successful in other contexts,

---

7. Interview by Eric Chin, David Goener, and Imme Kaschner with Nick West, in London, U.K. (Sept. 29, 2014).

law cannot be compared to any of those because of the unpredictable nature of legal matters, including actions and decisions of the client, other parties, courts, and regulators. This unpredictability, so the argument runs, makes it difficult to deliver outcomes within preset time frames and budgets that cannot accommodate the unforeseen. In the past, these uncertainties have been addressed by the risk being fully allocated to the client, that is, a law firm provided a comprehensive service on a matter based on its assessment of what was necessary at any given point, and payment was based on the time spent rendering that service. There was very little need for LPM in that system.

Now there is a strong and growing demand from clients to change the way fee risk is allocated. Law firms need to take on at least some of the risk through any number of alternative fee arrangements, necessitating finding ways to predict costs and allocate resources, and, in turn, be able to price in a profitable and competitive manner. (Chapter 9 provides details on alternative fee arrangements.) It is a misunderstanding that LPM is only suitable for highly consistent and predictable complex processes. To the contrary, it is about anticipating and clearly articulating uncertainties in multistakeholder processes, and preparing for those ahead of time as much as possible. LPM allows for each of the constituent parts of a legal matter to be provided in a standardized manner, and for possible alternative courses of action to be anticipated, resourced, and executed as necessary. This is known as "agile" project management, where instead of mapping out the entire project in the beginning, certain steps are charted, with follow-on steps added when the demands of the project become clearer as it evolves.[8] This connects to pricing strategies, since the specific steps should be priced in advance, and the anticipated costs communicated to the client. If there is a fixed budget, resource allocation can be adjusted between different steps as the matter progresses.

So LPM and LPI provide a high level of insight into, and define structured processes for, the predictable delivery of legal services. To reap these benefits, significant investments in mapping, analyzing, and redesigning processes are necessary, and there needs to be a willingness to fundamentally change the way that things are done within a law firm.

HOW (NOT) TO START WITH LPM

Legal project management expert Pam Woldow[9] provides insights into how to start when rolling out a project management initiative. While technology can be a valuable enabler of such initiatives, she cautions against relying on it for a start:

---

8. Lisa Damon, *Applying Lean Six Sigma Methods to Litigation Practice*, Prac. Law., Dec. 2013-Jan. 2014, at 28, 35.

9. *See also* PAM WOLDOW & DOUGLAS H. RICHARDSON, LEGAL PROJECT MANAGEMENT IN ONE HOUR FOR LAWYERS (ABA Law Practice Division, 2014).

Clients want consistent processes and repeatable outcomes. They want efficiency. They want predictable accuracy and projects that stay within budget. By and large, they are not getting these from their law firms. Law firms that are able to provide these value factors are the ones that are really doing very well—both with their clients and in terms of their own profitability. For LPM to work, to first take hold and then become an accepted part of "the way we do things around here," a strong commitment must come from the top of the firm. You then have to find client teams or practice groups within the firm who have an appetite for change. Frankly, usually this kind of sponsorship is triggered by pain points. I always talk about the forces that support LPM implementation by starting either with pain or gain. If you are about to lose a client, your market share, or your share of wallet with a client is slipping away you are at a pain point. And all of a sudden, you have a lot of interest in how to keep and please that client!

Some wise firms, unfortunately comparatively few, look at LPM's importance from a gain point of view. That is, they say, "We can build on LPM to go out and really grow our market share. We can get more work." That's pretty visionary and it takes a commitment that most firms don't have. They usually wait 'til they are in pain and then they call out for help. The most powerful way to roll LPM out is to focus on the people who are in pain, the practice group, or a client team. And when they start using LPM, they begin doing well, getting more work, more clients, winning RFPs, or whatever, others in the firm start to notice. Suddenly, LPM begins to look pretty good.

I see a real generational aspect to all this. Junior partners, those who are just starting to build their practices and books of business, are the ones who are most interested in LPM in a proactive way, perhaps even in a defensive way. They have got to build and keep every bit of business they have. They cannot afford to lose any. They are not the big rainmakers yet and so they have, I would say, a heightened interest in whatever steps will win and maintain clients. Many junior partners report that discussions about LPM are a great way to get client attention.

Interviewer: How do technology and technology platforms in law firms influence what you do in rolling out LPM?

PAM: The most honest answer is . . . inconsistently. But often the tools are already available. A lot of firms, particularly big law firms, have sophisticated suites of technology, some of which can be applied to LPM methods and processes, whether that is tracking the all-important "actual-to-budget" metric or monitoring how many hours timekeepers are billing. Almost all major law firms already have some ability to do the basic monitoring and tracking that a partner managing an engagement might need in order to keep track of where things stand and how they are progressing—against plan and against budget. True, this information may not be presented in the easiest format; it might be in a spreadsheet or something that is not quite as sexy as an integrated real-time project dashboard with multiple tabs for phases, tasks, team, time, actual-to-budget. Still, most of the big law firms have something they can use to support their LPM efforts.

But I must acknowledge my own prejudice: In implementing LPM initiatives, you should *never* start with technology or make the argument that great technology will result in smooth and effortless LPM use by all lawyers and project team members.

It is a mistake to bet the farm on technology. Every time a firm has focused on technology first, at least with LPM, the initiative stumbles out of the gate because what happens immediately is people say, "Well, this is just a tech or IT issue. As a practicing partner, I do not really have to change my mindset; someone in IT will do all the heavy lifting. Implementation will just take care of itself. I do not have to change the way I deliver my services, plan my work, lead my team, track progress, or communicate with the client. I can keep doing things the way I have for years, and the tech piece will be a bolt-on to what I have always done."

I will not take engagements with firms that approach me and want to start with sourcing and plugging in technology as the first step. I start with people first because making effective use of LPM requires a rethinking and relearning of the way we deliver services to meet client needs. LPM is as much about process as technology, and as much about interpersonal communication as it is about process. When all is said and done, LPM is a client-focused discipline (emphases added).[10]

So Pam sees the lack of change readiness as a huge obstacle to LPM implementation, more so than a lack of specific technology. Expertise in relation to the mechanics of process mapping is available through consultants, and they can work in tandem with the lawyers as matter experts for the process improvement. As with any major change initiative, the challenge is not so much designing and fine-tuning it, but rather to have the stakeholders adopt it in a lasting manner. If sufficient buy-in can be generated, the question is, what combination of aspects of project management will yield the best results for a specific firm.

CHOOSING THE TOOLS

LPM (like many other innovation strategies) is about bringing together people, process, and technology in an optimal manner. Any successful strategy needs to combine different approaches—for example, training people in a general (in project management) or specific manner (in using templates and applications); developing or buying technology-enabled systems that combine process maps, document templates, document generation, and dashboards; and integrating professional project managers—the possibilities are broad. Which specific strategies are going to be most profitable in any firm depends on a variety of factors, considering the desired and feasible degree of standardization. Are processes comparable across many groups and offices, so that practitioners would benefit from clear process maps, integrated with software-enabled templates, schedules, and document generation? Are large clients interested in identical client-facing communication portals or extranets across matters and offices, possibly even jurisdictions? Are there one-off complex transactions that would benefit from the involvement of dedicated project management staff, and should the firm invest in hiring their own project management professionals for teaching and implementation? Are there unique but

10. Telephone interview by Eric Chin and Imme Kaschner with Pam Woldow (Aug. 29, 2014).

smaller matters where training practitioners in charge of project management, and supporting them with applications that generate, track, and communicate project plans easily, would be an efficient solution? What pricing strategies does the firm want to offer, and how do they fit with LPM approaches? These and similar considerations aid in selecting which aspects of project management strategies a firm should implement.

PROCESS MAPPING

The diligent assessment of how certain matters are handled provides the basis for designing and implementing efficient work practices that can be employed for similar matters. Without such an assessment, it will be hard to identify how qualitatively similar or superior outcomes can be achieved faster, cheaper, and in a more predictable manner. Process mapping is also the basis for identifying what building blocks of legal services can be provided more efficiently by either non-lawyer professionals (such as for example paralegals, administrative staff, or project management professionals) or can be obtained from sources outside the firm.

The following graphic provides an example of an optimized process map that is a typical output of such a mapping and improvement process.

It is quite intuitive how such a defined process results in improved predictability (which enables confident pricing with an alternative fee arrangement), resource allocation, client communication, and timeliness over a one-off, reinvent-the-wheel approach to every matter.

Case Study: LPM Implementation at Gowlings (Canada)

The following case study, based on an extensive interview, provides an illustration of how the different aspects of change readiness, mapping, education, implementation, and connection to alternative fee arrangements can work in practice in a project management and process improvement initiative. The Canadian firm Gowlings has implemented LPM as part of their comprehensive innovation initiative under the name "Gowlings Practical." Mark Tamminga, leader of innovation initiatives and former managing partner of Gowlings' Hamilton, Ontario, office and Rick Kathuria, national director, project management and legal logistics, kindly provided detailed insights into the process.

MARK: I see project management as a code name for something much bigger. People think about, "How do you enter this redesigned wheel?". People have been trying to do it by way of process improvement. You can process improve until the cows come home and come up with beautiful process maps. Then they just sit in a drawer somewhere.

We needed a comprehensive collaboration tool that allows for the orderly conduct of what I call the *structured delivery of sophisticated legal services.*

FIGURE 11.1

Process Map Example

M&A Buyer Deal Process

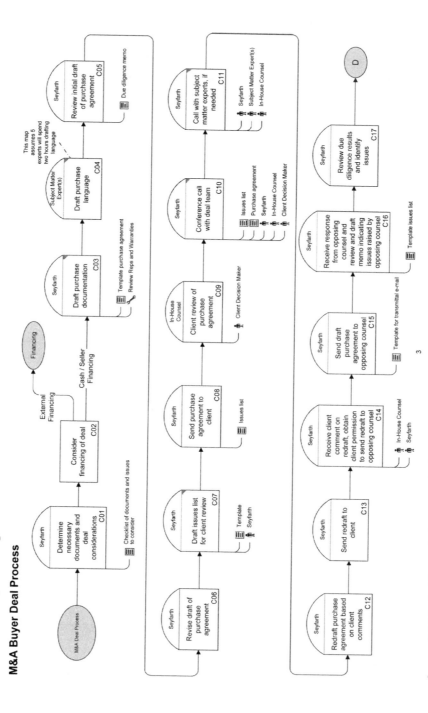

Source: Published with permission, copyright Seyfarth Shaw LLP.

That's what Liam [Brown, of nontraditional legal services provider Elevate] promised with their Cael™ project management tool. We realized early on that we needed somebody who actually understands the nuts and bolts of project management as a discipline and that was Rick [Kathuria]. Rick is a professional engineer, not a lawyer. He's also a project management professional. Most importantly, Rick is also very good with clients, and is very good at teaching lawyers about project management.

From the beginning, we have absolutely forbidden project management talk. There is no talk about Lean Six Sigma. There is nothing about agile. There is nothing about all of that jargon that irritates and alienates people; at least it irritates me. If people have questions about those things, we can answer them and explain how they fit in the framework, but that's only discussed with the people who actually want to know more.

That is how we landed on the name "Gowlings Practical." We simplified the project management cycle into four steps, which are intuitively obvious. Liam and I fastened on the concept of "just enough" project management. A light touch. It shouldn't take a lot of effort.

Ultimately, the central collaboration goal of project management was made clear to me by one of our partners in Vancouver. He said, "Look, here is my problem. I have a huge file. There's a complicated tax piece that I had to send to one of the specialists in our Toronto office. I think it's going to cost, say, $10,000. The tax lawyer gets to work on it. Does a good job. She is doing what she is supposed to do. She is a tax lawyer. But it ends up consuming much more than my $10,000 estimate.

I fail to look at the accounting system until it's way too late. Oh, and the tax lawyer by the way saw that there was a piece in Quebec, and so another whack of time gets consumed. I finally go back to the client saying "I know I said it was going to be $10,000 but it was more complicated than I anticipated and the account is now $70,000. Sorry about that." The client goes, "That is so stupid, there's no way I am going to pay you that." How do you solve that problem? You absolutely need a collaborative environment. A web-based project management tool that sends alerts when predefined thresholds are met simply makes that problem go away.

GEORGE: Could I ask what measures the executive committee of the firm relies on to gauge the return on investment that's been made? How is progress being measured? *What are your road map and milestones in this journey of Gowlings Practical?*

RICK: In the early days, when I started we didn't want to make it a numbers game. We wanted to deliver the right solution that would be used voluntarily. We did have to put some metrics in place, but that was to let us know how well we were doing and if we were on the right track. Our goal for this year was really more about firm education, firm buy-in, and more importantly, the firm's ability to accept the change.

Even though Mark and the executive team had done a fabulous job of getting the firm primed and ready to go, we had to make it real and keep them interested. One of the early things I had done when I started was to look at the whole concept in terms of what was being offered, what Liam [Brown, of non-traditional legal services provider Elevate Services] was providing. How it was all flowing and making sure that we kept it simple.

To that example, when I first looked at CAEL [Elevate's proprietary legal project management software], there were a number of things I did not like about it. I was pretty vocal with Elevate, saying, "We are not going to get lawyers using this—it's too complicated." I ran through it and knew what would likely work and what would not. I knew what it should do and should not do and what people would be willing to accept based on my previous experience in law firms and leading large initiatives.

I asked them to make a fair number of changes. To Liam's and Elevate's credit, they actually did. They said, "This all makes sense. Let's do it." Our goal at Gowlings this year is really about making sure people understand what it is and how simple it is. We wanted to continue to build on the early momentum.

The first milestone is the number of people who know what Gowlings Practical really is and can talk about it to their clients. We have been running these training sessions. I have a list of everyone in the firm who has attended any of these training sessions. As of today, I have been focusing on the professionals who do the billable work. I have 551 of them trained so far, and I have been here seven months. Our goal was to have them all trained by the end of the year. We did that by November 2014.

The other thing we set up as a metric is to recruit people who actually understand what the system is, and get them to use it to actually build out plans. It is not everyone at first, but we wanted people who are the most eager. We are making sure they have the training on using it, as they will be our ambassadors. We wanted to keep that enthusiasm going, so we wanted to make sure it was simple enough and that people would get it and run with it. We have got 100 people trained on that aspect already.

The other thing we wanted to do is pilot. We are very conscious of not doing a full rollout this year. We are not ready. We want to make sure we have some good stories that we can talk about. Here is what works. Here is what does not. Here is how it actually works in a real situation.

GEORGE: How do you involve the clients in this, Rick? Where do the clients come into the equation?

RICK: *Clients are really front and center.* Clients are asking for a project estimate. They are asking for a budget. They are asking for a fixed fee. Clients are asking our lawyers, "What have you got?" Our lawyers know enough to at least say, "We have something called Gowlings Practical. I do not know exactly how to do it myself, so I will call someone." Clients are coming that way.

. . .

We do not force our lawyers to go through training on how to build a process map. Instead, what we did was look at all of our typical types of matters. For our first pass, we got 22 of them. For each one of these matters we asked, what is the right process to go through?

Rather than having everyone do that, we took our experts who are people in the field who have done these types of matters very well many times and know exactly what should be done. After a detailed review by peer experts and myself, we created templates for each type of matter. For example, for a typical share purchase deal, a lawyer would have a good template with all the things they should be doing. By the way, this also saves them time and gives them a better result than starting from scratch.

The other thing we do about efficiency (and the clients really like this as well) is not to plan who specifically is doing the work, but what is the level and skillset of the person doing the work. *What you find in the old world of law: It is always the person I worked with the last five times who is going to do the same thing again, even though he was doing the stuff when he was a junior associate. Now he is doing it as a senior associate. That type of work should always be done by a junior associate.*

One of the things Gowlings offers that was not in Cael at the start, and I persuaded them to add it in, is to staff a matter by role and not by the name of a person. When you use the role, it comes out with a list of something like "I want a lawyer who is 9 to 14 years qualified in this, with this skill set, in this office." I can choose a specific office or not. It calculates the average rate for that; then I pick the specific person based on who is available at the time. I have my estimate. I have my whole plan. The tool actually helps build the firm as a whole because now I do not have to use that lawyer standing beside me. I can use that lawyer who has the availability when it's needed. It helps build firm-wide collaboration.

. . .

GEORGE: You referred to the other components of Gowlings Practical. May I ask what is inside the whole Gowlings Practical package?

RICK: Sure. The templates and building these up. The pricing of it. What it actually would cost if done the normal way. And what happens if we do it a different way, with a different kind of arrangement. It shows how it all works. And how profitable it is to the firm; there's no point in doing all this if we can't make money off it. Our clients want us to be around for the long-term, we need to manage our business and this helps us do it while meeting client demands.

GEORGE: Are there any parts of the firm that are resisting or not buying into Gowlings Practical? What are the lessons if there are any? And where is the resistance or reluctance coming from?

RICK: I would not say we are really seeing reluctance. There are some places where Gowlings Practical is not practical, so to speak. It does not make sense. I would not say it is resistance; it just does not make sense. For example, the patent practice. If you are filing a patent, that is more a portfolio than a project; it does not fit well in the project management world.

We are not seeing any practices pushing back. You will find people who say, "I am not sure it fits for me." What we are doing then is to explain it to them. That is the reason for our pilots; here is where it worked in so-and-so practice. I was doing one last week. The partner had not quite understood it. A client asked for some special pricing. He knew enough just to give me a call. I walked him through it and showed him, "We could do this three different ways. This is probably the one that makes sense." By the end of this conversation, he said,

"Wow. That was really useful. I can actually think of three more matters I've got where this would be more useful than the way I was doing it. I just didn't see it before." It is the experience and getting people to understand how it fits in their world.

Our training is very specific to the area in which each lawyer practices. When they go through that workshop, it is based on a real matter in their own practice area. Covering everyone at the firm is going to take a little longer, but we are getting there.

Back to the numbers, there is no rush to get everyone to do it, but if everyone understands it, when that matter comes up and the client asks them for something, the answer is "Yes, we can." If they can't do it themselves, they know who to call.

MARK: We have been very careful not to say this is mandatory. We know enough about our world that we have anticipated where there may be resistance. In our talks we use a rule of thumb. It is a definition that will change, but to merit project management treatment, the matter has to have more than two people on it, OR it has to involve more than one office OR it has to be worth more than $25,000. Those are arbitrary lines, but they put folks at ease because these are practical guides and they resonate with our people. Nonetheless, with our definition, we would still be targeting matters that represent a huge component of the firm's revenue.

. . .

GEORGE: How would you characterize the response from Gowlings' clients to these initiatives?

RICK: The clients are the ones who are asking for it, so it has been really favorable. The clients are saying "I get it; it makes sense." The clients also know that by putting a plan together before, it will cut the cost of their fees . . .. The clients see that and know they are getting more value. So the clients are all over it. The other thing is, Gowlings Practical is about *no surprises. That is one of our mottos for clients.* Right now, too many law firms give a bill to their client at the end of the matter that is higher than what the client wanted, which almost always leads to problems (emphases added).[11]

This description of the Gowlings Practical initiative by Mark Tamminga and Rick Kathuria provides a number of valuable lessons. The change journey started from the pain point of needing to be able to predict costs to be able to submit competitive, yet profitable bids. The firm responded to clients' demand for lower and more predictable costs. A comprehensive approach, combining initial mapping of frequent matters and leading to the provision of templates through specific software, was chosen, with the ability to support a range of different pricing strategies. The firm relied on a project management specialist and gave him significant leeway in setting up and implementing the initiative. In considering internal processes, a relationship with a legal services outsourcer was built, making use of the external expertise and proprietary software. Cooperation with a project management specialist with an engineering background

---

11. Interview by George Beaton with Mark Tamminga and Rick Kathuria, in Toronto, Can. (Sept. 19, 2014). Rick is co-author of a book on LPM; see *supra* note 2.

and a nontraditional provider of legal services are examples of an outcomes-focused collaborative approach that breaks down traditional "lawyer/non-lawyer" silo thinking.

The initiative was led by Mark, who had significant internal credibility through his tenure as partner in a profitable practice group and as a managing partner, and Rick, a recognized project management professional. There was clear support, including an allotment of "internal time" (time spent on the initiative considered equal to billed time) from the firm leadership. The rollout proceeded through pilot phases that were used to refine processes further. There was extensive training for fee earners and as-needed support to aid them in communicating the benefits of the initiative to clients. In fact, training was the initial metric for project success. There is obviously a clear realization that the "structured delivery of sophisticated legal services" is not a sprint, not even an endurance race like the ones that Mark is fond of, but an ongoing journey of improving services to meet changing client demands.

LPM AND UTILIZATION

Having a more structured and predictable approach to, and tracking and analyzing of, how work is done can also aid in smoothing utilization across different locations, which is a significant cost saving, as Mark Rigotti, joint CEO of Herbert Smith Freehills, points out:

> This is a hunch . . ., I don't know if this is right, . . . but I reckon our biggest cost is under-utilized lawyers. Our biggest cost is actually not our premises, it is not how much we pay our partners. Rather, it is underutilized lawyers.
>
> If three of us were in a partnership we would know who is busy, who is not, and we would self-correct as we went. For example, look at one of our smaller offices. Madrid has done phenomenally well with almost zero attrition and nearly 100 percent uniform utilization with a small spread. It is because there is a level of knowledge and accountability in a smaller environment with only 80 people.
>
> When you get large it becomes a cost of doing business that you have to wear . . . . Partners want their own people around them. There is a huge opportunity for the firm that is able either to do the same revenue with 20 percent less legal staff, or do 120 percent of your revenue with the same legal staff.
>
> I have a hunch there is a revolution here, if you could actually identify the work practices to smooth utilization really effectively. It is more revenue for no extra cost. [12]

So project management, beyond enabling the planning and execution of legal matters on time and on budget, offers firm-wide benefits beyond specific matters in planning for and aiding efficient resource allocation.

---

12. Telephone interview by George Beaton and Eric Chin with Mark Rigotti (Aug. 8, 2014).

METRICS

Once best practice processes have been settled and maps, templates, and work-flow management systems have been established, and LPM professionals added to teams, it is necessary to drive and monitor compliance for any project within the firm's agreed LPM ambit. Appropriate metrics help to assess if the planned gains in efficiency or other defined outcomes are achieved—and sustained—and what effect this is having on client engagement. Lisa Damon of Seyfarth Shaw LLP (quoted in chapter 8) affirmed the importance of quantitative analysis of LPM and LPI outcomes. So client satisfaction is clearly one element to measure when assessing the success of LPM initiatives. As the example of Gowlings Practical shows, an appropriate initial metric might be stakeholder participation in training, combined with a general proof of principle. Such a pilot project can be scaled up later. Proof of monetary return on investment in the first year is not necessarily a suitable predictor of the success of a long-term investment.

CONCLUSION

LPM and LPI are crucial in enabling a firm to work efficiently and predictably to meet the more-for-less challenge, partly through enabling accurate value-based pricing, and partly through defining the most efficient approach for each element that comprises a legal matter. Assessing the current status of how work is done; reinventing it in a standardized and efficient manner; and rolling out the tools, training, and measurement for this "structured delivery of sophisticated legal services" across the firm is a drawn out and resource-intensive process. However, law firms cannot afford to not make this investment in their future.

Chapter 12

Technology, Knowledge Management, and Analytics

Key Points

- Given the significant amounts that law firms spend on information technology (IT), they should aim to derive maximum value from this capability.
- Such maximum value can be achieved through an appropriate operating model, by structuring IT governance with senior management accountability and oversight, and by creating seamless IT integration across the operations of the firm.
- Information technology is already replacing lawyers to some extent. Artificial intelligence enables the analysis of vast amounts of complex, language-based data in a more consistent and efficient way than humans can, following an initial on-ramping process of system "learning". It is already being used in legal services.
- Knowledge management is enabled through technology, and appropriate tools that optimize search and retrieval can increase both quality of work and margins. Expert systems allow firms to broaden their services and leverage their expertise beyond custom-made individual advice.
- Analytics can enable law firms to provide more quantitative information relating to legal risk management. With increasing computing power and improved methods of data analysis, even high-volume, low data density information (big data) can be analyzed to reveal actionable patterns. Applying analytics to internal data enables law firms to mine their own data to improve internal processes.
- Legal advice should embrace visualization through the use of graphics and charts to illustrate data and concepts, supported by software. Visualization is an effective tool to improve communication of both qualitative and quantitative information in legal as well as other contexts.

INTRODUCTION

Legal technology encompasses many aspects. This chapter only considers technology use in the business model and strategic contexts, and certain technology-enabled ways of information processing, namely knowledge management, expert systems, visualization, and analytics. This selection allows us to focus on those areas we believe have greatest relevance in addressing the opportunities and challenges faced by today's law firms.

In economic terms, the importance of technology in generating legal services lies in the relationship between capital (equipment and facilities, including technology) and labor inputs (person hours) in determining total production. This relationship was originally expressed in the Cobb–Douglas production function.[1] The function shows that investment in technology can maintain constant productivity with decreased investment in labor. The Cobb–Douglas function and later studies indicate the economic argument for investment in technology as one of the ways of driving down fixed labor costs in law firms.

The more-for-less challenge faced by today's firms necessitates an appreciation of how digital disruption is affecting the legal sector, with legal information being freely available, and competition arising from a multitude of sources not limited to a "brick and mortar" presence in any particular location. Technology offers many opportunities when used consistently to support firms' strategies. A few examples: Technology supports transparent services through client-facing extranets, including dashboards. It allows for the delivery of commoditized instead of bespoke or custom-made services through expert systems. It supports project management. A simplistic view of legal IT as being limited to dealing with phones, computers, and software licenses will not encourage the development of innovative IT contributions to firms' productivity. To drive value from IT, its integration into business model modifications and overall strategy needs to be championed by top management, along with investment in it to support innovation.

Legal services is a knowledge industry. Firms sell legal knowledge to clients to address the legal dimension of their business needs. This knowledge is delivered mainly through language-based documents. Only a few decades ago, a lawyer would use printed books as source material for legal advice, and deliver it either orally in person or by telephone or in written form, typed on a mechanical typewriter. In some respects, it feels like not much has changed. Legal professionals still search for information such as statutes, regulations, and case law by keywords, but now in electronic libraries or internal precedents, and advice is delivered in written form, although usually in electronic documents.

As Richard Susskind and others point out, lawyers tend to be slow in embracing innovative technologies—the initial reluctance to embrace e-mail as a tool, cited in Susskind's *The End of Lawyers?*[2] serves as an example. Today there is a

---

1. *See, e.g.*, Paul H. Douglas, *The Cobb–Douglas Function Once Again: Its History, Its Testing, and Some New Empirical Values*, 84 J. POL. ECON. 903 (1976). For a brief and accessible overview, see *Cobb–Douglas Production Function*, WIKIPEDIA (last visited Jan. 6, 2015), http://en.wikipedia.org/wiki/Cobb–Douglas_production_function. *See also*, Daniel Martin Katz, Slide Show at the Legal Week Global Corporate Counsel Forum, in NYC. (Oct. 9, 2014) (for an interpretation of how this might apply to the legal services industry today), *available at* http://computationallegalstudies.com/2014/10/five-observations-regarding-technology-legal-industry-keynote-presentation-legal-week-global-corporate-counsel-forum-nyc-2014/.

2. RICHARD SUSSKIND, THE END OF LAWYERS? 21 (Oxford University Press 2010).

vast array of software and software as a service that aids, directly or indirectly, in the delivery of legal services, or even provides such services without lawyer involvement. This is occurring particularly in consumer law, for example through the generation of simple contracts, or software that guides couples through preparing the documents to file for divorce.[3]

The amount of information that legal professionals have to assess and distill to provide advice is too vast to be processed without technological assistance. Knowledge management tools that scan and retrieve information based on defined criteria, and deliver it in new formats by combining material from multiple sources (document generation systems) are crucial for today's commercial lawyers. These technological tools make a major difference to work efficiency, which in turn reduces the cost of production. This is particularly relevant when remuneration for services is based on criteria other than time worked. Knowledge tools are also used to capture expertise within a firm, and to make it available for others in the firm, or for clients, to adapt and re-use. Expert systems are becoming a means to deliver services to clients in a mass customized, rather than individual and custom-made manner. Given the increasing disintermediation and availability of self-service tools across many service industries, the trend toward commoditization of lower-complexity legal services is likely to accelerate.

The utility of legal advice partly depends on the clients' ability to comprehend and act on it. Advice that is more quickly or easily understood is therefore preferable from the clients' point of view. Visualization, that is, supplementation of text with graphic elements, can make complex information more accessible. Technology can enable the generation of graphics of a qualitative and quantitative nature from large amounts of data quickly and without graphic design skills or even human intervention being necessary. This improves the comprehensibility of legal advice.

Legal analytics is another technology-enabled response to vast amounts of data that are relevant to legal advice. Analytics deals with information in a quantitative manner, asking when, how often, how much, and in connection with what facts certain events occurred. Analytics, or (one way of putting it) the "discovery and communication of meaningful patterns in data,"[4] are relevant because they provide a basis for the formulation of probabilities and predictions about future events. This enables lawyers to advise on legal risks in a quantitative manner, which in turn enables client businesses to align legal assessments with business decisions.

Beyond applications to serving clients, analytics can also be used with internal data to enable firms to improve processes and bring them into line with business strategy, and price their work in a sustainable manner. Legal technology enables the processing of existing information in qualitative ways through knowledge

---

3. *See, e.g.*, www.lawdepot.com; Shake Law, http://www.shakelaw.com/about/; and www.mydivorce papers.com, but there are many similar services available.

4. *Analytics*, Wikipedia (last viewed Jan. 5, 2015), http://en.wikipedia.org/wiki/Analytics.

management tools to identify and retrieve specific information, and in quantitative ways through data analytics identifying probabilities. It remains to be seen if and how often applications commonly referred to as artificial intelligence (AI) will become able to identify legal questions from unstructured material and provide answers, particularly in areas that require synthesis of multiple distinct pieces of information.

LEGAL TECHNOLOGY IN NUMBERS

Law firms spend a significant part of their revenue on technology. A recent survey by the International Legal Technology Association (ILTA) found that in respondents' firms, technology spending was frequently between 2 and 4 percent of total revenue (48 percent of respondents), or even above (5 to 6 percent of revenue for 18 percent of respondents' firms, 7 percent of revenue or above for 7 percent of respondents' firms).[5] For the United Kingdom, the average spend as percentage of revenue reported in a survey of Top 100 firms was 4.1 percent.[6] Broken down as cost per lawyer in the ILTA *2013 Legal Purchasing Survey*, this meant annual costs of US\$ 8,000–17,000 for 43 percent of respondents, and costs of US\$ 17,000–20,000 for 13 percent of respondents, with a tendency for firms with over 50 attorneys to spend more per attorney on an annual basis than smaller firms.[7] Unfortunately, no more recent data has been made available.

There is evidence that lawyers feel that they are not getting value for their IT-related money. In a different 2013 survey, ILTA assessed both year-on-year changes in technology spending, as well as senior management's view of the law firm IT departments.[8] For IT capital budgets, expenses had decreased for 18 percent of respondents, stayed the same for 43 percent, and increased for 40 percent. For operating technology expenses, budgets had decreased for 12 percent, stayed the same for 46 percent, and increased for 42 percent. The results were similar to those obtained in surveys from 2010 to 2012.

These cost developments are probably a strong factor in the negative view that senior law firm management generally has of their IT departments (in the view of the respondents); 44 percent say that it is seen as an expense, with only 30 percent phrasing it more neutrally as an asset, and a mere 12 percent believing it contributes to the firm's revenue growth.

---

5. International Legal Technology Association, *2014 ILTA/Inside Legal Technology Purchasing Survey* 4 (2014), *available at* http://insidelegal.typepad.com/files/2014/08/2014_ILTA_InsideLegal_Technology_Purchasing_Survey.pdf.

6. Legal Support Network, *Legal IT Landscapes 2015* 12 (2014), http://www.legalsupportnetwork.co.uk/sites/default/files/Legal_IT_Landscapes_2015.pdf.

7. International Legal Technology Association, *supra* note 5.

8. International Legal Technology Association, *ILTA's 2013 Technology Survey: Analysis and Results* (2013), *available at* http://www.iltanet.org/MainMenuCategory/Publications/WhitePapersandSurveys/2013-Tech-Survey.html.

These views are a self-fulfilling prophecy; they are unlikely to lead to innovative ways of using technology to deliver better or different services. For legal technology to contribute to the execution of a firm's vision, there needs to be an appropriate operating system that enables the business model and is aligned with strategic goals.

STRATEGIC TECHNOLOGY USE

IT Delivers through Appropriate Operating Models

So how can a law firm's IT strategy shape legal technology into an asset that delivers positive returns on investment? Peter Weill and Jean W. Ross of the MIT Sloan School of Management's Center for Information Systems Research have published extensively on this subject in relation to companies, in addition to their earlier work with large law firms, and some of their insights are set out as follows. In their excellent book *IT Savvy: What Top Executives Must Know to Go from Pain to Gain* they point out that being "IT savvy" is not about the specific knowledge about the myriad of technical tools that exist, nor about the ability to choose the ideal software or device for a particular task. It is "a characteristic of firms and their managers reflected in the ability to use IT to consistently elevate firm performance."[9] It also is about viewing information technology as a tool with a reach that goes beyond solving the task at hand. It means making "a habit of executing disciplined processes and then applying the resulting data from those processes to both operational and strategic decision-making tasks."[10]

To consider how information technology best supports the strategic direction of a business, it is necessary to examine what information technology does in a fundamental sense. Weill and Ross narrow this down to two main aspects: Information technology delivers integration and standardization.[11] The combination of low or high degrees of integration and standardization results in four possible choices of operating model.[12]

Integration is about how much information is shared between parts of a firm or company. The crucial importance of general access to client and other information to provide the best possible services necessitates a high degree of integration; allowing different legal professionals to leverage existing knowledge and client relationships to the fullest, across locations, jurisdictions, and practice groups. Information has to be easily accessible to firm members, but how much of it can be made available to clients as a next step to further drive integration must also be considered. The need for a highly integrated business process platform for law

---

9. Peter Weill & Jean W. Ross, IT Savvy: What Top Executives Must Know to Go from Pain to Gain 4 (Harvard Business Press 2009).

10. *Id.* at 5.

11. *Id.* at 22.

12. *Id.* at figure 2-1, 35.

firms leaves only a choice between different degrees of business process standard-ization to determine the appropriate operating model.

The degree to which business processes can be *standardized* is based on an assessment of internal processes and a clear formulation of strategy. Generally, if the client population and their needs are fairly homogeneous, as might be the case for a boutique firm specializing in, for example, employment law or intellectual property law, a high degree of business process standardization is appropriate to achieve efficiency gains. For example, data to prepare a patent application would be retrieved from the same database in different jurisdictions, and would be used to populate different templates based on the jurisdictional requirements to file a patent application. If, on the other hand, client needs vary greatly in a firm with multiple distinctive practice groups across different jurisdictions, a low degree of standardization is more appropriate.

The Importance of "Plug-and-Play"

Regardless of whether what is delivered to the client across different client groups is uniform or varied, Weill stresses that it is necessary to deliver services in an integrated, "plug-and-play" manner.[13] "Plug-and-play" originally referred to auto-matic detection and configuration of computer components, compared to the ear-lier devices that necessitated connecting or even soldering multiple wires between different hardware components. In the context of today's information-intensive settings in a law firm or other business, it means the seamless (or as near as pos-sible) flow of information, and ease of access to it, without extensive set-up efforts on the part of the users. In a law firm, that can, for example, mean client-facing extranets to allow clients access to real-time information about their matters and matters' budget status.

In a corporate law department, it can mean having legal information embed-ded in business systems, and continuously collecting data about legal aspects of business transactions to identify areas where effort does not match potential gains (see the example of Axiom's IRIS system in this chapter's case study). The flip side of easy data access in any setting is of course an increased likelihood of a data security breach. Once the choice of the most appropriate IT operating model has been made, it needs to be implemented, and that needs considerable resources for the process itself and the change management involved. Chapter 13 discusses change management and addresses innovation initiatives that require people to change the way they do things.

---

13. Telephone interview by George Beaton and Eric Chin with Peter Weill, MIT Sloan School of Man-agement's Center for Information Systems Research (July 22, 2014).

IT Governance

Many partners feel out of their depth when trying to understand and use information technology and systems. A lack of confidence often leads to an abdication of responsibility in favor of experts.[14] But to rely on IT professionals without senior management oversight beyond a high-level budget more often than not results in a disconnection between IT and the strategic direction of the firm. The IT department is still too frequently seen as the people in charge of keeping the desktop computers running and the servers working, and no more than that.[15] This does not motivate IT professionals to consider how they can decrease maintenance spend to free up resources for innovative IT projects, such as, for example, better virtual reality conferencing that decreases the need for travel (with its cost and down-time for valuable staff), or ways to gather and code specialist knowledge of firm partners to build up expert systems quickly and efficiently.

Legal technology specialists on their own are also less likely to foster close collaboration with knowledge management professionals and legal professionals in ways that can generate gains in the quality or efficiency of delivered legal services. For an example of an innovative system to deliver better outcomes for the legal aspect of business problems, see the case study of Axiom's IRIS system. Gerard Neiditsch, former chief information officer of the Australian firm Allens Linklaters (the two firms work in an alliance), remarks upon the fact that if a law firm were a company built from scratch today, no one would structurally segregate lawyers and "non-lawyers" (the term itself indicates a certain mindset) in the way that mostly occurs in law firms today.[16] IT governance needs to be truly interdisciplinary and linked to overall firm governance, through bringing senior IT specialists to the table in a way that acknowledges their particular expertise, and incorporates IT into the firm's strategy.

In addition, there is a need for explicit and transparent processes for decision making, with final responsibility resting with senior management, rather than with IT specialists whose role is largely operational. This is particularly important for novel IT projects, to ensure alignment with the strategic direction of the firm and expected return on investment, both before and after implementation. Gerard Neiditsch advises firms to get used to the notion that IT projects will not all yield the desired results, and that it is important to establish desired milestones and outcomes, so that IT projects can be terminated to fail early and cheaply if necessary.[17] Chapter 13 will consider the problem of a perfectionist approach that stifles innovation in more detail.

---

14. *See, e.g.,* WEILL & ROSS, *supra* note 9, at 9–11.

15. E-mail management was the most frequently cited technology issue in the ILTA 2013 technology report; *see* International Legal Technology Association, *supra* note 8.

16. Telephone interview by Eric Chin and Imme Kaschner with Gerard Neiditsch, Chief Information Officer, Allens Linklaters (July 16, 2014).

17. *Id.*

Integrated Operational IT Governance

Beyond strategic governance, a lack of integration of IT departments in an operational sense means that if "IT problems" occur that necessitate a response from the entire firm, such as for example a data security breach, the firm will lack firm-wide capability to execute a concerted response quickly and effectively. The issue of data safety is beyond the scope of this book, but there can be no doubt that it is and will continue to be an increasing challenge for any entity that manages large amounts of confidential information, and needs to maintain quick and easy access to that information for business efficiency reasons. A recent well-documented customer credit card data breach provides just one example of poorly coordinated crisis management that was inefficient to prevent long-term customer loss, and thereby eroded value, significantly depressing the company's share price.[18] The first step in ensuring smooth operations is a clear reporting relationship between IT management and senior management. Such a relationship can yield initiatives such as playbooks and even drills for coordinated firm-wide responses to data security incidents, using a "hope for the best, plan for the worst" approach. It provides an established channel of communication to both prepare for foreseeable adverse events and deal with the unforeseen ones. Law firms need to assess what incidents might occur that necessitate firm-wide responses that include the IT department, be it data security breaches, natural disasters, or other events, and develop coordinated response plans.

In summary, to drive value from IT systems, law firms need to articulate an IT operating model based on their strategic goals, and implement it in a way that delivers plug-and-play services to their internal and external customers. IT needs transparent governance that is integrated into and informs the firm's overall strategy through close cooperation between senior IT specialists and top management.

OUTLOOK: ARTIFICIAL INTELLIGENCE?

But what about computers taking on a more fundamental role in lawyering? The argument is commonly made that it is impossible to replace lawyers with machines, and the Star Trek-style hologram lawyer (rather than medical doctor) advising clients is probably a good way off, in spite of 75 percent of respondents of ILTA's *Legal Technology: Future Horizons* survey expecting pioneer adaptation of holographic displays in the next six to ten years or even earlier.[19] Yet common applications such as sophisticated search engines, e-discovery, automated proof-reading, and document generation software are already making it much quicker for

---

18. *See* Vinayak Balasubramanian, *Cybersecurity and the Board: It's Not Just an IT Thing*, CORPORATE COUNSEL (June 2, 2014), http://www.corpcounsel.com/id=1202657397008/Cybersecurity+and+the+Board+Its+Not+Just+an+IT+Thing%3Fmcode=0&curindex=0&curpage=ALL.

19. International Legal Technology Association, *Legal Technology Future Horizons* 70 (May 2014), http://www.iltanet.org/MainMenuCategory/Future-Horizons.

lawyers to provide services, thereby decreasing the number of lawyers required to provide a certain level of service. Flex by Fenwick, the flexible resourcing arm of Fenwick providing "custom solutions for interim in-house legal needs," illustrates this in a slightly cheeky manner by listing FLEX-o-tron the Flex Bot as team member, including a "picture" of the robot and a "biosketch." FLEX-o-tron in action oversees a mini expert system app on the webpage aiding potential clients in deciding if they would benefit from the firm's offerings.[20]

IBM's natural language-enabled, cloud-based artificial intelligence system Watson also springs to mind, partly due to a well-oiled publicity machine, but also due to its advanced application in other comparable professional areas like medicine.[21] So far, Watson in the legal space has led to ROSS, a startup selling legal research services (after all, what is legal research other than a big game of Jeopardy?), but it is not quite clear to what level of client usability these services have evolved.[22] ROSS has recently joined forces with NextLaw labs, a collaboration between Dentons and IBM that aims to provide legal startups with access to multiple tools on a cloud-based platform.[23] Broadly, Watson is an enabler for lawyers and others dealing with unstructured information of a magnitude and complexity that defies meaningful processing in reasonable time frames by traditional human/computer teams because of its sheer size.

One project by Legal OnRamp using Watson illustrates how this can happen: Legal OnRamp uses large-scale natural language processing capabilities in developing "living wills" for large financial institutions, as required by post-GFC regulation. This necessitates the assessment of vast amounts of information, such as contracts and organizational structures, to be turned into a roadmap to dismantle the institution if necessary (comparable to the type of programmed cell death, or apoptosis, that leads to the orderly dismantling of a cell into little chunks from within, rather than the cell just dying and spilling everywhere, leading to widespread inflammation around it). The separate tasks to accomplish this are not overly complex, but the sheer number and the need for consistency and integration in categorization and analysis make this a task that is hard to achieve by lawyers supported by traditional computer applications. Watson can be used to apply complex structures, rules, and categorizations developed on a subset of the information consistently to the rest, without the need for additional human resources, and without any restrictions in simultaneously "keeping in mind" the requirements of a large number of rules simultaneously. This can enable organizations to come up with "living wills" that actually pass regulatory scrutiny, and may lead to vast

---

20. Flex by Fenwick, http://www.flexbyfenwick.com/about/.

21. For a discussion of IBM's plan for business cooperation, *see* Quentin Hardy, *IBM Is Betting That Watson Can Earn Its Keep*, N.Y. TIMES, Jan. 8, 2014, at B9.

22. Ross, see http://www.rossintelligence.com.

23. Dentons, *Dentons, NextLaw Labs and IBM Cloud Fuel Legal Tech Startups* (Aug. 7, 2015) http://www.dentons.com/en/whats-different-about-dentons/connecting-you-to-talented-lawyers-around-the-globe/news/2015/august/dentons-nextlaw-labs-and-ibm-cloud-fuel-legal-tech-startups.

efficiency gains down the track (by avoiding complex litigation in the case of an actual failure of the entity).[24]

There is no clear answer to the question of how artificial intelligence will shape the future of the business of law, but there is no question that it will shape it in significant ways. Some tasks completed by computers today such as face recognition or adaptive search algorithms would have been considered to be "artificial intelligence" in the early days of computing. As available computing power increases, and experimentation with using that power in legal services becomes more widespread, there will be ongoing advances. Firms need to monitor how they can apply such advances in the context of their own practices.

KNOWLEDGE MANAGEMENT

One area that has seen significant technology-enabled advances and changes in its scope is knowledge management (KM). KM involves obtaining, documenting, and delivering the knowledge that enables lawyers to produce legal advice that goes beyond their own personal knowledge. This knowledge is generated by third-party legal publishers and is also provided by the attorneys of the firm. It can be very specific in relation to a particular question of law, or more generally related to strategy for certain types of matters. Ron Friedmann, a lawyer and now legal consultant with extensive experience in the field, sees the knowledge management journey as one "from content to tools to productivity." He charts the development from physical sources to interactive productivity tools in his excellent and succinct overview *A Brief History of Legal KM*.[25] In essence, lawyers have moved from physical law reports and index files in the library to using search portals and their firm's online precedent banks to using firm-wide social media style platforms to identify relevant expertise beyond specific queries of the "how has this provision been interpreted in certain fact situations" type. KM is concerned with searching for and retrieving relevant information, as well as capturing the knowledge and expertise of firm members to make it identifiable and accessible for others. It extends to systems that assist in generating the final advice product, such as document assembly systems. KM beyond a certain level of complexity is simply not feasible without technology, since humans lack the facility to process information sufficiently quickly to deal with the sheer volumes. KM also extends to technology-free activities such as face-to-face mentoring session between senior and junior lawyers as a way of managing, in the sense of transmitting and preserving knowledge within a firm. These behavioral aspects of KM are not discussed in this book.

The relevance of KM arises from its intimate connection to the way that legal services are produced and delivered. In a simplified way, the typical workflow

---

24. Joe Calve, *IBM Watson: Its (Almost) Elementary*, Metropolitan Corporate Counsel (May 2015).

25. Ron Friedman, *A Brief History of Legal KM*, Prism Legal (Sept. 4, 2014), http://prismlegal .com/a-brief-history-of-legal-km/.

in legal matters goes like this: a lawyer receives instructions, obtains knowledge building blocks as needed beyond his or her own expertise, and drafts and delivers legal advice. The cost of information obtained through either subscription services or capture of expertise from other members of the firm, and the time necessary to retrieve that information, partly determine the production cost of the final advice, regardless of whether the final product is priced on production time or defined deliverables. Making knowledge available in faster and/or cheaper ways increases the margin on a fixed-price product, or allows for a lower price while maintaining the margin.

KM systems that minimize production costs by using technology increase a firm's competitiveness, and often benefit its margin, regardless of the basis of pricing. In-depth knowledge about what information is necessary to deliver what service, how it is identified, acquired, and modified by lawyers to add value, and how it is delivered to what clients provides a basis for commoditizing the final legal advice product through expert systems. Expert systems can be seen as "crystallized knowledge management," a phrase coined by Ron Friedmann.[26]

EXPERT SYSTEMS

Lawyers frequently balk at the notion of legal advice being anything other than a custom-made product delivered to the client by a highly skilled professional. But when was the last time, dear reader, that you used a travel agent to book a flight, hotel, rental car, or even a multiday cruise with a number of separate excursions, special cooking classes, and spa treatments? And if you did, did the agent add much beyond what you could have done yourself? Disintermediation, courtesy of the Internet, is occurring across all service and manufacturing industries, enabled by (more or less) easy-to-use search portals and free, ubiquitous information. An expert system is "a computer system that emulates the decision-making ability of a human expert,"[27] through rules, decision trees, if/then questions, and additional analysis based on applicable rules and regulations. The user is enabled to put in the relevant information to allow the expert system to answer a specific, narrow question (as opposed to the broader, more open, natural language-based search capabilities of the Watson-based applications).

Like the Shaker brethren hand-crafting large numbers of simple and functional chairs of a common type in the 1850s, like the artisans crafting prototypes for factory-produced chairs combining high functionality and aesthetic appeal at the German Bauhaus schools in the 1920s, and (more recently) like designers for the large furniture retailer Ikea (which sells mass-produced chairs for self-assembly under an extremely strong brand), lawyers can use their expertise to identify and

---

26. *Id.*
27. Peter Jackson, Introduction to Expert Systems 2 (Addison-Wesley 3rd ed. 1998).

create content for technology-enabled commoditized (possibly do-it-yourself) solutions to common legal problems.

One example of an expert system in action (developed in cooperation with Neota Logic) is Foley and Lardner LLP's Global Risk Solutions offering, a subscription-based integrated service to enable middle-market companies to comply with their obligations under the Foreign Corrupt Practices Act. The platform includes risk assessments and on-demand guidance through expert systems, manuals, and policies incorporating ongoing updates as necessary, training for employees, and access to legal advice and counseling if any compliance issues arise.[28] Littler offers a similar solution for compliance in the area of HR law.[29]

There is a good deal of room for the development of expert systems for specific areas of law, leveraging the areas of strength and the unique expertise of firms to deliver commoditized legal services in a customer-focused, easy-to-use format. Such services can incorporate the expertise of experienced lawyers as well as relevant current laws, regulations, and other material, and with search algorithms based on what experts know to be common issues in the relevant area. Based on the complexity of the desired system and intended interactions with a firm's own systems, client systems, or other databases, such systems can be developed in-house, or in cooperation with a developer of expert systems such as Neota Logic.[30]

CASE STUDY: ALLEN & OVERY ONLINE SERVICES

U.K. law firm Allen & Overy offers a number of subscription-based online information services relating to a variety of legal topics such as capital markets, derivatives, and debt and equity capital markets, but also human resources and antitrust law.[31] The information relates to a large number of jurisdictions, and some of the services contain document generation functionalities. From a client service point of view, there is a clear benefit to having topical information such as a "Dawn Raid Guide" (compliance with antitrust enforcement in an acute investigation situation) immediately available if and when needed. Allen & Overy has a strategy of having dedicated expert teams (frequently working in a dispersed fashion) developing the content for these services, rather than expecting the work to be done around direct client service responsibilities. The online services are part of Allen & Overy's extensive innovation portfolio also encompassing PeerPoint (a provider of on-demand legal professionals) and a captive legal services provider in Belfast, Northern Ireland. Senior partner David Morley refers to some unsuccessful innovation investments, and then sums up the experience with the online services:

---

28. Linda C. Yun, *Foley Introduces Industry's First Web-Based Affordable FCPA Compliance Solution* (Feb. 3, 2015) *available at* http://www.foley.com/foley-introduces-industrys-first-web-based-affordable-fcpa -compliance-solution-02-03-2015/.

29. Littler, *ComplianceHR, available at* http://www.littler.com/products-and-services/compliancehr.

30. Neota Logic, http://www.neotalogic.com/solutions/.

31. *See* http://www.allenovery.com/online-services/Pages/default.aspx (last visited Nov. 21, 2014).

Those initiatives were a relatively small failure—and an advantage of being a firm of our size is the advantage of scale. You can afford to place a few bets, and you are not betting the farm. And we placed other bets, for example, on online services, and that's turned out to be a big success, so that is generating £10+ million in revenue now. Purely subscription model online services.[32]

This is one example of a successful technology-enabled innovation strategy leveraging a firm's intellectual capital in a way that goes beyond custom-made services generated for an individual matter or client. Technology allows for such commoditized services to be provided (and paid for) with low costs beyond the initial setup and updates. Law firms are uniquely positioned to generate such services because of the expertise of their teams, and their general need to provide very specific and frequently updated information to their fee earners.

ANALYTICS

Analytics is another technology-enabled area that is becoming increasingly important for lawyers and firms.

Analytics has emerged as a catch-all term for a variety of different business intelligence (BI)- and application-related initiatives. For some, it is the process of analyzing information from a particular domain, such as website analytics. For others, it is applying the breadth of BI capabilities to a specific content area (for example, sales, service, or supply chain). In particular, BI vendors use the "analytics" moniker to differentiate their products from the competition. Increasingly, "analytics" is used to describe statistical and mathematical data analysis that clusters, segments, scores and predicts what scenarios are most likely to happen.[33]

In contrast, Wikipedia succinctly sums analytics up as "the discovery and communication of meaningful patterns in data."[34] By and large, the legal profession tends to rely more on verbal and qualitative methods to assess information, rather than on numerical and quantitative data analysis. Legal advice is all about managing risks—by providing for rare events through contractual clauses, for example, or by clarifying possible outcomes of a court case. Yet the relevant risks are rarely ever assessed in a quantitative way, unless, for example, a litigation funder sets a bar at a certain probability of success for supporting a party in a matter. Lawyers mainly go by gut feeling about chances of success for a matter, or the risks involved in a transaction. And there is some evidence that the predictions are frequently not as accurate as would be desirable.[35] Imagine the insurance industry operating without

---

32. Telephone interview by George Beaton and Eric Chin with David Morley, Worldwide Senior Partner, Allen & Overy (July 10, 2014).

33. *Analytics*, GARTNER IT GLOSSARY, http://www.gartner.com/it-glossary/big-data/ (last visited Nov. 23, 2014).

34. *Supra* note 4.

35. See Jane Goodman-Delahunty, Par Anders Granhag, Maria Hartwig, & Elizabeth F. Loftus, *Insightful or Wishful: Lawyers' Ability to Predict Case Outcomes*, 16 PSYCHOLOGY, PUBLIC POLICY, AND LAW 133 (2010).

an actuarial understanding of the probabilities that they are insuring against. Paul Carr, president of NewLaw provider Axiom, sees the assessment of risk as the big challenge for the legal industry:

> We are just starting to get a glimpse into the power of data and analytics. At a fundamental level the legal industry is an information industry, and it seems logical that for an industry that is information-based and that has seen very little application of technology, the handling and the manipulation and the analytics around that information surely has to provide a benefit.
>
> At Axiom, we think one of the big nuts to crack is developing a far more empirical understanding of legal risk. Legal risk is one of the biggest barriers to change because it is a black box. The peculiar thing about the way legal risk has been assessed traditionally is about credentials, that is, which law school or firm you went to: A lawyer with great credentials is less risky, while a lawyer with lesser credentials is more risky.
>
> Before joining Axiom, I was running an insurance business, and anyone who has worked in managing financial risk, credit risk, insurance risk understands there is science in how you measure it, and how you trade off cost and risk more empirically. One of the major challenges with law is that there is no analytic measurement of risk.
>
> We feel that one of the things that could really help accelerate evolution of the industry is getting a better handle on legal risk. At Axiom we are investing in data and data analytics as the way to better measure and manage risk, and therefore to put a set of tools and information in the hands of General Counsel to allow them to manage their functions in a more sophisticated way.[36]

And this strategy is paying off. In February 2015, Axiom announced a US$ 73 million deal with a large global bank to process the bank's "master trading agreements" such as the standardized contracts governing swaps. Obviously, there are risks involved in outsourcing such routine but nevertheless high-stakes processes, but the bank must have felt that the risks had been appropriately analyzed and addressed, and possibly insured against. Mark Harris, co-founder of Axiom, is reported as saying:

> By moving routine but still highly complicated transactions onto an electronic platform run by Axiom's team of lawyers and paralegals, the bank's lawyers and executives can focus on negotiating bigger, more customized deals as well as maintaining the bank's compliance with capital and other regulations. The incumbent model is largely artisanal. . . . It's perfect for novel challenges that are irreducibly complex, but it's not necessary for the bulk of commerce.[37]

---

36. Telephone interview by George Beaton with Paul Carr, President, Axiom (Aug. 8, 2014).

37. Daniel Fisher, *Legal-Services Firm's $73 Million Deal Strips the Mystery from Derivatives Trading*, FORBES BLOG (Feb. 12, 2015, *available at* http://www.forbes.com/sites/danielfisher/2015/02/12/legal-services-firms-73-million-deal-strips-the-mystery-from-derivatives-trading/.

Stephen Allen, head of market strategies for DLA Piper International, has a similar view on the importance of analytics, particularly to support a proactive and preventative, rather than the prevailing reactive, way of "doing law":

> Analytics is absolutely key . . . because it is around helping clients understand where the value risks lie, as a result of the potential risk of money going out, or not getting money in.
>
> . . .
>
> So where are the biggest areas of risk? If you think of a traditional risk model where you have the quadrants, and you have increasing likelihood of risk as your vertical axis and increasing value as your horizontal axis, most people look at the top right quarter. Actually, when you look at law, that is not necessarily where it is. We have discussed PPI (payment protection insurance, an insurance commonly sold as add-on to loans in the U.K. to cover repayment of the debt if the borrower becomes unable to service it as a result of death, illness, job loss or other circumstances) claims in the U.K. These run into billions of pounds of exposure for some of the U.K. banks. The individual claims are only 250 to 500 pounds each, but the sheer scale based upon the regulatory burden across this piece is huge. Data analytics can help in understanding the nature of risks when you get the small warning shot. You can then analyze what your potential exposure, roll it forward a number of years, and once you have a more sophisticated model, you understand what the causes and sources of legal demand are within a given business. They will be different in any given business. You can start to look at whether there is a predictability or a probability that if x, y, and z happens, the likelihood of large legal exposure is increased, and therefore, you want a warning when x, y, and z might happen, so that you can pick up on it.[38]

Law firms need to build significant numeracy and analytics skills throughout their ranks, to both provide commercially relevant advice that goes beyond qualitative risk assessment to their corporate clients, and to be able to critically examine the costs and benefits of the service that they provide. The following is an example of applied analytics in the context of contract management.

CASE STUDY: AXIOM'S IRIS SYSTEM

At this point, it seems that the large investments necessary for sophisticated analytics systems are more commonly made by nontraditional providers of legal services that have the option to monetize them by offering the service to multiple parties, not just their own client base. Axiom's cloud-based IRIS analytics and contract management system is one example. IRIS has been implemented for multiple clients, including telecommunications giant BT Group. Nick West of Axiom describes IRIS's purpose and operation:

---

38. Telephone interview by George Beaton and Eric Chin with Stephen Allen, Head of Market Strategies, DLA Piper International (July 29, 2014).

There is a big vision behind IRIS. We want to change how organisations manage contractual risk. It begins with the idea that in this day and age, it is frankly outrageous that most organizations cannot answer questions like "How many contracts do we have," or "What is our contractual exposure to a global crisis such as Ebola in West Africa or a potential Greek Euro exit," or "What is our overall contractual position on X, Y, or Z?" . . . To be able to get answers like that, you need a well-organized process to ensure contracts are drafted and negotiated in rigorous compliance with standard terms, that all the contract terms are marked up consistently and stored in a single repository that can be analyzed. We use IRIS as the technology platform to make that happen.

. . .

Let me break that down a bit. IRIS is essentially a platform with several components. The first component is a client front-end, through which business teams can request contracts. The next component is a portal that an Axiom team leader uses to receive those client instructions and delegate to a member of the Axiom team. Then, there's a document creation tool, containing templates and clause libraries, pre-agreed with the client, which our legal professionals use to draft a contract, using dropdowns to select approved terms and an Axiom Word ribbon to carry out certain tasks.

Here's where it starts to get interesting. The business team might want a five-year term, but the standard is two years and the Axiom professional only has authority to go to three years in certain circumstances. For a five-year term, the Axiom professional has to escalate back to a designated senior business approver. IRIS contains workflow tools which our team can use to seek approval from the business, right from within the Word environment—an email will be sent to the approver, containing the clause, seeking approval for the longer term. The approver either agrees or declines and that decision is stored in the database alongside the clause, creating an audit trail. If approved, the contract gets finalized and then the Axiom professional negotiates with the counterparty, clearly logging changes to the contract along the way, seeking approval where required. Once the contract is executed, it is stored in a central database.

From here, we can create incredibly insightful analytics. Because all the contracts are executed through the identical system, using identical mark-up, all the data entities are comparable—what I mean is that we can compare terms at the clause level very easily across different types of contracts. So, it's easy to work out average contract duration or the proportion of contracts which include France as a jurisdiction. Or the time elapsed in negotiation. And we can segment that data by contract type, or business unit, or whichever individual in the business is making the request. That allows us to help the business look at more strategic questions like "How many contracts contain an XYZ clause?" and compare for business unit A vs business unit B. Or how long does it take on average for business unit A to conclude a particular type of contract, compared to business unit B.

. . .

Here are a couple of real life examples. Many of our clients' primary goal is to speed up the contracting process, to be able to book revenue quicker. Using IRIS, we now have the data to tell them how to do that by saying, "You know what? Your business units in country A and country B both negotiate these X, Y, Z documents. But do you realize that country A does it three times faster than country B?" "Why is this?" "Well, look how much time is spent on clause 17—one team spends three times as much time on it as the other. And you know what—the outcome is almost always identical in any case—both teams have to give up that clause roughly 20 percent of the time. So, just tell country B to let go of this obsession with negotiating clause 17." There are loads of other things you can do—at the macro level, you can build a picture of how much risk you have in your contracts—that's obviously critical where the contracts cover financial products. On a more micro level, you can remove or modify clauses depending on likely outcomes or show the business how much time and effort (and therefore real cost) is actually involved in low value contracts. All of this kind of analysis can only happen if you have a closed system.

Right now, very few organizations do anything like the above. Most of the time, when a business person wants a document, they just go off and do whatever they like—and that is that. No one has got any line of sight into what is happening. How can you expect to make strategic decisions in this setting? Changing how contracting is done is part of Axiom's mission.[39]

Axiom's IRIS enables the application of analytics to the contracting process and later events in the contract life cycle. This leads to actionable suggestions for aligning contract negotiations and contract clauses with business goals. Lex Machina provides another practical example of how analytics can aid client decision making in intellectual property litigation.

BIG DATA

"Big data" is a term commonly applied to data that because of its huge volume and low density of relevant information defied analysis and interpretation in an earlier era of computing power. Today's sophisticated search algorithms make big data analysis readily available to many users. Gartner offers the following definition for big data: "High-volume, high-velocity and high-variety information assets that demand cost-effective, innovative forms of information processing for enhanced insight and decision making."[40]

Big data therefore needs specific analytic approaches that rely on extensive processing power and sophisticated analysis. Commonly used descriptive business intelligence, such as sales data, costs of materials, or customer demographics, is regularly used to inform business decisions. In contrast, big data needs to be analyzed with an open mind as to the insights that its patterns might yield when interrogated in creative ways. Compared to business intelligence, for big data the

---

39. Interview by David Goener, Eric Chin, and Imme Kaschner with Nick West, Managing Director, Axiom U.K., in London. (Sept. 29, 2014).
40. GARTNER IT GLOSSARY, *supra* note 33.

work starts with formulating propositions about existing patterns and then testing these through data analytics.

EXAMPLE: LEX MACHINA

One provider of quantitative data that aids in the generation of comprehensive legal advice in the area of intellectual property law is the U.S.-based company Lex Machina.[41] The company uses publicly accessible intellectual property litigation information to collect and analyze data about patents, judicial decision-making patterns, law firm activities in the space, costs involved in the proceedings, and other relevant facts, and makes this information available through a subscription-based offering—and partly free for some public interest entities.

Lex Machina uses sophisticated search algorithms to capture the information and structure it in a way that can easily be searched based on criteria such as judge, law firm involved, type of patent, and any number of other criteria. Lex Machina has recently released additional offerings that allow for the generation of customized reports visualizing strategic data in relation to cases identified based on a number of specific search criteria.[42] Lex Machina allows practitioners to assemble, query, and visualize quickly relevant cases and the track records of judges and opponent clients or firms. It also yields quantitative data that is relevant to risk assessment such as costs and damages awarded in similar cases, and time frames for interim or final decisions. Being able to quantify the business risks that arise through litigation beyond the direct legal costs, as well as the time frames for any expected risks to crystalize, adds value to legal advice because it allows the client to align the litigation strategy with business goals.

In addition, Lex Machina reveals probabilities of certain litigation strategies succeeding based on past cases. In a less structured way, similar considerations certainly inform the litigation advice that an experienced practitioner will give, but the human capability to process large amounts of data within short periods of time is necessarily limited. Using technology to efficiently search and collate relevant data to use in combination with a practitioner's experience allows for the practitioner to focus on crafting the most sophisticated legal strategy. Lex Machina's evolution illustrates the rise of data and analytics as basis for legal decision making.

INTERNAL LAW FIRM DATA

Large law firms have billing and practice management systems that generate large amounts of data, but this data is not necessarily coded in a way that lends itself

---

41. *See* www.lexmachina.com.

42. Press Release, Lex Machina, Lex Machina Launches Custom Insights: Personalized Analytics for Unprecedented Insights into Cases, Motions, and Trends (Nov. 12, 2014), *available at* https://lexmachina.com/media/press/lex-machina-launches-custom-insights//.

to analytics for practice improvement. The right technology is essential to capture and measure efficiently what work is done, how, and by whom, as a basis for any changes such as instituting alternative pricing strategies (see chapter 9) or instituting legal project management (see chapter 11). Toby Brown, chief practice officer at Akin Gump, elaborates on some of the problems with using data from legacy systems for analytics:

> We are in our infancy of trying to embrace any sort of meaningful data analytics. The most typical one that comes up is analytics around billings.
>
> In my significant experience of analyzing data billings, the data is not structured well for what people are trying to accomplish by looking at it . . . . What they think is that they can look at past billings and that will tell them how much legal work should cost. And I know that does not really tell you that.
>
> It might give you a really broad range of fees, but it is not going to tell you for the matter you have in front of you what the market-based cost is. This goes back to my point about the nature of the billing data: What that is about is writing narratives that the client reads and says, "Okay, that was worth two hours of the lawyer's time, I will pay the bill." It was not centered around what type of work it is; the metadata we have around those time entries is not very useful for determining costs or prices.
>
> I was talking with a provider recently about how we might use the same technology that is used for predictive coding in discovery on our time entries and our documents so that we could predict metadata about that content. For instance, one of my big challenges right now is what I call matter type codes. I think we are going to have a hard time understanding any budget data until we actually understand what we are selling. And by that I mean most law firms will have a few hundred matter type codes that were developed probably in the 1990s. So we do not even have good data structured around the type of work we do. So back to the main point, I think we are in the very early stages of trying to figure out how data analytics can improve the management of practice.[43]

While there is usually plenty of data about law firms' internal workings, usually going back many years, identifying patterns in this data to optimize work flow or to guide pricing decisions is problematic, and mostly needs specialist expertise. There is clearly a need to assess if current systems in a firm capture metrics in a way that point to desirable improvements.

COMMUNICATING THE DATA: VISUALIZATION

When using analytics and quantitative, as opposed to qualitative, methods of analysis as the basis of legal advice, one challenge that arises for the verbally skilled

---

43. Telephone interview by Eric Chin with Toby Brown, Chief Practice Officer at Akin Gump Strauss Hauer & Feld LLP (Aug. 8, 2014).

but often less mathematically literate lawyer is to communicate the findings and the advice based on those findings in a clear and intuitively powerful manner. This challenge is not necessarily limited to advice based on data as opposed to qualitative information, though. It has been realized that visualization (a useful definition is one offered by Michael Curtotti and Eric McCreath: "the use of graphics, images, or symbols—other than words themselves—to enhance the communication of meaning contained in or associated with (legislative) text")[44] can aid in communicating complex matters to an audience, particularly if the audience is less familiar with the topic than the writer. Visualization might be as simple as adding illustrative graphics and charts of a low complexity to a legal text.[45] The need for improved visualization of legislative materials as a matter of access to the law led to "innovations" such as section numbering and breaking up legislation into paragraphs in the pre-IT age.[46] Technology enables the quick completion of much more complex charts and graphs through templates or even dedicated programs incorporating complex information.

Visualization Example: Encompass

Visual elements enhance readibility of a complex, fact-heavy text, regardless of whether the recipient posesses legal knowledge or not. One example of effective visualization is provided by the offerings of Encompass.[47] The company uses information from the Australian Securities and Investments Commission register (the main source of information related to Australian companies), the bankruptcy register, land title information including mortgage information, data from the Personal Property Security Registry (registering of securities on this national register is necessary to establish priorty of any securities in case of limited liquidity or bankruptcy), and the Australian Business Name Register.

Encompass's proprietary portal allows for the quick creation of adaptable visual representations of structure, ownership, assets, and security interests relating to Australian companies and other businesses. The graphic representations can be rearranged and modified, and include automatic updates as relevant information changes. Customization through linking additional documents to parts of the chart is possible.

The sample chart reveals an intuitive way to present complex information that would otherwise take a long time to assemble from the various sources, and to communicate. This tool adds value to commercial legal advice by providing factual

---

44. Michael Curtotti & Eric McCreath, paper presented at the 2012 Law via the Internet Twentieth Anniversary Conference at Cornell University: Enhancing the Visualization of Law (Oct. 2, 2012), *available at* http://ssrn.com/abstract=2160614 or http://dx.doi.org/10.2139/ssrn.2160614.

45. For some examples, *see* Adam L. Rosman, *Visualizing the Law: Using Charts, Diagrams, and Other Images to Improve Legal Briefs,* 63 J. Legal Educ. 70 (2013).

46. Curtotti & McCreath, *supra* note 44.

47. *See* www.encompasscorporation.com (last visited Nov. 24, 2014). The webpage contains a brief animation of the search functionalities and opportunities for customization of the Encompass graphics.

FIGURE 12.1

Visualization Example

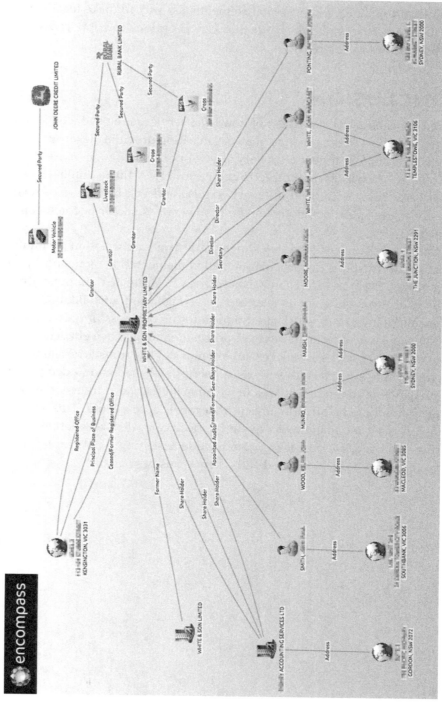

Published with permission, copyright by Encompass; some content has been intentionally blurred.

information in a way that can be quickly understood and communicated to parties by the client.

So whether it is to aid in the communication of data relevant to legal advice, or to illustrate complex fact scenarios in a way that is easier and quicker to understand than text only, adding visual elements is a way to make legal advice better, and there are scores of different technological options to support visualization of varying degrees of complexity.

CONCLUSION

Technology shapes every aspect of how legal services are produced and delivered. A significant part of the revenue of an organization providing legal services is spent on legal technology. It generates very large opportunities to increase the efficiency and quality of legal services directly and indirectly. Artificial intelligence solutions are already being employed in legal services, and will become more widespread as more ready-to-use solutions for the legal services sector become commercially available.

Deriving value from the investment in a firm's information technology infrastructure necessitates the articulation and implementation of an appropriate operating model. Effective governance has to align IT strategic direction with the goals of the firm through senior management oversight and accountability, facilitating the seamless integration of IT operations into the business processes of the firm.

Knowledge management offers opportunities to improve efficiency and quality of service. There are many successful examples of law firms leveraging their expertise widely through offerings such as subscription-based knowledge portals.

Analytics is an important area in which law firms need to become proficient in order to continue to provide advice on legal risks to clients. This includes using results of external analytics to quantify specific legal risks relating to outcomes such as costs and awards. It can also include assessing repetitive legal processes to optimize results to be aligned with clients' business goals.

Chapter 13

Partners, Innovation, and Change

Key Points

- The pace and nature of the ubiquitous change in the legal services industry necessitate transformational rather than incremental change in law firms.
- Change happens at an organizational level in the stages described by Kurt Lewin — unfreeze, transform, and refreeze. The process often invokes considerable negative emotions from stakeholders. Jeanie Duck refers to this as the "change monster".
- Lawyers tend to be conservative and risk averse in their personality traits, and their quest for perfection is at odds with the experimental approach that sees failure as a necessary part of development and change.
- Innovation—or *remaking* in keeping with the title of this book—must be an integral part of a firm's strategy, starting in small ways and including an assessment of the risks involved in building a manageable portfolio of innovation initiatives.
- Application of considerable resources is necessary to design and execute sustainable change initiatives in a law firm. A firm needs to proceed by creating a shared understanding and shared experiences for its people, and by using tools that facilitate the process and address the emotional as well as rational arguments for change.
- Success in the "refreezing" stage of change implementation depends on monetary and nonmonetary signals, that is, partner performance management and compensation.
- Any change journey needs strong leadership. It ain't easy, and BigLaw firms need to start their journey sooner rather than later.

INTRODUCTION

The previous chapters have set out ways in which a BigLaw firm can improve its capacity to serve clients and as a result improve its competitive position. Implementing any of these strategies necessitates major changes in the way that partners and staff work. It will be disruptive and costly. There are no silver bullets to provide immediate benefits, and positive long-term outcomes are anything but guaranteed. But clearly, *not* to innovate and remake the firm is *not* an alternative.

"The people side of change" is a major factor influencing the success, or arguably more often failure, of any change initiative. The discipline of change management has developed in response to this realization. Successful change implementation is not as common as one might think (while this obviously depends on the specific circumstances, the Change Management Institute suggests an overall success rate of only 30 percent of all change initiatives in all types of organization).[1] Any change process in a law firm must address the general change averseness commonly found in the legal profession, as well as other factors likely to hinder the particular initiative.

So how can partners be persuaded that there is a burning platform in the legal services industry and in their own firm in particular? How can firm leadership facilitate consensus around the way forward in the face of considerable uncertainty? And how can a firm make innovation a normal part of doing business? This chapter gives answers to these questions because, as Kenneth A. Grady of Seyfarth Shaw LLP points out,

> [o]ne of the biggest opportunities for BigLaw firms comes out of the complacency of other law firms with the same business model. Law firms and lawyers seem content to wait for extinction, rather than to implement ways to avoid it. For each law firm, this complacency offers a tremendous opportunity. If a large law firm could overcome the issues of trust and culture, organize its services at levels and price points that clients want, embrace technology, and become proactive in tackling the large market for more routine legal work, it could take a commanding lead over other law firms. This first-mover advantage would give a firm the rare opportunity to position itself in a way that would take other law firms a long time to match if they finally decide to move.[2]

THE CASE FOR CHANGE IN BIGLAW FIRMS

There can be no question that the legal services industry is experiencing major changes. The establishment of legal services providers operating with business models distinct from traditional partnerships, deregulation allowing law firm incorporation with public ownership (in the United Kingdom and Australia at the time of publication), and an increasing uptake of technological tools and management strategies geared toward increasing efficiency by members of the legal profession are all indicia of far-reaching change. As Kenneth A. Grady puts it:

> The corporate legal services market is changing, but not as fast or as dramatically as many people predicted. From the law firm side, there was an expectation we would see large firms collapsing (or at least merging) at a record rate. While it

---

1. Change Management Institute, The Effective Change Manager: The Change Management Body of Knowledge 21 (Vivid Publishing 2013).

2. E-mail from Kenneth A. Grady, Chief Executive Officer of SeyfarthLean Consulting to George Beaton (Aug. 14, 2014) (on file with authors).

seems the rate of law firm mergers is tracking at about the same level each year, we are not seeing any dramatic change. The drama seems to be less about what is happening, than how these changes compare to years of stability.[3]

Stuart Fuller, global managing partner at King & Wood Mallesons (an international firm with strong Australian, Chinese, and U.K. roots), points out that "if you look back five years and you see the changes that have happened and the scale of the events and extrapolate that forward, it is going to happen very quickly."[4]

Simon Harper of alternative business model U.K. firm Lawyers On Demand (LOD) links the change dynamic to the millennial years:

> This era for law firms keeps reminding me of things I was seeing with our clients in the dot com era between 1997 and 2001. In the legal industry it feels like we're now in the period where the new players and traditional players have both realised something is going on that's here to stay. We have gone beyond the denial phase. Everyone is trying different things and there are so many ideas out there. The next stage will be to see how it all shakes out.[5]

But not all observers and analysts hold views as moderate as those of Grady, Fuller, and Harper. Edwin B. Reeser, a former BigLaw managing partner and now industry analyst and adviser, sees it this way:

> The change we've seen in the last ten years has not been operational. The change that we have seen in large law firms over the last ten years has been structural, and it's the worst kind, because it's rearranging chairs—deck chairs on the Titanic. It gives the impression that we're actually engaged in change when we're doing no such thing. Somebody says, "We're playing musical chairs, and now instead of going clockwise, we go counterclockwise," the classic example, in business, of frenetic motion, and wasted energy and resources.
>
> Meanwhile, the operational change to improve the value proposition of what we do for the client has been ignored for the most part. We have clients who continue to have dissatisfaction at an increasing rate and lawyers that profess to be doing everything possible. The disconnect between the two forces is clear, just read the legal press.[6]

There is evidence that many clients similarly feel that law firms are not doing a lot to change service delivery models: A 2014 Altman Weil survey asking Chief Legal Officers about how serious they thought law firms were about changing service delivery models to provide greater value found a median rating of three (with zero = being not at all serious and ten = doing everything they can).[7]

---

3. *Id.*

4. Telephone interview by George Beaton with Stuart Fuller, Global Managing Partner, King & Wood Mallesons (Sept. 8, 2014).

5. Telephone interview by Eric Chin and Imme Kaschner with Simon Harper, Co-Founder, Lawyers on Demand (Sept. 2, 2014).

6. Telephone interview by George Beaton with Edwin B. Reeser, President, Edwin B. Reeser: A Professional Law Corporation (Oct. 10, 2014).

7. Altman Weil, *2014 Chief Legal Officer Survey: An Altman Weil Flash Survey* 25 (2014)..

Perhaps Aric Press best captures the need for change and for remaking the traditional law firm business model in his analysis and essay based on a detailed review of trends in the AmLaw 200 firms over the period 2004–2013:

> There are at least two things to say about the future. First, we're optimistic about BigLaw firms, but not about every BigLaw firm. And second, that for all the broad market changes trends, each firm stands essentially as its own microclimate, with its own market challenges. As a result, each firm needs—immediately—to assess where it stands and where it seems to be headed.[8]

To Aric's admonition we would add: And do something strategic and sustained about where it is headed. Now.

One can see these trends as an invitation to commercial law firms to start remaking themselves—or at the very least start to realize the need to do so. Charles Handy, author of *The Empty Raincoat*, offers some apposite insights in relation to individual career strategies. He points out the danger of persisting with one set of ideas, strategies, and competencies on an individual level, since he predicts that both performance and job satisfaction are invariably bound to decline beyond a certain peak if strategies are not changed to accommodate changing circumstances, as his classic s-curve shown in Figure 13.1 suggests. Handy explains point "A" of the rising curve is the optimal time to innovate, reinvent, or remake because waiting until "B" leaves too little time and the individual or organization is irreparably weakened.

FIGURE 13.1

Handy's S-Curve

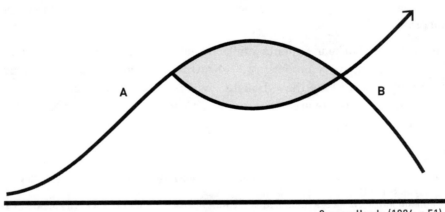

Source: Handy (1994, p.51)

---

8. Aric Press, *Big Law's Reality Check*, THE AMERICAN LAWYER BLOG (Oct. 29, 2014).

Handy suggests an approach that willingly accepts a certain decline in performance as new competencies are learned and acquired. But in Handy's way of viewing lasting and effective change, this eventually leads to a level of both performance and professional satisfaction that surpasses the plateau, and avoids the otherwise inevitable ensuing decline.[9] This is illustrated in Figure 13.1 by the new curve that starts at "A," dips, and then rises above what would have been the peak of the old trajectory, hence the moniker "Handy's S-Curve."

The corollary is, of course, that to continue the upward journey, repeated learning and relearning efforts are necessary. Handy's concepts about the need to step down to move forward can readily be applied on both organizational and individual levels. But it is important to realize that the letting go of established ways of doing things is fraught with challenges and frustration.

HOW CHANGE HAPPENS

Change is constant in life. One prominent thinker of managing change was Kurt Lewin.[10] He created a model of change consisting of the three stages of unfreeze, transform, and refreeze in order to help organizations to move successfully from one point of (relative) stability to another.

The stages can commence once the need for change is established, and they work through incorporating new processes into parts of the old routine. However, some level of resistance is inevitable, and unfreezing refers to identification and reduction of such resisting forces. This is followed by the implementation of new and aligned values, behaviors, systems, and processes that together constitute the transform stage. Lastly, the new behaviors need to be refrozen, the change needs to become the new routine for a lasting effect.

Jeanie Duck, formerly of the Boston Consulting Group, identified three essentials of working though change: strategy, execution, and sensitivity to emotional and behavioral issues. She personified the emotions and fears of those faced with change by coining the term "change monster."[11] The important insight is that while change readiness and implementation partly depend on the adequate communication of relevant facts to stakeholders, there is more to it. To paraphrase the common saying, written is not read, and read is not agreed. Bringing the partnership and the rest of the firm along on the change journey will need more than a detailed memorandum, or even a few town hall meetings, about what changes are necessary and why. Following Duck's imaginary bestiary, another literary example comes to mind. Bilbo Baggins was not exactly eager to join the band of dwarves at first.[12]

---

9. Charles Handy, The Empty Raincoat 49 (Arrow Books 2002).

10. K. Lewin, Field Theory in Social Science; Selected theoretical Papers 7 (D. Cartwright ed., Harper & Row 1951).

11. Jeanie Daniel Duck, The Change Monster: The Human Forces That Fuel or Foil Corporate Transformation and Change (Crown House Publishers 2001).

12. J.R.R. Tolkien, The Hobbit or There and Back Again 15–36 (HarperCollins Publishers 1993).

Yet, after a night of feasting and singing dark and beautiful songs about faraway places and dragon gold, he rushed off after them without even a handkerchief, ready to face trolls, Smaug the dragon, and come what may. And he never looked back. And if you, dear reader, now feel transported to a more innocent time when you first read Tolkien, or at least spent an enjoyable evening at the movies, you will understand the point that change readiness needs to be addressed through emotional as well as intellectual avenues.

INCREMENTAL AND TRANSFORMATIONAL CHANGE

Law firm partners frequently talk about changes that they have recently implemented, thinking that minor adaptations will be sufficient to position their firm for the future in a mature market.[13] However, in times of fast-paced and fundamental change in the environment, transformational, as opposed to incremental, change is needed. Management strategist Herbert Kindler succinctly summed up this important distinction in organizational strategy:

> The more familiar and commonly used strategy for change is incremental: step-by-step movement or variations in degree along an established conceptual continuum or system framework. Incremental change is based on precedent; it is intended to do more of the same, but better. An underlying assumption is that the conceptual or material system is adequate to satisfy the planner's objectives . . . .
>
> [T]ransformational change is a variation in kind that involves reconceptualization and discontinuity from the initial system.
>
> A transformational change strategy generally takes more time and energy than an incremental approach. Because it represents a departure from tradition, more risks are involved. This higher investment and vulnerability may be justified when: (1) incremental change fails to yield an acceptable level of improvement; [and] (2) discontinuities appear in the nature of the problem or in available means for dealing with it . . . .
>
> All change involves resistance, which stems from habit, norms, insecurity, dependence, or vested interests. However, transformational change invokes resistance from two sources: fear of separation and fear of failure in attempting a creative leap.[14]

There is frequently a "nip and tuck" approach to change in law firms, that is, strategies are limited to incremental change of various kinds. The hope in these firms is that it might suffice to adapt slowly to changing external conditions, and thereby avoid the strategic drift that results from simply not doing anything much beyond persevering in once-successful patterns of behavior. Nipping and tucking

---

13. As one experienced partner and law firm CEO aptly put it "Most partners think a nip here and a tuck there is all the change they need to stay beautiful."

14. Herbert S. Kindler, *Two Planning Strategies: Incremental Change and Transformational Change*, 4 GROUP AND ORGANIZATION MANAGEMENT 476, 477–78 (1979).

will not suffice in meeting the major current and future challenges firms face. As an example of such a burning platform, that is, a situation necessitating immediate and decisive action, Mark Tamminga of Canadian firm Gowlings shared some of the events leading up to a major initiative to introduce legal project management (Gowlings Practical) in the firm (discussed in detail in chapter 11):

> In terms of coming up with better ways of delivering legal services, most of our senior people were saying, "There's got to be a better way because this is really beginning to suck. We can't deliver the services at the prices our clients want in a way that's profitable for us. There's got to be something else."
>
> That realization, combined with some big write-offs in 2012, wasn't exactly a crisis for the firm, but it was the minor heart attack that causes the smoker to quit permanently. In effect, we got religion. Over the course of the summer last year, we got to "We're going to do this."[15]

So a major challenge to the firm's stability was used to facilitate partnership buy-in to drive a transformational change initiative. It was a quintessential burning platform.

A PORTFOLIO APPROACH TO INNOVATION

Among many senior law firm partners there is little tolerance for failure and small risk appetite and willingness to experiment. There is plenty of anecdotal evidence about examples where failed initiatives were sufficient to dissuade firms from future innovation attempts, in spite of the losses being financially irrelevant in comparison with the firm's overall profit. This could be the result of "ego discomfort," or a more general disquiet with imperfect outcomes among partners. Beyond firms, failures of nontraditional providers in the legal services market may be wrongly interpreted as evidence that innovation and change are unnecessary, rather than as a normal occurrence in a dynamic market.[16] If a majority of partners subscribes to such views, it will be difficult, if not impossible, to introduce major changes such as universal fixed fee arrangements or alternative sourcing. Yet, in a dynamic and changing market, the choice to refrain from change initiatives in the face of surrounding competitive innovation is itself a risky decision. Any proposed initiatives have to include an assessment of likely outcomes and the consequences if the perceived risk or opportunity prompting change is *not* addressed. Change averseness should not be masked and justified as risk averseness. The goal should not be to avoid failure at the cost of not moving at all, without assessing the specific risks that arise from doing nothing. Instead, the risk of failure has to be managed by building change portfolios on the basis of quantified and balanced risks.

---

15. Interview with Mark Tamminga, Leader, Innovation Initiatives, and Rick Kathuria, National Director, Project Management and Legal Logistics, Gowlings, in Toronto, Can. (Sept. 14, 2014).

16. See, e.g., Jordan Furlong, *The Failure of Legal Innovation*, LAW21 BLOG (May 29, 2014), http://www.law21.ca/2014/05/failure-legal-innovation/.

Specifying clear milestones allows for projects to fail early and at predictable costs, if failure cannot be avoided. The willingness to consider circumscribed failure acceptable and potentially valuable learning is a competency that needs to be built as precondition for effective change management.

Encouraging and incentivizing small-scale experimentation can most readily achieve this. Not every firm is in a position to have dedicated research and development people and resources, as, for example, the well-known legal innovator Seyfarth Shaw LLP does. Nevertheless, law firms have to turn their minds to innovation and transformational change at whatever level they can afford as part of their strategy, and therefore have to commit resources to formulating, and implementing, innovative strategies.

Another important precondition for any major change or innovation initiative is a willingness to embark on the journey, even if the exact way to achieve the desired outcome is not clear at the start. Hindsight, of course, always has 20/20 perfect vision, but to demand a complete and perfect plan for any change initiative, as opposed to a general sense of direction including an assessment of major risks, is simply not an option if any relevant change is ever to be made.

CASE STUDY: HOW INNOVATION HAPPENS AT DELOITTE

Peter Williams is chief edge officer at the Centre for the Edge, Deloitte Australia. The Centre's mission is to identify and explore emerging opportunities related to big shifts that are not yet on senior management's agenda, but ought to be. While it is focused on long-term trends and opportunities, it also considers implications for near-term action, the day-to-day environment of executives. Pete describes the Deloitte approach to innovation:

At Deloitte we have an innovation overhead charge, just putting a small annual percentage of revenue into a cash bucket. It's not allocated at the start of the year; rather it's allocated as ideas come through, and that can be as simple as one process we use, called micro-funding. If somebody puts up an idea that we like, we'll review their progress every two weeks, along the lines of "Hey, we like that idea. Here are a couple of people who can help you. Here's what we think you need to be thinking about in terms of taking this idea to the next level, and somebody will sponsor you through it." We make those decisions on the spot. Then if something starts to fly or looks as though it would be expanded, then we've still got that money to be able to do the expansion. It's not a huge percentage of our revenue, but that's where all the innovation that you see at Deloitte comes from, just about all of it comes out of that process.

It starts off with delivery innovation, and also some unstructured, organic ideas that people come through with, and that gets them to franchise and create their partnerships. I've never seen a law firm do that. This sort of model is all about increasing the speed of what you do, the notion of being able to take ideas and rapidly learn and test them in a market. At Deloitte, we have the target that 30 percent of revenue comes from stuff that we weren't doing two years before, and that's a hefty target, but right now we're running somewhere between 24 and 28 percent. That's a real innovation machine![17]

Such an approach might seem foreign for a law firm. But developing a mindset that considers ongoing innovation and investment in it are a crucial part of any successful business strategy.

THE CHANGE-AVERSE "LAWYER PERSONALITY"

Much has been written about the "lawyer personality" as it comes to the fore in law firm partnerships. Stuart Fuller sums up the challenge:

> Partnership is both the best model and the worst model rolled into one. Best in terms of if you can get it to work, you get a strong alignment of ownership and management, and partners in the business who can then lead the teams. The worst because partners are change resistant.[18]

The discussion of the lawyer personality here will be limited to evidence that is relevant when crafting efficient change management strategies for lawyers. Lawyers overwhelmingly display the "thinking" preference in the Myers–Briggs Type Indicator® (MBTI). The thinking mode tends to deemphasize harmony and personal relationships. Individuals with this preference have a high tolerance for conflict. In two studies of personality types among lawyers,[19] the most frequent types were INTJ (exhibiting preferences of introversion, intuiting, thinking, and judging), ISTJ (introversion, sensing, thinking, judging), and ESTJ (extraversion, sensing, thinking, judging).[20] In short, lawyers are skeptical people who value individual achievements over group consensus, and dislike change for the uncertainty that it brings, rather than valuing it for the opportunities that it provides.

Although the MBTI differences between lawyers and the general population are pronounced, corporate executives are similar to lawyers in MBTI terms. Like lawyers, top corporate executives overwhelmingly prefer thinking (95 percent) and judging (87 percent).[21] The most frequent types among successful corporate executives are INTJ, ISTJ, and ESTJ. These similarities suggest lawyers are equipped to understand and relate well to the executives, not just in-house lawyers, in their

---

17. Telephone interview by George Beaton with Peter Williams, Chief Edge Officer at the Centre for the Edge, Deloitte Australia (Sept. 3, 2014).

18. Fuller, *supra* note 4.

19. L. Richard, *How Your Personality Affects Your Practice: The Lawyer Types*, 79 A.B.A. J. 74 (1993); Vernellia R. Randall, *The Myers–Briggs Type Indicator, First Year Law Students and Performance*, 26 CUMB. L. REV. 63 (1996).

20. L. Richard, *supra* note 19.

21. Susan Swaim Daicoff, Lawyer, Know Thyself: A Psychological Analysis of Personality Strengths and Weaknesses 35 (Am. Psychological Ass'n 2004).

corporate clients. The similarities also suggest that the general MBTI preferences of lawyers are not the only contributor to change resistance.

Using another assessment tool, the Caliper Profile, Larry Richard has demonstrated that there is a much higher level of skepticism in lawyers compared to the general population. Skepticism combined with an efficiency-driven approach contributes to the tendency to overlook the need for more open-endedness in strategy design and implementation, and the importance of experimentation in defining new strategies.[22]

People who score high on skepticism are inclined to be questioning to the point of being argumentative and judgmental. They trust in themselves, rather than in a team, and consider their views the most rational view of the world. Lawyers in the sample scored on the 90th percentile for this trait, compared to the population average of the 50th percentile[23]—making law firms what former Harvard Business School professor and author of the pioneering 1993 book *Managing the Professional Services Firm*[24] David Maister calls a "low-trust environment."[25] This does not bode well for situations where team consensus is necessary to alter direction to meet changing client demands. These high levels of skepticism explain the difficulties in trying to generate consensus about business model changes in a firm, since lawyers are likely to question both the information that is the basis for decision making as well as any suggested changes that are the result of a situational analysis. While this ability to scrutinize and question complex information is obviously an advantage in carrying out legal tasks, the trait is less beneficial where consensus within a team is necessary to move forward—but lawyers will unfortunately not simply switch it off. Mark Tamminga commented:

> I left the firm's management team at the end of my first term, even though it is common to stay on for an additional period. I found the role endlessly interesting, but difficult for me personally. It's really hard to manage partners and their strong personalities. They are very good at arguing their point. I lost a lot of sleep doing the tough things I had to do.[26]

Maister offers anecdotal evidence of the unwillingness of lawyers to trust in others and abdicate control, quoting one senior partner as saying "[a]ll your recommendations are based on the assumption that we trust each other and trust our executive or compensation committees. We don't. Give us a system that doesn't

---

22. Larry Richard, *Herding Cats: The Lawyer Personality Revealed*, http://www.managingpartnerforum.org/tasks/sites/mpf/assets/image/MPF%20-%20Herding%20Cats%20-%20Richard%20-%203-5-121.pdf; 29(11) Altman Weil, Report to Legal Management 2 (Aug. 2002), *available at* http://www.managing partnerforum.org/tasks/sites/mpf/assets/image/MPF%20-%20WEBSITE%20-%20ARTICLE%20-%20Herding%20Cats%20-%20Richards1.pdf.

23. *Id.*

24. David Maister, Managing the Professional Services Firm (Simon & Schuster 1997).

25. David Maister, Strategy and the Fat Smoker: Doing What's Obvious but Not Easy 231 (The Spangle Press 2008).

26. Tamminga, *supra* note 15.

require us to trust each other."[27] Maister quotes another partner pointing out that "[i]t's not that I don't trust my partners . . . . It's that I don't want to have to trust them."[28] So there is a low willingness and desire to build strategic consensus based on trust in law firms, and any change management initiative has to take that factor into account.

Another aspect of lawyer preference is a high level of perfectionism, which makes them unwilling to embark on initiatives that might not be successful, particularly since they usually operate in a comfort zone of high personal expertise (as any successful partner in a commercial firm necessarily does). At this level, occasional project failure is seen as personal failure indicative of an individual's lack of competence (resulting in "ego discomfort," as Patrick McKenna dubs it),[29] rather than as a necessary consequence of attempts at innovation. A perceived lack of professional competency will also decrease an individual's authority among the peers in the firm that largely derives from technical and commercial success. Gerry Riskin of Edge International points out that as a result of this change-averse behavior, law firms are

> [b]eing paralyzed by the tedious, never-ending and totally ineffectual process of divining the perfect strategy accompanied by the perfect tactics. These firms are tied so firmly to the pier that no matter how well steered, they go absolutely nowhere. . . [T]heir biggest claim to fame is that they hit no icebergs—few ships do from the pier.[30]

David Perla, former co-founder and co-CEO of legal services outsourcer Pangea3, and now president of Bloomberg BNA Legal, links barriers to change in the legal industry to the ownership and capital structure:

> The hardest thing in this market is the perception, rightly or wrongly, that the lawyer absolutely has to be right all the time. So, they see quality as binary. To be wrong is to be fatal. And part of that is impacted by the capital structure. So, if you look why is it different in the U.K. or why is it different elsewhere, when you have outside capital, you can afford to take risks and make certain mistakes. Just like at Pangea3, we made mistakes and we weren't always right, and we could afford it. A law firm distributes its retained earnings every year. So, they cannot ever be wrong.[31]

---

27. Maister, *supra* note 25, at 231.

28. *Id.*

29. Interview by Nerly East with Patrick J. McKenna, *McKenna on Leading Change in Your Law Firm,* *available at* http://www.patrickmckenna.com/pdfs/McKenna%20On%20Leading%20Change.pdf (last visited Dec. 18, 2014).

30. Gerry Riskin, *Seven Immutable Laws of Change Management,* EDGE INTERNATIONAL REVIEW 28 (Summer 2006).

31. Telephone interview by George Beaton with David Perla, President, Bloomberg BNA Legal Division/Bloomberg Law (Aug. 14, 2014).

THE PRECEDENT MINDSET

Beyond personality traits that are prevalent in people who choose to become lawyers, and lead to a general reluctance to embrace change among members of the profession, there is also the additional learned element of tried and established courses of action over new courses of action. At least the common law is based on precedent, and lawyers throughout their work learn to model beneficial strategies on previous successful cases. Legal arguments are based on a clear and detailed understanding of applicable precedents, and the ability to identify cases that were resolved in a manner that would be favorable to the client if applied, as well as to distinguish those that were not. Creative new strategies for resolving legal issues are a tricky thing—they are well placed in the context of a law reform commission, but will not result in runs on the board for the lawyer who offers them in court or in a transaction.

Toby Brown of Akin Gump identifies this as one of the barriers to change in law firms: "I call it the paradigm of precedent. The entire industry, its mindset and approach to everything is based on precedent."[32] Basing change on precedents in a "more of the same but better" way leads to incremental change, as Kindler points out. There can be a dangerous presumption that strategies that have been employed successfully in previous challenging situations will be sufficient when a new crisis arises, limiting the ability of law firm leadership to react to novel and unprecedented crises. Stuart Fuller points to the challenge that this poses for executive leadership:

> The challenge of the chief executive or managing partner or chairman of law firms is to bring the outside world into the firm. A good deal of my role is to bring those external forces into my firm and to advocate for the ideas. The counter to that is there are often generations of partners resisting changes who have come through under difficult circumstances in the external environment.[33]

In order to develop the competency of change readiness in lawyers, the precedent mindset needs to be identified, and the burning platform necessitating transformational change has to be clearly distinguished from situations where the precedent mindset does indeed yield good results.

CHANGE MANAGEMENT AND CHANGE LEADERSHIP

Before going into more detail about change implementation, it is important to point out the difference between change management and change leadership.

---

32. Telephone interview by George Beaton with Toby Brown, Chief Practice Officer at Akin Gump Strauss Hauer & Feld LLP (Aug. 8, 2014).
33. Fuller, *supra* note 4.

Management author and Harvard Business School Professor Emeritus John P. Kotter succinctly summed up the difference between management and leadership in general:

> Management is about coping with complexity. Its practices and procedures are largely a response to one of the most significant developments of the twentieth century: The emergence of large organizations. Without good management, complex enterprises tend to become chaotic in ways that threaten their very existence.
>
> . . .
>
> Leadership, by contrast, is about coping with change. Part of the reason it has become so important in recent years is that the business world has become more competitive and more volatile. . . . The net result is that doing what was done yesterday, or doing it [five] percent better, is no longer a formula for success. Major changes are more and more necessary to survive and compete effectively in this new environment. More change always demands more leadership.[34]

Law firm change therefore needs to be spearheaded and clearly supported by the firm leadership, but also needs to be managed on a daily basis by professionals that have built this competency, and these are not necessarily the firm's partners. Kenneth A. Grady discusses the problems and the need for interdisciplinary cooperation that arise in the change management context:

> Most firms do not have the experience or skill sets to implement change management. As with most areas of firm management, lawyers do not have training in change management nor have they spent time during their careers learning how to implement change management. Lawyers come to firm leadership, typically at some point when they are partners and have practiced for ten or more years, with nothing more than an interest and a demonstrated aptitude for building a legal practice. Lawyers also tend to be "cut from the same cloth." If you go to a culture session in an organization, and they sort the attendees into different personality types (typically four different groups), each group is filled with individuals from areas of the organization that mesh well with their personality type. Finance typically goes into one quadrant, HR in another, and senior executives in a third. If you do the same exercise at a law firm, almost all of the lawyers group into one quadrant. Without diversity of management expertise and skills, law firms are poorly positioned to implement any strategies.[35]

In short, successful change implementation needs committed leadership, as well as competent management by professionals—not necessarily lawyers.

---

34. John P. Kotter, John P. Kotter on What Leaders Really Do 52–53 (Harv. Bus. Rev. Books 1999).

35. E-mail from Kenneth A. Grady, Chief Executive Office, SeyfarthLean Consulting to George Beaton (Aug. 14, 2014) (on file with authors).

WINNING HEARTS AND MINDS: LEADING UP TO THE CHANGE JOURNEY

Any change initiative within the firm will only be able to proceed from a willingness to engage in common endeavors that have evolved beyond the "low trust" and high autonomy environment as discussed previously, and a shared understanding among the stakeholders that is built on consensus about the issues to be addressed. Law firms are fortunate in that there is a strong common denominator among stakeholders—as Lisa Damon of Seyfarth Shaw LLP put it, "we tap the desire to serve as professionals; it motivates our people. . . . Part of change is tying into what people are passionate about".[36] Stuart Fuller describes partners' desire to improve their firm: "The word stewardship is not a word all in the industry use. But I think there is an inherent pride amongst partners to leave the firm in a better position than when they came into it."[37] A willingness to improve the firm, however, does not necessarily equate to consensus about how that is to be done. If, on the other hand, there is client demand for the service that is the product of the proposed initiative, the motivation changes radically. Simon Harper, driving force behind the United Kingdom's alternative legal services provider LOD, describes a key experience:

> The journey with the clients started off with me, as a commercial and technology partner, talking to a number of clients I worked with, before we launched LOD, hypothesizing the idea and if they were interested. There were generally good responses, but one particularly telling moment was when two clients called separately soon after I'd shared the concept and requested this service. I had to explain that we weren't quite ready and that it was just an idea. The fact that the two clients called us about something that was just an idea felt like a revelation for me as a lawyer. And calls continued to come in after we launched LOD, and they were new clients inviting us to talk about the service. The idea of clients ringing the lawyer, and new clients too, requesting a service was very exciting.[38]

Pam Woldow, LPM specialist and consultant, vividly describes the difference that client pressure makes to LPM implementation, as it does equally to other law firm change initiatives:

> Whether with LPM or any other major change initiative within a firm, there is tremendous resistance from the boots-on-the-street level lawyer. The resistance is so pronounced because lawyers have established ways of doing things. If it has worked, if they have been successful in the past, they make the leap of faith that because it was successful, the way I do things must be **good**. It must be efficient. It must be value laden. Therefore, when you come to them and say, "We have got to rethink the way we deliver services to clients," they are really not terribly

---

36. Telephone interview by George Beaton with Lisa Damon, National Chair, Labor & Employment Department, Seyfarth Shaw LLP (Aug. 21, 2014).
37. Fuller, *supra* note 4.
38. Harper, *supra* note 5.

interested because their answer is "It's always worked this way." To counteract this inertia, if I may use a metaphor from physics, you have to change both the lever and the leverage. You have to exert a strong and irresistible push from a new direction. From what I have seen, the most effective way to get lawyers to change is through pressure from their clients.

When clients demand LPM efficiency, if they say, "We are rethinking the law firms and lawyers that we use because we need lower costs, more efficiency and more predictability," you suddenly get a lot of religion inside of the practice groups that find themselves under the gun. The best LPM training I've ever seen was in hands-on workshops with client-side participants in the room. The clients served as a looming presence to keep the firm lawyers from kidding themselves or lapsing into denial. They sat on the edge of their chairs, nodding their heads and exclaiming "Yes! That's exactly what we want. We want to know the workflow. We want to know what's efficient. We want you to reuse your prior work and not re-invent the wheel with every task. We want to be able to access and measure where you stand and how you're doing." When you don't have the clients in the room, many lawyers sit with their arms crossed over their chests, huffing away: "Spare me all this process crap. I just want to practice law. Let me just do it my way."[39]

Pam Woldow's comments illustrate the profound and immediate influence that clients' demands and involvement can have on lawyers' willingness to change. But firms should be careful to not to change only in response to direct client demands. Susan Hackett, former senior vice-president and general counsel of the Association of Corporate Counsel (ACC), puts it in her inimitable style:

I think that is where the real disconnect comes in. Clients get really sick of having firms say either, "my clients aren't demanding new ways to deliver their services," and "they haven't told us what they want and how they want it, so why should we change our practices," as if *clients* are responsible for building better or more responsive law firms.

Unless you're Paris Hilton, you do not go to a lingerie store and tell them what kind of underwear you would like to have so that they can go off and make it. Regular customers expect that a really good store will stock a good selection of the best products and advise them on what will work best based on their expertise, since they are the underwear specialists. Customers expect to have lots of different kinds of underwear to choose from, and they expect to find what they want, and at the price they want it, or they'll go to another store. So it is with clients and law firms in this emerging marketplace where the client (and not the firm) is king.[40]

Susan's point and Pam's perspective illustrate the need to closely interact with clients to be able to *anticipate* their business needs and challenges using a variety of points of contact and methods from open-ended conversations to systematic surveys (see chapter 7). Mel Anderson, head of information and insights at Grant

---

39. Telephone interview by Eric Chin and Imme Kaschner with Pam Woldow, Principal & General Counsel, Edge International (Aug. 29, 2014).

40. Telephone interview by Eric Chin and Imme Kaschner with Susan Hackett, Legal Executive Leadership LLC (Sept. 4, 2014).

Thornton Australia, and former director of benchmarks at Beaton Research + Consulting, explains the important difference between client feedback and other client-derived information:

> Often firms talk about client insights, but what they mean is client feedback. So they are talking about matter debriefs, or satisfaction with the firm or with the performance on a particular project. But in the future, for firms to be ahead of the game, they need to use insights to drive their decision-making, their strategy. Insights around what the future challenges are that face client businesses, or the challenges in the broader market, and using these to drive strategy.[41]

Irrespective of whether the change readiness is built through client demands or from within the firm in anticipation of future client demands, consensus around specific change initiatives has to be built and consolidated, and efficient media use is an essential part of that.

MEDIA AND COMMUNICATION TO BUILD CHANGE CONSENSUS

The multifaceted, busy, and dispersed nature of a large, modern law firm makes it harder to build consensus through personal contacts. It becomes necessary to engage members in ways that are consistent with the technology-enabled cooperation that they use in their daily practice. Trust is built on knowledge and shared experiences. Channels of communication through firm-based social media or proprietary platforms can provide a degree of interaction and common experiences in the absence of personal interaction—think about how well-known cartoons or a recent sports game provide a shared experience with complete strangers. There is no question that building and improving trust in a law firm is difficult—but implementing lasting change is simply not possible without it.

Once channels of communication have been established, they can be used to deploy information about change initiatives, always keeping in mind that the status of the sender will influence the responses—the higher up, the more likely to have the desired effect. The information needs to be simple and sufficiently attractive to appeal to the audience in an emotional as well as intellectual manner, prompting responses that differ from the skeptical and argumentative "lawyerly" approach. Initial steps for the project should be set out in detail to generate interest and buy-in and opportunities for coverage of initial successes.

Animated presentations and short videos, with a lead-in of short messages to set the scene, are well suited for this. Think of a well-run propaganda campaign vividly painting the present and desired future, while maintaining an intellectual level appropriate for the target audience. One example of the successful use of

---

41. Interview by George Beaton with Mel Anderson, then Director, Benchmarks at Beaton Research + Consulting, in Melbourne, Australia (Jan. 12, 2015).

simple and graphically supported materials was the presentation of the Mont Fleur scenarios canvassing options for political change in South Africa (during the transition from the apartheid regime) in a newspaper insert and a short, partly animated film.[42] The materials facilitated high-stakes discussions between diverse parties that ultimately led to a mostly peaceful compromise solution in the political transition. Stakeholder buy-in to start negotiations that led to transformative change depended on simple, evocative and clear communication, not detailed analysis as first step, as the Mont Fleur example illustrated.

One potential aid in building the shared language and understanding necessary to launch a change initiative is scenarios, that is, narratives of a potential future, as discussed in the preceding paragraph (and the subject of chapter 5). The Kaleidoscope scenario sets out envisaged developments in the legal services industry that support the need for the changes we describe. This material can focus the discussion about the need for change, and viable options if the developments come to pass. Other possible strategies include discussion rounds with external speakers, client sessions to amplify the voice of the client within the firm, dedicated chat groups, or internal competitions soliciting change proposals.

This "ripening" of issues needs to proceed until there is a grassroots demand from the majority of individual partners to institute change in defined areas, rather than a top-down decision to do so. This is an example of the covert leadership competency that Professor Empson of Cass Business School has identified as crucial for effective law firm leaders.[43] A by-product of proceeding in this manner is an increased willingness on the part of the partners to engage in the continuing change project once implemented, since they already feel a sense of ownership for having driven it thus far.

THE ALTERNATIVES: STEALTH INNOVATION AND SKUNKWORKS

Sometimes it might be simply impossible to build majority consensus around a major change initiative in a firm where the precedent mindset has never been substantially challenged. In that case, feasible alternatives are to practice "stealth innovation," or to build a formal skunkworks project outside the parent entity, assuming of course approval and, more importantly, funds can be secured.

---

42. For part of the animated sequences and a general discussion of the Mont Fleur scenarios, see the short movie Mont Fleur Scenarios (Part 1/3), *available at* http://www.youtube.com/watch?v =f92RYCZMwEk&index=2&list=PLQ6-nobwfFu9KZODVAYkUq7cHa1nPtysi (last visited Dec. 19, 2014); see also Adam Kahane, Transformative Scenario Planning: Working Together to Change the Future 9 (Berrett-Koehler Publishers 2012).

43. Laura Empson, *Reluctant Leaders and Autonomous Followers—Leadership Tactics in Professional Services Firms* 18 (Cass Business School 2014), *available at* http://www.cass.city.ac.uk/__data/assets /pdf_file/0018/222723/Reluctant-Leaders-EMPSON.pdf?bustCache=46494072.

The term "stealth innovation" seems to have been coined by professor Paddy Miller of IESE Business School and Thomas Wedell-Wedellsborg of Innovation Architects in their 2013 *Harvard Business Review* article "The Case for Stealth Innovation—When It's Better to Seek Forgiveness Than Ask Permission."[44] The authors use the term to describe innovation initiatives that do not go through established corporate channels for new projects, including budgeting and sign-offs. The motivation to innovate in this way can be manifold, and includes the desire to generate some proof of principle prior to the proposal facing the full scrutiny of the partnership, or the concern that direct approval is unlikely because of the prevailing culture and processes in the firm.

Miller and Wedell-Wedellsborg suggest that covert innovation projects need four elements:

- Stealth support, that is, support by managers a level above the innovator, with control of sufficient resources to be helpful, but not at the very top. This has the advantage of a larger pool of potential sponsors.
- Stealth testing, meaning that the goal at this stage needs to be generation of clear proof of feasibility, and data supporting a business case, not mere innovation for intellectual enjoyment.
- Stealth resourcing, suggesting that often there is room to divert some manpower and other resources from other projects, possibly by bartering superfluous resources under the innovator's control—and this is intimately connected to the fourth and last element.
- Stealth branding, meaning a simple and credible cover story for the stealth activities to remain "under the radar" until stealth testing has been achieved.

Overall, something of a maverick mindset is necessary to effect stealth innovation successfully. The hierarchical and highly structured nature of work in a law firm does not make it any easier, but it is worth trying.

A skunkworks project, on the other hand, needs formal approval from within a firm, but since the innovative project happens outside established structures, it is often seen as less threatening than within-firm initiatives.[45] The term "skunkworks" goes back to aircraft maker Lockheed utilizing separate facilities and a specialized team within the company to develop innovative types of airplanes during World War II. The group was nicknamed after a factory for illegally brewed liquor in the comic strip Lil' Abner, but there is also the possible double entendre of the physical separation of the group's research facilities, as might have been done to combat the olfactory remnants of a skunk encounter.

---

44. Paddy Miller & Thomas Wedell-Wedellsborg *The Case for Stealth Innovation—When It's Better to Seek Forgiveness Than Ask Permission,* HARVARD BUSINESS REVIEW 91 (Mar. 2013).

45. The potential for applying the principles of skunkworks in law firms was pointed out to George Beaton by Professor William D. Henderson in Chicago, September 2014.

Simon Harper of the U.K. firm LOD discusses "stealth innovation" in the context of a law firm, referring to the *Harvard Business Review* article.[46] LOD has several hallmarks of a skunkworks project, since it was set up as an entity offering flexibly working lawyers for both in-house law departments and law firms. This was done from *within* traditional model firm Berwin Leighton Paisner, which provided an early strong co-branding effect, but the new brand can also be considered something of a firewall to avoid any tainting of the core brand. Simon comments on both the advantages of stealth innovation and skunkworks projects:

> [I]t made me smile more and more with recognition as I turned over each page. The essence in this piece (the *HBR* article) was about taking a more pragmatic approach on innovation in a large organization. It was effectively saying—start something under the radar and let people see if it works. Once it works, you can start to slowly put it out there. . . . It would be lovely to say LOD was beautifully planned to be exactly like it is now. However, the reality is reflected in that piece, though it was written years after our launch. LOD was an incremental and pragmatic approach to things we were seeing in the market. On one hand the clients being eager for an alternative and on the other hand friends, colleagues and other lawyers wanting to work differently. There was an element of stealth, or maybe accidental stealth.
>
> . . .
>
> The firm has always embraced new ideas and new things. The senior management team at Berwin Leighton Paisner was always very open to my LOD concept. I remember well before LOD's launch, the firm's managing partner, Neville Eisenberg, was giving a talk to staff and one of the things that struck me was him saying "Try new stuff. We know some of things will go wrong but try new stuff." And that really spoke to me. It is an indication of the culture of permissiveness to innovation. And this was really important.
>
> The other side of this of course is that lawyers like proven things that work. The joy of doing things a little quietly to start off with is you have created your precedent. You have proof that it worked, proven the idea and not broken anything disastrously.
>
> . . .
>
> The people required to change were from outside of the organization essentially. It required change from the clients and it required change from the people who were working in LOD, who were not Berwin Leighton Paisner lawyers. It didn't require big organizational change from Berwin Leighton Paisner. . . . The lawyers we recruit for LOD are self-selected and are given a completely transparent view on what it means to work this way.[47]

So if change initiatives cannot be agreed upon through consensus within the firm, the covert option of stealth innovation, or the less confronting option of

---

46. Miller & Wedell-Wedellsborg, *supra* note 44.
47. Woldow, *supra* note 39.

skunkworks initiatives, might be the way to make inroads toward building a culture of change readiness.

INVESTING IN LEGAL START-UPS

Yet another option if a law firm is willing to invest is to possibly cooperate with legal start-ups looking for investment. As Professor Henderson of the Maurer School of Law points out, this can be a win–win giving the start-up a steady stream of work and an option to test their innovative ideas in the real world, and allowing the law firm access to technology, systems, and services that they would otherwise not be able to access:

> The legal start-ups are going to get rolled up, either into Thomson Reuters or into firms such as K&L Gates and the like. Peter Kalis would probably disagree with me, but it makes sense for him to begin shopping for legal start-ups, take a small position in them and begin to use their products because the client needs value. You might as well start using, start sourcing, these things. We are going to see these start-ups getting uptake from the global law firms because it makes a lot of sense for the globals to start in this way.[48]

It might of course be easier said than done to find the right start-up match for the right price at the right time.

CHANGE AND COMPENSATION

Whether a change initiative will be successful depends on the way that the build-up and implementation are managed, but the long-term "refreeze," that is the permanent establishment of new processes, is a function of the long-term motivation of participants to adhere and contribute to the new way of doing things.

Motivating factors can be divided into the monetary and the non-monetary, and successful initiatives should be built around both. But significant changes in how the work is done at a law firm, particularly if that means accepting structured processes that limit an individual partner's discretion, will necessitate changing the firm's compensation system in a way that incentivizes the new way of working. The compensation system obviously goes to the heart of a firm's "operating system." Modifying it to drive and maintain other changes is therefore another Catch-22. As Mark Tamminga of Canadian law firm Gowlings puts it, "I think the biggest cultural change we could make would be compensation."[49] The relevance of the compensation system for the operation of a law firm is also illustrated by the comments of Kenneth A. Grady:

---

48. Telephone interview by George Beaton with William D. Henderson, Professor of Law and Val Nolan Faculty Fellow, Maurer School of Law (July 31, 2014).

49. Tamminga, *supra* note 15.

I believe those lawyers dissatisfied with the situation that Mr. Maister described (the low-trust environment and cumbersome decision-making processes in law firms) increasingly leave BigLaw firms and in some instances leave the profession. The lawyers remaining at BigLaw firms either do not have viable options or are content to live in low growth, no growth or even shrinking revenue environments. Their dominant focus is on their personal income level, not on wealth creation for the firm or themselves.

Contrast this with corporate leaders. Most of their income comes from wealth creation. They drive the value of their institutions higher, and the value of their equity rises with the value of the institutions. Their yearly income (salary) is a small part of their overall compensation. As a result, they focus on driving enterprise value. They also receive that value over time. For example, most equity grants vest over three to five years. BigLaw partners think in terms of immediate income, with all of their compensation tied to the immediate year and paid out shortly after the end of the year. As a result, BigLaw partners think of now, not the future.[50]

Kenneth identifies the traditional partnership culture combined with a conventional compensation system as the key reasons why long-term value creation is neglected in BigLaw firms. Innovation initiatives are a specific form of long-term investment. One common reason for failed initiatives in our experience is a lack of connection with established reward structures. Lawyers will not be able to spend time on learning new processes or developing and running pilot projects, for example to build applications or legal knowledge platforms, or to invest in building working relationships with efficient external legal services providers, if they are expected to bill the same amount of time as they otherwise would. This can be addressed by setting up internal equivalents of billable time, allowing for time spent on certain projects to be recognized as equivalent to billable time for the purpose of compensation (a strategy successfully utilized for example by Gowlings in implementing their Gowlings Practical initiative). But that results in a smaller piece of pie for everyone, and therefore again needs partnership approval (remember, there is always a catch . . . Catch-22 . . .).

CHANGE AND GOVERNANCE

This chapter has shown how common traits and mindsets of individual lawyers contribute to a general culture that is less than innovation-friendly in law firms—the general "vibe" in a firm.[51] But beyond culture, law firms are characterized by more formal, though not necessarily always written, structures of internal

---

50. Grady, *supra* note 2.
51. See the Australian movie THE CASTLE (Village Roadshow 1997), a perennial favorite among Australian lawyers, particularly intellectual property lawyers. In the movie, a barrister refers to "the vibe" of the Australian constitution in trying to convince the court that the expropriation of his client's house was unconstitutional, unfortunately citing for support s 51 (xviii) of the constitution, the head of power that sets out the federal parliament's entitlement to legislate in regard to various forms of intellectual property; https://www .youtube.com/watch?v=wJuXIq7OazQutube link.

governance. Each firm has its own unique way of formulating its future course of action, and enacting it, engaging partners in various ways throughout the process. Compensation is one aspect of this. One experienced practitioner put it this way, "A law firm is like a marriage . . . unique, and you really cannot know how things work from the outside." Both unwritten rules and codified governance structures have a major influence on how change initiatives are implemented in a firm. Governance structures, including compensation systems, are a reflection of a consensus about how financial surpluses should be allocated, particularly in regard to investment versus immediate distribution. Stephen Mayson sums up this dichotomy in law firm culture:

> [T]he choice is between the "reality" of custodian equity in an institution, where firm-specific capital is the continuing bedrock of future growth and development, or the "ownership" of individual capital in a firm that may be successful for its immediate owners but which is just as likely to destroy itself by its own inherent weakness or lack of cohesion.[52]

An "all profit today" mentality is a hindrance for long-term investments, including those in change initiatives discussed in this book. Where "all profit today" is present, only a truly burning platform, that is, circumstances that will result in a systemwide implosion save for immediate action, has a chance to lead to change consensus.

If there is an acknowledgement that a certain level of investment in the future is necessary (because a genuine sense of stewardship prevails, or as a matter of sound business practice, or because of a combination of the two), the question becomes one of working within the firm's governance structures to shift resource allocation toward specific new change initiatives. If well-established structures of effective decision making exist, change implementation needs leadership buy-in as a first step to make significant resources available for the initiative. In a firm that is consensus driven, with the majority of decisions being made through plenary votes, general acceptance is a prerequisite for committing resources for change initiatives. In such a setting, starting with very small initiatives, usually by stealth, to gain traction and broad-based buy-in is a better way to gain consensus for allocation of meaningful change resources.

THE CHANGE JOURNEY

Once stakeholders' emotional buy-in and in-principle approval have been achieved, the project needs to proceed with visible initial steps to create a positive feedback loop. Process needs to be monitored against preset milestones, and stakeholder concerns need to be addressed as and when they arrive. This is the stage when the

---

52. Stephen Mayson, Making Sense of Law Firms: Strategy, Structure and Ownership 472 (Blackstone Press 1997).

change monster is most likely to rear its ugly head for a number of reasons. After the initial well-orchestrated enthusiasm, the project is now being implemented, and both anticipated and unforeseen problems will arise. The momentum wanes as members of the group are being asked to change how they do things in earnest, moving out of their comfort zones of established expertise for more than a short period of time. This is unpleasant, and people are likely to resist it, even if they generally believe in the necessity for change. This is where the going gets tough, and projects fail if the commitment and resources for implementation are not sufficient.

Doing things the new way is initially harder, even if it is a better solution long-term. And for some lawyers and other staff, it might not be. Some team members will find themselves unable to make and sustain the changes, and might have to go. In addition, carrying the change through means that eventually even the most change-averse firm members, who had resisted so far, now need to buy into the initiative. This is the point where the change project might fail because, using Lewin's terminology, the transformation, and the subsequent "refreeze" to establish the new ways of doing things are not being achieved across the board.

To overcome these challenges effectively, a change manager needs to address the operational implementation issues (for example, people having to learn new skills, or new resources not being available as needed, or parts of the planned goal not being achievable) along with the personal, emotional barriers that make people unwilling to embrace the change. Struggling team members might need support, possibly in peer groups, to aid learning. Others who remain unwilling to change might benefit from compassionate exits. Throughout the project, progress needs to be made visible, and successes celebrated, while failures on the way should be used as learning opportunities, without apportioning blame. Appropriate person-to-person and mass communication needs to address both factual and emotional aspects of the change implementation. One "change journey example" is set out in the following case study. Another example relating to LPM at Canadian firm Gowlings may be found in chapter 11.

Case Study: The Change Journey at Allen & Overy

David Morley, worldwide senior partner at Allen & Overy, describes the circumstances around setting up the firm's captive center:

> We opened [our captive center] in Belfast three years ago. The back office move from London to Belfast meant 300 people would be made redundant as a result. It was a bit of a leap into the unknown. The night before we made the announcement, Wim Dejonghe came into my office and said "I think we will have to pull the plug on this because the objections are so loud, I had so many people telling me it will not work, the quality of what we do will suffer, we are not being true to our culture by making people redundant." There was just a wall of objections and issues that were raised. We talked about it and reassured ourselves.

> It was very tough, having to tell 300 people they will be losing their jobs. Three years later Belfast is our third largest office with 400 people employed, and expanded to include legal services with 50 lawyers. Two months ago the firm won a very large transaction, the work will go on for five years, against fierce competitive tenders. The client wrote a letter saying there were four reasons Allen & Overy had won, the third being our Belfast offering and what we could do. The problem now is to get sufficient resources into Belfast, which is a good problem to have. The partners now see Belfast as a success and off the back of that, are giving the management an informal mandate to try other things.
>
> Part of being able to innovate successfully in a law firm environment is to be able to demonstrate success from the things you have tried. You might not be successful at all things you have tried but having a track record of successes will provide tangible evidence for partners to support new initiatives.[53]

And eventually, if the people aspects are sufficiently addressed along with the other facets of change management, the change will become the new normal, likely looking different from what was envisioned at the beginning of the journey, and probably just in time for it to be in need of another round of improvement. What remains is the need to assess and document the project learning, specifically, which substrategies worked, which ones did not, and what if any other areas in need of change were identified in the process. Beyond the specific change, the firm has improved its core competency of change readiness, which can be applied to the next project. Well done!

CONCLUSION

The success of any change initiative in a law firm depends on the ability to successfully address the emotions, concerns, and project-related needs of stakeholders such as clients, partners, and other legal professionals. As a group, lawyers tend to be risk-averse. They are also loath to engage in projects that are outside their comfort zone, that is, their area of experience and expertise, and that carry a risk of failure. The strongest change motivator for lawyers in a private practice firm is clear evidence of client demand. Effective planning and information management create the cohesion and momentum that are necessary to implement changes in the way that lawyers work, but the need for significant and sustained resourcing of change management should not be underestimated. To "refreeze" new modes of doing legal work, there needs to be a connection to the compensation system. If it is not possible to build change consensus initially, a stealth innovation approach may allow for proof of principle and the collection of data to build a business case. Ultimately, building the competency of change readiness in a firm might be the most important strategic priority, since it underlies a firm's ability to implement any strategic change in response to altered circumstances.

---

53. Telephone interview by George Beaton with David Morley, Worldwide Senior Partner, Allen & Overy (Oct. 21, 2014).

Chapter 14

Outlook

We have traversed the *why* of remaking law firms, starting with the legal services industry of today, moving on to the clients of tomorrow, further on to the 2025 kaleidoscope scenario, and concluding with the diagnostic tool. We proceeded to the *how*, beginning with design of a firm's business model, and covering branding, pricing, sourcing, LPM, technology, and innovation readiness and change.

This is our research-based view of where the legal services industry stands today and where it is heading, as well as our understanding of how law firms can remake themselves to continue to serve their clients and prosper in that future. Thank you for coming on the journey. You might vigorously disagree with our view of what is happening in the legal services industry and what firms should do about it. In that case, consider reading *Remaking Law Firms* an entertaining interlude, and continue doing what you have always done. To say it with an old Shakespeare favorite:

> *If we shadows have offended,*
> *Think but this, and all is mended, —*
> *That you have but slumber'd here*
> *While these visions did appear.*[1]

That was easy.

Or maybe you agree with (however much of) our assessment. You have reached the conclusion that the traditional law firm business model is not sustainable into the future unless significant changes are made to it. You might feel inspired, and ready to take remaking action in your firm. Hold that feeling. If you haven't done so already, go back to chapter 6 and use the self-assessment tool as a guide to where to start. Forget thinking about everything that could possibly go wrong, and why it will not work, and why it is all just too hard. Then ask yourself, supposing you knew for a fact that whatever change you want to effect was possible, how would you go about making it happen?

---

1. Shakespeare. *A Midsummer Night's Dream*, act 5, sc. 1, at 301 (Barnes & Noble, 1994).

Next, find a way to amplify the voice of your clients into the firm. No, those voices are not just in your head; things will never be the same if you listen deeply to clients. Major client organizations have drawn lines in the sand. Ask. Listen. Listen more. Be willing to take in the possibly inconvenient truth about how the work that you deliver may not be the best way to meet client needs. Try to put yourself in your clients' shoes and think what you could do better, and then check with them if they agree. Bring the clients in to share their ideas about possible innovations with the firm. Remember that doing better does not necessarily mean spending more time and more dollars. All too often, it may be exactly the opposite, another inconvenient truth.

Once you have identified the area in which you want to start, consider what resources can be made available for whatever it is you are planning, since this will partly determine the scale of your initiative. Smaller is usually better to start with, but not so small as not to make a noticeable difference. Do the numbers, for both best- and worst-case scenarios. Talk to people who have done similar things. Roll out your public relations machine, and relentlessly proselytize about the project, unless you have decided do take a stealth innovation approach—in that case, build your smokescreen. Then start doing it, whatever it is. Be ready to be wrong, to start again, and to do that over and over. Remember the old joke about why they call it REsearch? And be infinitely patient. Godspeed!

Appendix

Interviewees and Contributors

Stephen Allen

Stephen has worked as a lawyer both in private practice and in-house. During his early career he crossed the board table to become managing director of two divisions of Orange-France Télécom in the United Kingdom and Continental Europe. Uniquely, he combines that deep business and legal understanding to address the demands of the current legal market—notably being the architect and implementer of multi–award winning Managed Legal Service for Thames Water, the first ever multiyear, fixed-price deal for legal services.

Stephen set up and led PwC's legal market advisory practice, internationally, advising and delivering value-led change programs for law firms and corporate legal functions.

At DLA Piper, his remit is strategic: Reimagine the firm so that it may win more work, from clients internationally, through being able to offer a seamless full service offering, which delivers more for less and offers clients value through innovation.

Author of the widely read and followed lexfuturus.com blog, Stephen prides himself on and has a long track record of making the complex simple and the simple effective. He sits on a number of advisory boards and is a permanent commentator for the FT Innovative Lawyer Awards™.

Mel Anderson

Mel is head of Information & Insights at Grant Thornton Australia. In the past she has been director of Benchmarks at Beaton Research + Consulting and a client insights consultant at law firm Allens Arthur Robinson. Mel has worked extensively with professional service firms, drawing on her data-driven insights to address particular business needs. She holds an MBA from Melbourne Business School in The University of Melbourne and a bachelor of arts and bachelor of commerce from Monash University.

Liam Brown

Liam is founder and chairman of Elevate Services, Inc. He has spent over 20 years providing consulting, technology, and services to law firms and Global 1000 corporate legal departments. As an advisor and consultant, Liam has guided law firm leaders and general counsel through a variety of strategic decisions focused on improving effectiveness and efficiency. He founded Elevate in 2011, a next generation legal service provider with the mission to help law firms and corporate legal departments operate more effectively. He was the founder, president, and CEO of Integreon, Inc., which he led from startup in 2001 to annual sales of nearly $150 million by 2011, before he sold his stake to private equity investors in order to launch Elevate. Prior to Integreon, he was president, COO, and co-founder of Conscium, Inc., a leading Web 1.0 virtual deal room business serving lawyers and bankers, which he sold in 2001 to then-NYSE-listed Bowne & Co. (now RR Donnelley Venue) and NASDAQ-listed Merrill Corp (now Merrill DataSite). Liam is also an active investor in Web 2.0 and Cloud technologies in the legal sector, and is an executive coach for founders of startups.

Toby Brown

Toby is the chief practice officer for Akin Gump. In this role, Toby works with firm partners and clients in developing pricing arrangements and service delivery models that drive successful relationships. This includes practice management, pricing, legal project management, practice innovation, and alternative staffing approaches. Prior to this, Toby served as the director of strategic pricing & analytics for Akin and served in similar roles for both Vinson & Elkins and Fulbright & Jaworski. At Fulbright he also drove knowledge management (KM) initiatives and various marketing efforts. Before joining Fulbright, Toby served as the communications director for the Utah state bar, and as the CLE, access to justice and programs director.

Toby was named to *The National Law Journal*'s 2013 list of legal business trailblazers and pioneers and received the Peer Excellence Award, the President's Award, and the Anne Charles Award from the National Association of Bar Executives.

Toby maintains the ABA award-winning 3 Geeks and a Law Blog with two colleagues at www.geeklawblog.com. He is active on Twitter as @gnawledge and can be found on LinkedIn.

Richard Burcher

Richard is a former practicing lawyer and managing partner with over 35 years of experience. Now based in London as the managing director of Validatum™, Richard is widely regarded as one of the leading international authorities on pricing legal services. Widely published, his pricing consultancy services and speaking engagements take him throughout the United Kingdom, Asia, India, Europe,

Australasia, and North America, working with a broad cross-section of law firms ranging from ten partners to over 400 partners and turnovers of £5 million to £500 million. Projects include in-house pricing training for partners and senior associates, large pitches, pricing support retainer arrangements, and pricing capability recruitment advice and training.

Paul Carr

Paul is the president of Axiom, the world's largest provider of tech-enabled legal, contracts, and compliance solutions for large enterprises. The firm's unique solutions combine legal expertise, technology, and data analytics to deliver work in a way that dramatically reduces risk, cost, and cycle time.

At Axiom, Paul oversees the firm's global sales, service, solutions, and delivery teams and is responsible for geographic expansion as well as service line development. Having joined in 2008, Axiom has quadrupled under Paul's leadership and now employs over 1,200 people across 16 locations around the world.

Before joining Axiom, Paul was the general manager of American Express' international insurance business including all underwriting, reinsurance, and distribution activities. The business sold over $500 million in premiums annually across 22 international markets. Prior to that role, Paul served as Amex's global head of strategy. Before his tenure at Amex, Paul was a partner at The Boston Consulting Group working in a number of offices including Chicago, Seoul, Sydney, Paris, and London. Paul received his undergraduate and MBA degrees at the University of Melbourne.

Eric Chin

Eric is an associate at Beaton Capital where he works closely with senior management in law and accounting firms on strategy, M&A, and business model innovation engagements across Australia, New Zealand, Hong Kong, Singapore, and other markets in the Asia-Pacific region. He introduced the "NewLaw" neologism as the business model antithesis of traditional law firms. The industry and the Twittersphere have now adopted NewLaw terminology. An astute student of the professions, Eric has written on this subject in the *Australasian Law Management Journal*, *Global Legal Post*, *Managing Partner Magazine*, and *Asia Law Portal*. He has coauthored book chapters on the topic and contributed to the e-book *NewLaw New Rules*.

Lisa J. Damon

Lisa is a recognized leader in innovation and value in the profession of law. She serves on the Executive Committee and as the national chair of Seyfarth Shaw's 350-attorney Labor & Employment Department. She also shares executive oversight of SeyfarthLean®, the firm's proprietary, value-driven client service model, which combines the core principles of Lean Six Sigma with process improvement, project management, and tailored technology solutions.

Lisa has been named one of the most innovative lawyers in the United States by the *ABA Journal* and *Financial Times*. She has been honored as an ACC Value Champion, a fellow in the College of Law Practice Management, and was named Employment Lawyer of the Year 2012 in the inaugural Chambers USA Women in Law Awards.

Leon Flavell

Leon leads the PwC Global Legal Services Network, which comprises over 2,500 lawyers in over 85 countries. Prior to leading PwC's Global Legal Services Network, he led PwC Legal's business in the United Kingdom, having joined that business shortly after its formation in 1996. Leon started his legal career at the bar in London, and prior to joining PwC Legal he worked as a corporate lawyer (specializing in private equity) at Frere Cholmeley, Clifford Chance, and Pinsent Curtis (as partner). He is based near London and is married with two children. Outside of work and family, his interests include sports (particularly horseracing, football, and tennis), ancient history, and archaeology.

Ron Friedmann

Ron is a consultant with Fireman & Company. He improves law practice efficiency and law firm business operations. He is a lawyer and former BigLaw CIO. His areas of expertise include knowledge management, legal project management, legal and business process outsourcing, e-discovery, process improvement, online legal services, legal vendor marketing, and technology for law practice and law firm operations. Ron believes that to achieve legal efficiency and improve value, changing the business model for a law firm is not enough; lawyers must also change the way they practice law, sometimes doing less law. He blogs at www.prismlegal.com.

Stuart Fuller

Stuart is global managing partner of King & Wood Mallesons, a global law firm headquartered in Asia. Stuart is responsible for the development and implementation of the firm's global strategy, overall development of its practices and global client program, as well as the functional integration of the firm.

His role encompasses the firm's operations in over 30 offices throughout China, Hong Kong, Australia, Europe, the Middle East, Japan, and the United States. Stuart is a member of the BCA's Global Engagement Taskforce, the Advisory Council for the Asia Society, and the Law Society of New South Wales.

Tahlia Gordon

Tahlia Gordon was the inaugural research & projects manager at the Office of the Legal Services Commissioner (OLSC) in Sydney, Australia. Tahlia also lectured regularly to the profession, students, and the general public on ethics, regulation, and professionalism. Prior to joining the OLSC, Tahlia was the executive director of the Legal Profession Advisory Council in Sydney and policy officer at the NSW Bar Association.

Tahlia has also worked at the Australian Mission to the United Nations in New York. She is the secretary general of the Australian Section of the International Commission of Jurists. In August 2013, Tahlia established Creative Consequences Ltd. with Steve Mark.

Tahlia has a bachelor of social science with honors and a bachelor of laws from the University of N.S.W. and a master's in human rights law from the University of Notre Dame, Indiana, U.S.A.

Kenneth A. Grady

Ken is lean law evangelist for Seyfarth Shaw LLP and the former Chief Executive Officer of SeyfarthLean Consulting, LLC, a subsidiary of Seyfarth Shaw.

A recognized thought leader, Ken is a frequent speaker in and outside the United States on legal industry issues and trends, including innovation, leadership, efficiency, and change management. Ken's articles and posts have been featured in many online and print media publications, and he is the editor and principal author of the blog SeytLines.com. He has also earned a number of accolades during his career, including being named to the Fastcase 50, which honors the law's "smartest, most courageous innovators, techies, visionaries, and leaders" and was honored by the *Financial Times* for innovative leadership of in-house counsel/outside counsel relationships.

Ken helped pioneer techniques in the legal industry, such as value-based fee arrangements, project management, and process improvement, netting impressive results including reducing legal department expenses by as much as 50 percent while at the same time supporting high-growth companies. Ken's training in lean thinking includes studies at the famed Japanese consulting firm Shingijutsu Co. Ltd. under Yoshiki Iwata, an original member of the Toyota Autonomous Study Group that developed the Toyota Production System.

Andrew Grech

As group managing director of Slater & Gordon Lawyers, Australia's first incorporated and publically listed law firm, Andrew focuses his time on the achievement of Slater & Gordon's goal—to provide easier access to world-class legal services for everyday people. Andrew joined Slater & Gordon in 1994, and worked as a lawyer in most of its litigation practice areas before becoming managing director in 2000. Andrew has been instrumental in implementing Slater & Gordon's growth strategy in order to create a leading international consumer law firm that provides a wide range of consumer legal services. Slater & Gordon employs 1,300 people in over 70 locations in Australia and 1,300 people in 20 locations in the United Kingdom. Andrew's contribution to the legal industry has been recognized over the years with awards such as the Lawyers Weekly Managing Partner of the Year Award in 2011 and the American Lawyer's Innovators Award in 2013.

Susan Hackett

Having served for more than two decades as the general counsel of the Association of Corporate Counsel, Susan is one of the world's leading experts on in-house practice in its many forms: across industries, geographies, and subject matter. She is now the CEO of a consulting firm specializing in law department and law firm leadership and management: Legal Executive Leadership, LLC. She likes to point out that corporate clients don't have legal problems; they have business problems. To serve them well, you must be more than a good lawyer; you must be a good business executive.

Simon Harper

Simon Harper co-founded alternative legal services provider Lawyers On Demand (LOD) in 2007 while an equity partner at Berwin Leighton Paisner, where he led the firm's technology and media practice. He stepped down from the partnership in 2012 to focus on leading LOD. A long-time fan of creative lawyering, he was named by *American Lawyer* magazine as one of the 50 most innovative lawyers of the past 50 years.

LOD helps in-house legal teams and law firms manage changing workloads more efficiently, and offers talented lawyers different ways of working. With a team of more than 300 talented freelance lawyers, LOD has won multiple awards for innovation and client service.

William Henderson

William (Bill) teaches law and business law courses at the Indiana University Maurer School of Law, including corporations, business planning, project management, and the law firm as business organization. From 2009–2014 he served as the director of Indiana Law's Center on the Global Legal Profession. Henderson's scholarship focuses on empirical analysis of the legal profession and legal education. In addition to his scholarly works, his pieces appear frequently in national publications such as *The American Lawyer*, *The Wall Street Journal*, *ABA Journal*, and the *National Law Journal*. In 2014, *National Jurist* magazine named him the most influential person in legal education. Henderson is a research associate with the Law School Survey of Student Engagement (LSSSE) and a principal in Lawyer Metrics, a research company that focuses on the use of data for better strategic decision making.

Silvia Hodges Silverstein

Silvia researches, teaches, writes, and speaks on topics related to purchasing decision, metrics, marketing/business development, and change in law firms. She is the executive director of the Buying Legal Council, the organization of procurement professionals tasked with sourcing legal services. She is also a lecturer at

Columbia Law School and an adjunct professor at Fordham Law School, where she teaches law firm management. Silvia co-authored the Harvard Business School case studies GlaxoSmithKline's legal procurement and new model law firm Riverview Law. She is the editor of the *Legal Procurement Handbook* as well as a number of books on law firm management.

Rick Kathuria

Rick is national director, Project Management and Legal Logistics at Gowlings. In this role, he leads the firm's business transformation agenda and project management strategy (Gowlings Practical), applying process optimization and project management principles to the delivery of sophisticated legal services.

Rick has over 15 years of experience working on large international projects at top-tier consulting firms. A noted authority on legal project management (LPM), he co-authored the book *Project Management for Lawyers*. He is on the executive committee of the Project Management Institute's LPM initiative, promoting the education and adoption of LPM around the world.

Eduardo C. Leite (Foreword)

Eduardo is chairman of Baker & McKenzie's Executive Committee. A partner since 1986 and an accomplished energy, infrastructure projects, and M&A lawyer, Mr. Leite served on Baker & McKenzie's Executive Committee from 1999–2003, and he chaired the firm's Policy Committee in 2005. Prior to being elected chairman, Mr. Leite was the managing partner of the four offices in Brazil, a position he held for seven years. From 1999–2003, he was chairman of the Latin American Regional Council.

Mr. Leite has spent several years working in Baker & McKenzie's Chicago and Miami offices since joining the firm in 1979. He has also led the firm's Global Energy, Mining & Infrastructure Industry Group. Mr. Leite is married and the father of two daughters.

Michelle Mahoney

Michelle is the executive director of innovation at King & Wood Mallesons and is responsible for the design and delivery of the innovation agenda and portfolio for the firm. With a deep understanding of the professional services industry, first to market services, continuous improvement and design thinking practices, Michelle is able to design and deliver legal products and services that are driven by what clients value. She is a Prince 2 project management practitioner, a Prosci Change Management practitioner, d.school Design Thinker, and a Lean Six Sigma Black Belt. Michelle is a fellow of the College of Law Practice Management and she has been specializing in the legal sector for in excess of 20 years. Michelle can be followed on Twitter @michmahon.

Steve Mark

Steve is a lawyer and former president of the New South Wales Anti-Discrimination Board from 1988–1994. He was appointed legal services commissioner when the office was established in 1994. In 2013, Steve established an international consultancy, Creative Consequences, which is engaged regulatory design, and developing ethical culture in the legal financial and security professions.

Steve holds various other appointments. He is chairman of the Australian Section of the International Commission of Jurists, chair of the Council of International House at The University of Sydney (since 2013), and registrar, Australasian Register of Security Professionals.

In 2011, Steve was appointed Technical Committee member of ASIS International, setting an auditable standard for private security companies in the United States. In 2013, Steve was appointed chair of the Standards Australia/ASIS Mirror Committee to adopt the ISO Competency Standard for Private Security companies into Australia.

Steve is also a founding director of Midnight Basketball. In 2014, Steve was awarded an AM for his contribution to law, regulation, indigenous rights, and community service.

David Morley

David is Allen & Overy's worldwide senior partner, a role akin to executive chairman. He joined Allen & Overy as a trainee in 1980, qualifying as a solicitor in 1982 after obtaining an MA in law from St John's College, Cambridge University. He is a banking lawyer with 25 years of transactional experience. In 1998, he became global head of the banking practice. He was elected worldwide managing partner, a role akin to CEO, in May 2003; elected worldwide senior partner in 2008; and reelected for a further four-year term in 2012.

David is a member of the Mayor of London's International Business Advisory Council and a member of the Best Lawyers Advisory Board. He is chairman of Prime, the U.K. legal profession–wide initiative to provide fair access to quality work experience. In 2012, he was listed as one of the ten most influential lawyers in the United Kingdom by *The Times* newspaper. In 2013, he was recognized as one of The Top 50 Big Law Innovators of the Last 50 Years by the *American Lawyer*.

Alastair Morrison

Alastair is head of Client Strategy at Pinsent Mason, and the executive board member with overall responsibility for the firm's client and sector strategy. He is the relationship partner for some of the firm's largest clients and has firsthand experience of the challenges general counsel and their teams are responding to.

His own client experiences and those of his colleagues have been central to the development of his firm's strategy and in the creation of a range of innovative legal delivery models. Alastair has spoken at international conferences on the challenges being faced by clients and how these challenges are shaping his firm and the legal profession more widely.

Gerard Neiditsch

Gerard has been CIO at three major law firms in Australia: Allens Linklaters, Norton Rose Fulbright, and King & Wood Mallesons. He is currently a Research Associate at St. Gallen University in Switzerland. Gerard has a track record of transformation management at large professional services organizations. For more than two decades, he has been working in applying innovative technology and leading large-scale work practice changes at leading legal, advisory, and accounting firms. He was also the co-founder of a leading eDiscovery software company, and is the co-inventor of a new electronic filing technology. He has a reputation for building high-performance teams and for enabling sustained change in industry-leading firms. Gerard has worked in Switzerland, the United States, and in Australia in local, regional, and global roles.

David Perla

David is president of Bloomberg BNA's Legal Division. He plays a key leadership role in the continued growth of the company's Legal business, which includes legal, legislative, and regulatory news analysis, and the flagship Bloomberg Law® legal and business intelligence research system. He drives the growth strategy for Bloomberg BNA Legal and oversees the development of distinctive content and products characterized by Bloomberg BNA's renowned editorial excellence and Bloomberg's reputation as a technology leader.

Before joining Bloomberg BNA, David served as chairman and CEO of Matterhorn Transactions and co-CEO and co-founder of Pangea[3], the globally known legal process outsourcing provider. Prior to forming Pangea3, he was vice president—Business & Legal Affairs for Monster.com.

David received a BA from the University of Pennsylvania, and a JD from the University of Pennsylvania Law School. He began his legal career as a corporate lawyer at the law firm Katten Muchin Rosenman LLP.

Andrew M. Perlman

Andrew is a professor at Suffolk University Law School, where he directs the Institute on Law Practice Technology and Innovation as well as the Concentration on Legal Technology and Innovation. He has served as the chief reporter for the American Bar Association's Commission on Ethics 20/20 and as the vice chair of the American Bar Association's Commission on the Future of Legal Services.

Edwin B. Reeser

Edwin is a business lawyer with nearly 40 years of experience. He focuses on representation of law firms and lawyers in lateral movement, withdrawal agreements, strategic alliances, mergers, drafting partnership and shareholder agreements, forming new law firms, and complex ethics and conflicts issues. He also advises on compensation systems, succession planning, partner capital, policy manuals, partnership structure, and agreements with of counsel, income partners, and associates. As a business lawyer, he has specialized in structuring, negotiating, and documenting complex real estate and business transactions for international and domestic clients, including choice and structure of entities. Edwin is the author of more than 100 published articles on law firm management, leadership, operations, and economics.

Mark Rigotti

Prior to becoming joint CEO (with Sonya Leydecker) of Herbert Smith Freehills, Mark was a partner in the Banking & Finance group where he focused on the leveraged and project finance areas. He has been a member of the management team for some time, having led different practice groups at different times and having been involved in a range of leadership and management matters before taking on a role managing the firm's client portfolio.

Mark is a member of the firm's council, co-chairs the Global Executive, and is chairman of the Global Diversity and Inclusivity Group. Mark is a member of the Business Council of Australia and the Financial Services Institute of Australia.

Michael Roster

Mike was managing partner of Morrison & Foerster's Los Angeles office and co-chair of the firm's Financial Services Practice Group worldwide. He subsequently served as general counsel of Stanford University and Stanford Medical Center and then of Golden West Financial Corporation. Mike has been a director and chair of the Association of Corporate Counsel, an outside director and vice chair of Silicon Valley Bank, chair of the Stanford Alumni Association, and chair of several startups. He is currently co-chair of the ACC Value Challenge, an adjunct professor at the University of Southern California, and a director of MDRC in New York.

Jeremy Szwider

Jeremy is a principal and founder of Bespoke, a NewLaw firm. As a pioneer of the NewLaw revolution, Bespoke turns the conventional wisdom of the traditional legal market on its head by combining in-house and private practice principles. The result is high-quality, pragmatic legal solutions with a value-based pricing model. The outsourced business model does away with fixed overheads, bureaucratic large firm processes, and inflexible fee agreements. Instead, Bespoke provides a network of experienced lawyers working with clients with a unique "in-house philosophy" and who are available to provide outsourced in-house counsel services, without watching the clock. Jeremy is a recognized leader in the legal industry and has been instrumental with his entrepreneurial flair in pushing the boundaries of the NewLaw movement.

Mark Tamminga

Mark Tamminga is a partner at Canadian firm Gowling Lafleur Henderson LLP, practicing in the area of real estate and mortgage collections. He is a former managing partner of the firm's Hamilton office and is currently Gowlings' Leader, Innovation Initiatives. Mark has a particular interest in the area of practice automation tools for lawyers, having automated the Gowlings Recovery Services practice and having designed and built a number of additional practice systems for debt collection, loan placement, and civil litigation. He is currently deriving a great deal of satisfaction from leading the firm's transformational Gowlings Practical process improvement and project management program.

Richard Tapp

Richard is company secretary and director of Legal Services at the U.K.-based company Carillion plc. Carillion is a major support services and construction company, with revenues exceeding £4 billion, more than 50,000 employees, and an in-house team of some 25 lawyers focusing on the provision of innovative business solutions. Richard led the restructuring of Carillion's legal resourcing to refocus the internal legal function and to form the Carillion Legal Network of law firms, which serves the group's legal needs. His accolades include Most Innovative European In-house Lawyer as recognized through the *Financial Times* Innovative Lawyer Awards 2013. He is the co-author of *Managing External Legal Resources* (ICSA Publishing) and the *In-House Lawyers' Toolkit* (Law Society Publishing).

Thomas Thoppil

Thomas is vice president and deputy general counsel for Asia Pacific and Japan, Hewlett-Packard Company, Singapore. In this position, Thomas is the region general counsel leading a team of more than 100 attorneys in the Asia Pacific and Japan region, and is responsible for all legal matters affecting the business of Hewlett-Packard Company.

Thomas joined Hewlett-Packard in 2002 as country counsel for India and subsequently was appointed as lead counsel for South East Asia and South Pacific. Thomas assumed the role of region general counsel for the Asia Pacific and Japan region in July 2013. Prior to joining HP, Thomas worked as an in-house legal counsel with Wipro Ltd, ICICI Ltd, and Industrial Development Bank of India (IDBI). Thomas started his professional career as a litigation lawyer in the High Court of Kerala, India.

Thomas earned a bachelor's degree in law (LLB) from the University of Kerala and a master's degree in law (LLM) from the University of Georgia, Georgia, U.S.A.

Steven M. Walker

Steven is associate general counsel and South Pacific region counsel, Hewlett-Packard. He manages HP's Office of the General Counsel in Australia and New Zealand and is company secretary for HP's local corporations.

He spent eight years of his career in private practice, as an associate with Norton Rose in London and later as a senior associate with Baker & McKenzie in Sydney. He joined Electronic Data Systems in 2007 and remained with Hewlett-Packard during the HP/EDS integration.

HP's Office of the General Counsel (OGC) is committed to legal services innovation. In the last two years, the OGC has implemented revolutionary legal services initiatives, tools, and technology, including the deployment of a cloud-based contract management, workflow, and analytics tool. Steven has been evaluating "next generation" LPO-style solutions for commoditized legal work and is leading the deployment of legal project management methods in service delivery.

Peter Weill

Peter is the chairman of Massachusetts Institute of Technology's Center for Information Systems Research and senior research scientist at the MIT Sloan School of Management. Peter's work centers on the role, value, and governance of digitization in enterprises and their ecosystems. Peter is currently working on exploring how boards become pivotal players in developing the role of digitization within their organizations.

His award-winning books include *IT Savvy: What Top Executives Must Know to Go from Pain to Gain* (2009); *Enterprise Architecture as Strategy* (CIO Insight's #1 must-read for 2009); and *IT Governance: How Top Performers Manage IT Decision Rights for Superior Results* (2004). Peter's journal articles and case studies have appeared in the *Harvard Business Review*, *MIT Sloan Management Review*, and *The Wall Street Journal*. In 2008, Ziff Davis recognized Peter as #24 of "The Top 100 Most Influential People in IT" and the highest ranked academic.

Peter works regularly on digitization issues with executive and MBA programs as well as with organizations such as Aetna, AMP, ANZ, BBVA, BCG, BT, Commonwealth Bank of Australia, France Telecom, IBM, McKinsey, Microsoft, Oliver Wyman, Origin Energy, Raytheon, State Street Corporation, TCS, Unibanco, Woolworths, and World Bank. He conducts workshops for high-level conferences, including for Microsoft, Bill Gates' CEO Summit, and SAP's CEO Summit.

Nick West

Nick is the U.K. managing director of Axiom, the world's largest and fastest growing nontraditional provider of legal services. The firm's unique solutions combine legal expertise, technology, and data analytics to deliver work in a way that dramatically reduces risk, cost, and cycle time.

Axiom serves nearly half of the Fortune 100 through 14 offices and five delivery centers globally with 1,200+ employees, including legal professionals, technologists, project managers, solution designers, and delivery managers.

Prior to Axiom, Nick held a number of senior executive roles at LexisNexis in London, New York, and Paris; was a consultant at McKinsey & Co.; and started his career as a lawyer at Linklaters.

Geoff Wild

Geoff is the director of governance and law at Kent County Council, United Kingdom. He heads up one of the largest teams of local authority lawyers in the United Kingdom, with 125 lawyers serving over 600 public sector clients and generating over £2.5 million profit annually. It is designed and managed to run as a fully traded business along private sector lines, while retaining a strong public sector ethos.

Geoff was named Most Innovative European In-House Lawyer at the FT Innovative Lawyer Awards 2014. He was also named Leader of the Year at the Law Society Awards 2011, where the judges described him as "someone who has made a dynamic contribution to legal services in the public sector."

Peter Williams

Peter is chief edge officer for the Centre for the Edge, Deloitte Australia, and a board member at law firm Hall & Wilcox. He is a recognized thought leader and practitioner in innovation with a particular focus on digital innovation. Peter founded Deloitte Digital, a business pioneering the delivery of professional services online, and has been the chairman of Deloitte's Innovation Council since 2004. The Centre's mission is to identify and explore emerging opportunities related to big shifts that are not yet on the senior management's agenda, but ought to be.

Pam Woldow

As principal and general counsel of the global legal consulting firm Edge International, Pam has earned widespread recognition for her pioneering work in transforming law firm–client relationships. She has been named a "Legal Rebel" by the American Bar Association—a provocative change catalyst for innovation in the legal profession.

Pam specializes in providing advice to general counsel and chief legal officers on law department operations, cost management, litigation management, and management of outside counsel, as well as advising law firms on Legal Project Management, business development, and all aspects of counsel–client relationships. She is a certified master coach, co-author of the ABA-sponsored book *Legal Project Management in an Hour for Lawyers*, and author of the award-winning legal blog focusing on LPM, *At the Intersection*.

David Worley

As a managing director in the marketing and sales organization of PwC, David is the firm's West region business development leader. He is responsible for the integration of marketing and sales strategies across all business units and industries, connecting marketing with both sales and client service to ensure that PwC delivers a differentiated experience for its key stakeholder groups. He is client-facing, routinely interacting with clients to learn from them and ensure the firm is delivering solutions to meet their needs.

David has over 30 years of experience as a thought leader who specializes in building and strengthening global, high-performance sales organizations competing in business-to-business, sales, and relationship-management environments. His experiences give him a unique perspective on strategically managing large organizations.

List of Abbreviations

ABS   Alternative Business Structures

ACC   Association of Corporate Counsel

ACLA   Australian Corporate Lawyers Association

AFA   Alternative Fee Arrangement

AI   Artificial Intelligence

BD   Business Development

CEO   Chief Executive Officer

CFO   Chief Financial Officer

CIO   Chief Information Officer

CLO   Chief Legal Officer

CRM   Client Relationship Management

GC   General Counsel

HR   Human Resources

IT   Information Technology

ILP   Incorporated Legal Practice

ILTA   International Legal Technology Association

KM   Knowledge Management

LPI   Legal Process Improvement

LPM   Legal Project Management

LPO   Legal Process Outsourcing/Outsourcer

LSO   Legal Services Outsourcing/Outsourcer

MBTI   Myers Briggs Type Indicator

MIT   Massachusetts Institute of Technology

PPP   Profit Per Partner

PSF   Professional Services Firm

R&D   Research and Development

RFP   Request for Proposal

Index